250 YEARS OF STEAM

BY THE SAME AUTHOR

Your Book of Traction Engines
Steam Engines at Bressingham
Published by Faber & Faber

Locomotives of the Great Western Railway
Locomotives of the Southern Railway
Locomotives of the London, Midland & Scottish Railway
Locomotives of the London & North Eastern Railway
Locomotives of British Railways
Published by Jarrold Colour Publications

250 YEARS OF STEAM

Alan Bloom

WORLD'S WORK LTD

Acknowledgements

My thanks to John Ravenscroft for his work both in researching and
procuring photographs and for writing many of the captions.
Thanks are due also to those who lent photographs free of charge, and
especially to Mr. Ronald H. Clark, A.H.I. Mech. Eng. I must record my
appreciation to the publishers for the help given to me by Mr. David Elliot,
Mr. Robert Aspinall and Miss Jo Shepherd, over some of the more
difficult hurdles concerning both the text and illustrations.

Index compiled by R. C. Raper

Published by World's Work Ltd
The Windmill Press, Kingswood, Tadworth, Surrey

Printed in Great Britain by BAS Printers Limited
Over Wallop, Stockbridge, Hampshire

SBN 437 01400 2

CONTENTS

List of illustrations
Introduction

Steam pioneers
Some famous locomotive designers
Museums, steam centres and preserved buildings
Books for further reading
Index

LIST OF ILLUSTRATIONS

All illustrations are from the author's collection, except where stated.

Introduction

The Steam Age has ended. As a direct source of power over a period of two centuries steam was supreme. It was the greatest single factor in the Industrial Revolution, usually dated from 1760 to 1860, spreading out from Britain to the rest of the world wherever it could be applied. Its ability to turn load-bearing wheels far surpassed the efforts of men and horses, which for countless centuries before were the only sources of power, apart from the wind and gravity.

From the first crude attempts to harness it for power, steam has been a source of intense and widespread interest, often amounting to wonderment. Its attraction was probably less during the period when steam engines were commonplace, than in its early stages of development, or at present, when only those in preservation can be seen. Far more people are now taking an intelligent or nostalgic interest in

steam engines than was the case fifty years ago, probably for much the same reason that crowds flocked to witness engine trials and exhibitions of a hundred or a hundred and fifty years ago.

The truth is, however, that the working of steam power has always evoked a fascinated interest, and I believe this springs from basic factors concerning the birth and growth of the human evolutionary process. The two principle elements with which early man had to contend were fire and water. Having learned how to make fire and to use water for survival, he learned also how best to control these elements and to avoid the harm resulting from their becoming bad masters, instead of good servants. Water could extinguish fire, but fire could boil water for cooking, could make pottery and fashion metals into tools and weapons. If the rising vapour from boiling water was not seen as a possible source of power, it was because no means of harnessing it existed.

When the steam engine finally became a reality, a power affecting life

and work, it must surely have stirred a deep-seated emotion in many a human breast. For here was a great and spectacular evolutionary achievement, a triumph over two elemental forces of nature. One element had been made to combine with the other; fire forced water to produce steam under pressure and anyone could see how the seeming miracle was performed. There were awesome moving cranks, beams and wheels, to prove that steam held a power infinitely greater than any made or induced by man ever before. 'Iron Horses'—the name given to the early locomotives was in itself emotive. They were to be seen at work by the general public more often than were the massive stationary steam engines which were by that time providing power for industry. But they were both inspiring proof that, by mastering the power of steam, the door was open through human ingenuity to a vast new field of achievement and wealth.

It is far from true that the steam engine was invented by James Watt as a result of seeing how steam heaved up the lid of a boiling kettle. Inventions

are not often spontaneous creations or discoveries, leading directly to prompt and useful application. Almost always they are the result of variations or improvements on the work of others, and the first principle of generating power, which Watt used as a basis, was evolved over a century before his time. This principle was of creating a vacuum within a confined space, by means of a piston within a cylinder. This was the beginning, and the cylinder and piston remained basic for the whole of the steam age, except for the much later development of the steam turbine. James Watt's improvements to the steam engine were none the less an outstanding achievement. It led to the direct force of steam pressure being employed, not only for his stationary engines for industry and drainage pumps, but to road and railway locomotives, to ships, steam rollers, navvies, cranes, winches—and not least to farming.

This book covers all these aspects of steam power, based almost entirely on the original principle of a piston being forced back and forth within a cylinder.

On this theme there were almost infinite variations concerned with the transfer of steam power to serve whatever need or purpose arose. Once development was under way during the upsurge of industry in Britain, it became a classic example of necessity mothering invention, if only because of its broad field of application. In addition the necessity, as well as the advantage, of gaining the maximum power for a given purpose at the least cost in terms of fuel and maintenance, were a constant incentive to further invention. So was the safety aspect, when dealing with a vapour potentially far more dangerous than either of the two elements which produced it. Steam could sometimes be lethal in its early years of development, and explosions had to be avoided by making boilers, pipes and valves of metal strong enough to contain the pent-up pressures.

In describing the many aspects and applications of steam-powered engines, I have had in mind the vast number of people whose interest has been or can be aroused, simply because it stirs in them an emotion. It may be

basic, as I have suggested, or it may simply arise out of interest in things mechanical. For many, it is pure nostalgia. The object of this book is, therefore, to record the saga of the steam age in narrative form, with its principles, practices and developments simply described. Considerable emphasis is placed on where examples of the many types of steam engines may still be seen. The first steam engines to be used successfully were British inventions. But if Britain was among the first industrial nations to invent or adopt other means of power to replace steam, it has at least the distinction of possessing the largest and most comprehensive range in the world of relics of the steam age. They form a very important part of our national heritage, and this book is designed to give this fact the prominence it deserves. But because steam has so many ramifications, the book cannot rank as anything more than an introduction to the subject.

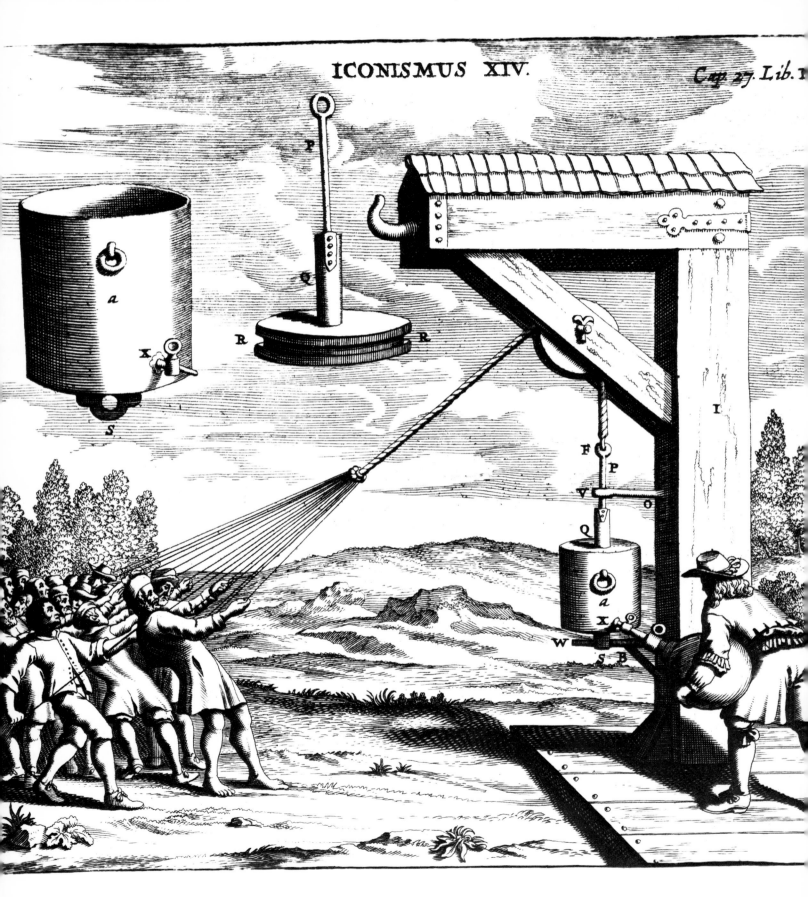

EARLY PROBINGS, PRINCIPLES AND PRACTICES

Steam and the Industrial Revolution

Steam power should be seen as the effect rather than the cause of the Industrial Revolution. True, it was the greatest single factor in that revolution which changed Britain from being principally an agrarian and seafaring nation to an industrial one in the hundred years from 1760 to 1860. But its development as a source of power should be primarily linked to the basic physical and natural resources of food and mineral-producing land, along with the resources of the human mind. Scientific enquirers and potential inventors had been intrigued by notions of untapped sources of power long before the steam era began. But it was not until the 18th century that economic and sociological pressures made clear a vital need for power.

The combined effect of an increasing population, improving agricultural techniques, and the widespread enclosures of land, set the stage for the eruption known best as the Industrial Revolution.

Population increase in the first half of the 18th century can be taken as the first link in a chain reaction. It was due

In 1654 Otto Von Guericke built an apparatus to demonstrate the power of atmospheric pressure. When air was pumped out of the cylinder below the piston, atmospheric pressure forced the piston down despite twenty strong men pulling on ropes to prevent it. However, this method of creating a vacuum was cumbersome, and in 1690 Denis Papin applied condensed steam to produce a vacuum more simply.

mainly to improving hygiene and medical knowledge, and it led automatically to the need for increased food production. Haphazard and uneconomic farming methods were steadily replaced, when it was found that Jethro Tull's seed drill produced much better yields, as did 'Turnip' Townsend's system of crop rotation. Robert Bakewell's improvements to livestock by selective breeding, and the provision of winter fodder, put an end to the wasteful autumn slaughter. All this fitted in neatly with the change from open strip farming to fields of an economic size. This process, begun in later Stuart times, accelerated under the Hanoverians, and was effective not only in getting more food from the land. It made many a yeoman and peasant landless and drew him into the expanding towns for work, along with those who had left or were leaving because the new horsedrawn machines and implements reduced the need for human labour.

The change from a land-based to an urban-based population should not be over-emphasised. It was a slow process which has continued ever since—over two centuries, during which the population of Britain has increased more than fourfold. The gradual drift from the land to the towns was natural, and made more inevitable by changes which called for labour in the towns. Prior to 1760 or thereabouts industrial production was based largely on what might be termed a domestic system. This was widely practised where employers, such as those concerned with textiles and the smaller metal products, contracted with home-based families. It was a system conducive to workers being very dependent on their employers, and was wide open to abuse and harsh bargaining.

The first factories

The domestic system was also one which precluded the adoption of machinery; but employers were quick to grasp any advantage to themselves of any new machines which could increase production and profit. The textile industry was in the forefront of mechanical development. Kay's 'flying shuttle' and Hargreaves' 'spinning jenny' became available in the first half of the 18th century.

These were followed by other devices, but the most effective spur to the revolutionary change from the domestic to the factory system in textiles came from John Arkwright's improvements in and use of cotton-spinning machines. Using the River Derwent for power, he built a factory in 1784 near Matlock for his Musson Mill, for spinning yarn.

The advantages of having a concentrated labour force at the source of power for mechanised production put this venture far ahead, in terms of economic and profitable output. It set the pattern which others were quick to follow, revealing as it spread the need for reliable power with which to drive machines for many other purposes than textiles.

These were some of the factors leading to the Industrial Revolution. They were interdependent sociological and economic factors and they were taking shape scarcely noticed by the unaffected majority. But there was a tiny minority, with visionary or inquisitive minds, who were aware of changing times, and a very few of these believed steam to be capable of filling the need for power.

The theorists

Although the steam engine was essentially a British invention, it could be said to have had its origins in the minds of 17th and 18th century philosophers who were probing the secrets of natural forces. Galileo in Italy was an early investigator, and soon others in Germany, France, Holland and England were testing their novel theories. Their chief aim was to establish principles, with very little thought or knowledge of what others were doing, or of any practical application of the discoveries they made. A lack of rapid communication, and of suitable tools and equipment, confined their efforts to expounding theories in isolation from each other. So half a century passed before anyone produced even a crude model capable of proving a new-found principle.

It was the discovery that the atmosphere had pressure and weight that led Otto von Guericke of Magdeburg in 1650 to demonstrate his new invention of an air pump capable of lifting a weight. He is credited as being the first to use a piston inside a cylinder. After extracting air from the cylinder to create a vacuum under the piston, the weight or pressure of the atmosphere was found to be great enough to force the piston down and to raise a weight above ground. This was a momentous discovery; though it still did no more than establish a principle, news of it was enough to spark off other experimenters.

A model, made by Desaguliers, of Savery's 'fire engine'. This was the first, though inefficient, apparatus to raise water by steam power. Steam alternately entered two vessels connected to a pit sump. It was then condensed, causing atmospheric pressure to force water from the sump up into the vessels through a non-return valve. Admission of fresh steam forced the water up the outlet pipe.

Pumps and pistons

Robert Boyle, assisted by Robert Hooke, succeeded in making the first English air pump. It was based on von Guericke's idea, as was that of the Dutch scientist Huygens. He later concentrated on a more effective means of creating a vacuum under the piston than that of merely extracting air, by using a small charge of gun-powder.

This expelled the air through self-sealing leather glands, and as a demonstration of the latent power of atmospheric pressure, it worked quite well. But the main obstacle to it having any practical application was that of obtaining an automatic, reliable repetitive action.

It was not until 1690 that condensed steam was tried as another means of producing a vacuum. Denis Papin, a French Huguenot physicist, had worked under Huygens, and had at times been in close touch with the English experimenters. His belief was that steam had an expansive property, but he was far from imagining what power it could exert under pressure. The

working model he produced demonstrated that unpressured steam, entering a cylinder beneath a piston, created a vacuum on being condensed. Papin also believed that his principle could be adopted for draining waterlogged coal and tin mines. With the growing importance of mining at increasing depths, this appeared as an objective worth pursuing, but there was no-one to take up the challenge.

There were ample reasons why Papin's invention was not taken up. For long enough there had been a wide gap between theory and practice—between the discoverers of principles and those with practical skills and materials with which to exploit them.

During the 17th century this gap narrowed to some extent, with the increase of commercialism. But skills, tools and materials unheard of at that period would have been needed to build a working engine. The techniques of using brass and copper were at an infant stage. Iron could only be forged in primitive smithies using the charcoal-smelted product, and although screwing and soldering had been invented, such pipes as were made were mostly of wood. Boilers simply boiled and steam rising from water was seen merely as a vapour, wafting and condensing in the atmosphere above.

Savery and Newcomen

But in the 1690s those with mechanical minds became alert and willing to take up as a challenge to their ingenuity for commercial gain what the scientists had demonstrated. Foremost were two West-countrymen, Thomas Savery and Thomas Newcomen. Both were aware of the pressing need for pumps capable of ridding the Cornish tin mines of water. Neither had heard of the early experiments of von Guericke, but Newcomen had at least been in correspondence with Hooke in the early 1690s regarding Papin's experiments with steam. Although known to each other, they began working independently to produce an efficient pumping engine. Savery was the first to complete a working engine, and was granted a patent for it in 1698. Newcomen had been working on different lines and his engine was well advanced. But Savery's initial success prompted Newcomen to drop his own work and throw in his lot with Savery, protected as he was by Royal Patent. Two heads, they decided, were better than one; but both had the fixed idea that atmospheric pressure alone held the secret of mechanical power.

This was a turning point in the history of mechanics. The initiative had passed from the philosophers and theorists to those with practical ability,

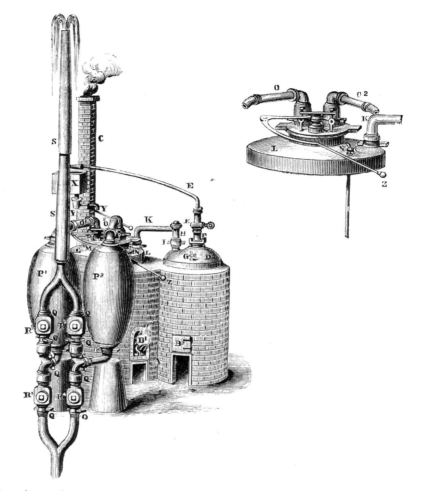

Savery's pumping engine of 1702 worked with limited success by a partial vacuum created when condensing steam was replaced by air. With a high consumption of fuel it was able to raise water slowly to 80 ft. 'Fire engine' was the term used in these early experiments.

the first true mechanical engineers. Savery's pumping engine worked by the power created when a partial vacuum from condensing steam in a receiver was replaced by air. It was not generated by the piston-cylinder principle, but it was able to raise water and push it upwards via a non-return valve. Because of this departure from Papin's principle, the Savery engine was not an ancestor of the steam engine; and if it worked reasonably well, its scope was very limited. Its boiler consumed an enormous amount of coal to provide the steam, and it could lift water but slowly a mere 80 feet, while some of the Cornish tin mines went down to 350 feet. Savery suggested a series of such engines and boilers at intervals down a

mineshaft to overcome this disability, but history has no record of such a scheme being applied. Had it been tried, there would no doubt have been some spectacular catastrophes.

The successful 'atmospheric' engine

Savery's engine proved inadequate, to say the least, and he encouraged Newcomen to resume work on his own ideas. His engine was completed and put to work in 1709. It was simple and reliable—and Newcomen had overcome the difficulty of obtaining a steady, repetitive stroke action. Above the vertical cylinder, which was open-topped, there was a heavy rocking wooden beam to which the piston rod was connected at one end. The other end of the beam was connected to a working force pump of traditional design. When steam at minimal pressure entered the cylinder, the piston was drawn upwards by the weight of the pump rods. When steam was cut off, that in the cylinder was condensed by a jet of water, leaving a sufficient vacuum for atmospheric pressure to force the piston down; with the condensate ejected through a 'drum cock' or exhaust valve, a complete, repeating stroke was made.

It is worth noticing that the first customers for Newcomen's engines were the owners of coal mines. These too were becoming deeper and greatly troubled by water, but the main reason why their owners rather than the Cornish tin mine operators took them up was that the latter had no access to coal supplies for raising steam. Sea-borne coal was taxed, whereas at the pit-head coal in plenty was on hand.

Newcomen's engine was installed near Dudley Castle in 1712, enabling the coal miners there to delve more deeply. It was a little less extravagant in the coal it consumed than was Savery's, but coal consumption was not then a vital consideration enforcing more economic methods of turning water into steam. The link between coal mining and the demand for New-comen engines set off a process whereby the demand for coal greatly increased, not only because water-free mines made for a cheaper product, but because the engines themselves consumed so much of it.

The Newcomen atmospheric engine. These huge ponderous engines were increasingly used from 1712 until Smeaton and later James Watt improved the design many years later. They served a vital need in keeping mines clear of water, and contributed to the birth of the Industrial Revolution. Practically all of this type of engine had to be built with its brick or stone housing as a unit.

REFERENCES

By Figures, to the feveral Members.

1	The Fire Mouth under the Boyler with a Lid or Door.
2	The Boyler 5 Feet, 6 Inches Diameter, 6 Feet 1 Inch high, the Cylindrical part 4 Feet 4 Inches, Content near 13 Hogfheads.
3	The Neck or Throat betwixt the Boyler and the Great Cylinder.
4	A Brafs Cylinder 7 Feet 10 Inches high, 21 Inches Diameter, to Rarifie and Condenfe the Steam.
5	The Pipe which contains the Buoy, 4 Inches Diameter.
6	The Mafter Pipe that Supplies all the Offices, 4 Inches Diameter.
7	The Injecting Pipe fill'd by the Mafter Pipe 6, and ftopp'd by a Valve.
8	The Sinking Pipe, 4 Inches Diameter, that carries off the hot Water or Steam.
9	A Replenifhing Pipe to the Boyler as it waftes with a Cock.
10	A Large Pipe with a Valve to carry the Steam out of Door.
11	The Regulator moved by the 2 Y y and they by the Beam, 12.
12	The Sliding Beam mov'd by the little Arch of the great Beam.
13	Scoggen and his Mate who work Double to the Boy, Y is the Axis of him.
14	The great Y that moves the little y and Regulator, 15 and 11 by the Beam 12.
15	The little y, guided by a Rod of Iron from the Regulator.
16	The Injecting Hammer or F that moves upon it's Axis in the Barge 17.
17	Which Barge has a leaking Pipe, befides the Valve nam'd in No 7.
18	The Leaking Pipe 1 Inch Diameter, the Water falls into the Well.
19	A Snifting Bafon with a Cock, to fill or cover the Air Valve with Water.
20	The Wafte Pipe that carries off the Water from the Pifton.
21	A Pipe which covers the Pifton with a Cock.
22	The Great Sommers that Support the Houfe and Engine.
23	A Lead Cyftern, 2 Feet fquare, fill'd by the Mafter Pipe 6.
24	The Wafte Pipe to that Cyftern.
25	The Great Ballanc'd Beam that Works the whole Engine.
26	The Two Arches of the Great Ballanced Beam
27	Two Wooden Frames to ftop the Force of the Great Ballanced Beam.
28	The Little Arch of the Great Ballanc'd Beam that moves the No 12.
29	Two Chains fix'd to the Little Arch, one draws down, the other up.
30	Stays to the great Arches of the Ballanc'd Beam.
31	Strong Barrs of Iron which go through the Arches and fecure the Chains.
32	Large Pins of Iron going through the Arch to ftop the Force of the Beam.
33	Very ftrong Chains fixed to Pifton and the Plugg and both Arches.
34	Great Springs to ftop the Force of the Great Ballanc'd Beam.
35	The Stair-Cafe from Bottom to the Top.
36	The Afh-hole under the Fire, even with the Surface of the Well.
37	The Door-Cafe to the Well that receives the Water from the Level.
38	A Stair-Cafe from the Fire to the Engine and to the Great Door-Cafe.
39	The Gable-End the Great Ballanc'd Beam goes through.
40	The Colepit-mouth 12 Feet or more above the Level.
41	The dividing of the Pump work into halves in the Pit.
42	The Mouth of the Pumps to the Level of the Well.
43	The Pump-work within the Pit.
44	A Large Cyftern of Wood 25 Yards or half way down the Pit.
45	The Pump within the Houfe that Furnifhes all the Offices with Water.
46	The Floor over the Well.
47	The Great Door-Cafe 6 Feet fquare, to bring in the Boyler.
48	Stays to the Great Frame over the Pit.
49	The Wind to put them down gently or fafely.
50	A Turn-Barrel over the Pit, which the Line goes round, not to flip.
51	The Gage-Pipe to know the Depth of the Water within the Boyler.
52	Two Cocks within the Pit to keep the Pump work moift.
53	A Little Bench with a Bafs to reft when they are weary.
54	A Man going to Replenifh the Fire.
55	The Peck-Ax and Proaker.
56	The Centre or Axis of the Great Ballanc'd Beam. that Vibrates 12 times in a Minute & each ftroke lifts 10 Gall of water 55 yards perpend.

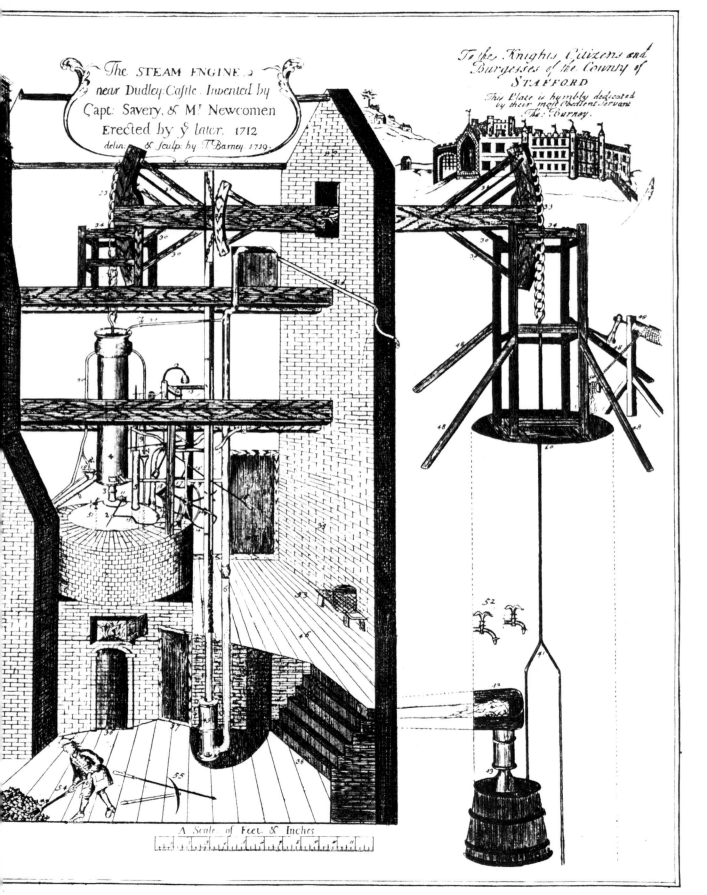

The STEAM ENGINE near Dudley Castle. Invented by Capt: Savery, & Mr. Newcomen. Erected by ye later. 1712

delin. & sculp: by T. Barney. 1719.

To the Knights, Citizens and Burgesses of the County of STAFFORD

This Place is humbly dedicated by their most Obedient Servant The. Barney.

A Scale of Feet & Inches

11

Coalbrookdale

Such a development was bound to lead to new technologies and inventions even if the atmospheric engine was to hold sway for another generation or two. Although beaten copper was used by both Savery and Newcomen, as was brass for small castings, these were expensive. Iron was relatively cheap; and at about the time Newcomen was installing his first engine, Abraham Darby began his new blast furnaces at Coalbrookdale in the West Midlands. His method of smelting iron, using coke instead of charcoal, with the aid of forced draught, produced iron of much better quality. These blast furnaces were complementary to Newcomen's engines, for not only did they provide iron for their construction, but Darby made use of the engines to provide the blast. Cast iron was now available for such vital components as cylinders, and was used by Newcomen from 1723. The Coalbrookdale principle of making iron by using banks of furnaces and taking it through the smelting, casting and fettling processes was an outstanding technological achievement. Happily Coalbrookdale is preserved as a museum in its own right.

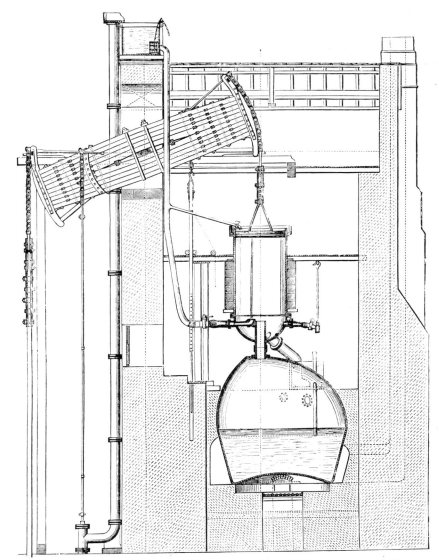

This sectional diagram shows how the atmospheric engine worked within its specially constructed housing. In the cylinder above the boiler, the cold water jet effects condensation, which draws down the beam, raising water as the pump suction rod is drawn up.

Improvements on Newcomen's engines

Although the patent on Newcomen's engine expired in 1733, neither he nor anyone else brought out any major improvements on his basic principle for a considerable time. Improvements based on trial and error were made as more widespread use was made of the engines. There were also considerable variations in their size to suit individual needs, from providing water for stately homes, to pumping it out of the larger coal mines, especially those around Newcastle. Power was dependent on the diameter of the cylinder; one was installed at the Walker Colliery about 1760 with a bore diameter of 74 inches. There were three waterjets to condense the vacuum-making steam, whose production took $6\frac{1}{2}$ tons of coal a day. The pumps were arranged in three lifts to raise water from a depth of 522 feet.

It was about this time that John Smeaton, a civil engineer, began experiments with the atmospheric engine. The many Newcomen-types in use were ponderous, slow-acting machines with only 8 to 10 strokes per minute, and Smeaton believed that greater efficiency could result from smaller-bored cylinders and longer strokes. But his first engine in 1765 proved nothing. Further experiments on the relations between cylinder proportions, power output, and coal consumption pointed the way, and his findings translated into practice resulted in almost doubling the average lift of water. Smeaton went on to explore the properties of the metals used, and found that iron produced by the Darby method had better conduction than the softer, quicker-wearing brass, thus making condensation more rapid within a cylinder. Cast iron thus became standard for cylinders and pipework. But boilers were still made of copper while both brass and copper served for such fittings as cocks and valves. Other inventions to Smeaton's credit were the use of a grooved wheel and chain instead of the direct action rocking beam, and the fitting of a spherical firebox inside a boiler.

Mechanical power had fired the imagination of many others during what might be termed the gestation period of the steam engine proper. Sometimes successful developments were the direct result of past failures, but occasionally an inventor would improve an existing arrangement. For instance, the effective working of a Newcomen engine depended on the alternate opening and closing of two valves; one for steam entering the cylinder, and the other for the condensed steam to escape lest it hinder the returning piston. They required a boy to act as a valve operator, working precisely with the stroke of the engine fourteen times every minute. Lacking, understandably, the necessary concentration over long periods, one bright youth, Humphrey Potter by name, contrived a means of operating the valves by attaching their handles to the rocking beam above. He used string, but when it was seen how effective such automatic valve control could be, metal rods were used and their fitting became a standard practice in engines made by one of Newcomen's actively inventive contemporaries, Henry Beighton of Newcastle.

Beighton and Smeaton were by no means the only men concerned with steam, during its early stages of development. Nor were stationary engines their only interests. As early as 1737 Jonathan Hulls issued a pamphlet suggesting what appeared to be an ingenious but simple means of adapting an atmospheric engine to propel shipping.

But in 1737 there was living an infant, born the previous year, whose genius was later to show to a remarkable degree the imperfections of the atmospheric engine, compared with his own achievements. His name was James Watt.

The properties of steam

This is probably the appropriate point to remind ourselves of the properties of steam. If 1760 can be taken as roughly the date for the start of the Industrial Revolution, it will also serve as one when the pressure of steam by itself was first seen to hold the secret of reliable and economic power. The atmospheric engine had been based on the weight or pressure of the pervading air, amounting to about 15 pounds per square inch. Steam rising uncontrolled from boiling water has no greater pressure than the atmosphere, and it is both dry and invisible until it comes into contact with the air which begins to condense it into the familiar white vapour. Water converted by boiling into steam becomes 1,700 times greater in volume, and a cubic inch of water becomes nearly a cubic foot of steam under normal atmospheric pressure. But given the means of confining steam, its pressure rises with continued boiling of water as its density builds up. And this pressure makes it a potentially explosive force. Securely confined, steam under pressure is elastic and its temperature and its density rise. Not until steam reaches a pressure of 3,650 lb per square inch does it become so compressed as to return to the density of water from which it evaporated.

The upper limit of the explosive force of steam, being entirely governed by the strength of the vessel which contained it, was quite beyond the imagination of those who saw it only as a means of creating a vacuum by condensation. James Watt was not aware of it either, but at least it was he who first made direct use of steam under pressure, even if he came to frown on pressures of more than two or three times that of the atmosphere.

Watt's first design for an oscillating engine.

James Watt and Matthew Boulton

James Watt was born in Greenock, and at an early age showed outstanding qualities in the variety of work he undertook, from instrument-making to dredging and civil engineering. In 1763, when aged 27, he undertook the repair of a model of Newcomen's original engine for Glasgow University, and having done so was struck by its wasteful use of coal and steam. This wastage was due to the use of cold water to condense steam within the cylinder in order to create a vacuum. A year later he had contrived a separate condenser. The cylinder was lagged, and the heat remained concentrated; the piston, working its pump-rods, at once became more efficient, and used much less fuel in relation to the amount of power produced. His sytem represented a radical improvement on the purely atmospheric engine.

Having overcome the bogey of heat loss within the cylinder, Watt set about making demonstration models, prior to obtaining orders for working engines. But within two years he was heavily in debt with no orders to cover his outgoings. In 1767, Dr. Roebuck, one of the founders of the Carron Ironworks near Falkirk, decided to sponsor Watt. This enabled him to develop his engine until it could be secured by patent and this was granted early in 1769 for 'A New Method of Lessening the Consumption of Steam and Fuel in Fire Engines'.

Construction of a full-sized engine was hampered first by inaccurately bored cylinders, but when it was at last built and tested, a saving of 50% in fuel over the Newcomen engine was achieved. Another setback occurred at this vital point so close to success, when Dr. Roebuck was declared bankrupt. But already Watt's fame was spreading, and it so happened that one of Roebuck's creditors was an enterprising engineer named Matthew Boulton, who had not long since expanded onto a new site at Soho, near Birmingham. He realised the value of Watt's patent and discharged Roebuck's debt, in return for the share he had held in it. An agreement was drawn up in 1773, making Watt a partner with Boulton. The engine Watt had built in Scotland was dismantled and he followed it to Soho, to begin work anew in 1774.

By early 1775 Boulton had arranged to have the cylinders bored by one of the new ironmasters, named John Wilkinson, of Bilston in Staffordshire. He was nicknamed 'Iron Mad Wilkinson' and achieved notoriety by making in readiness his own coffin and headstone of iron. The result of his precision boring was that the performance of the engine with its separate condenser was further improved, calling for an extension of the patent. This was effected and it amounted to a monopoly to run for 25 years—until 1800.

In 1776 two of the new breed of atmospheric engines were put to work. One pumped water from the Bloomfield Colliery at Tipton, Staffordshire;

James Watt's engine showing his sun and planet method of obtaining rotative motion on a wheel from the overhead beam. This enabled engines to be used for purposes other than pumping, and with Watt's separate condenser, showed a marked saving in fuel over those of Newcomen.

the other powered the bellows at John Wilkinson's ironworks. They created such interest that the order book became quickly filled, for fuel consumption figures proved that the new engines were much more efficient than the old Newcomen type. Watt had also invented a stroke counter, which accurately recorded the number of strokes made by each engine in a given space of time.

The engines built during the next few years by Boulton and Watt were nevertheless still on the atmospheric principle. Orders came simply because they were so much more efficient and

economic to run than the cumbersome Newcomen and Smeaton engines.

But the very fact of creating a new demand—bearing in mind that industry was beginning to expand—to some extent deflected Watt from other ideas, not only that of making use of pressured steam as the direct means of power, but of widening its scope. He saw the need for engines to do work other than on the vertical plane for pumping. Smooth, continuous rotative motion became his goal, and one of his early proposals was to have two engines, acting separately on cranks set on the same axis at 120 degrees to each other, with a balanced flywheel to equalise the reciprocating weight of moving metal.

Rotative motion

Watt's two-engine proposal did not materialise, and when in 1782 he could no longer wait to grapple with the problem of rotative motion, he came back to using a single engine to drive a flywheel by means of his novel 'sun and planet' motion, but it is not certain if Watt used it for preference. At that time, the cranked shaft was already an established principle, but a patent by James Pickard, another mechanic, taken out in 1780, was deemed to cover the crank as well. It is believed that Watt decided not to contest Pickard's patent, and in any event he considered his 'sun and planet' was now more suitable for a single-acting engine than was a crank, because it allowed double the speed of the flywheel as compared with that allowed by a crank for the same piston-stroke.

There was a demand for the single-acting engine with power transferred to the flywheel by the 'sun and planet' method until about 1800. But in March 1782 Watt had patented his reciprocating double-acting engine. The problem of achieving an equal thrust during each half revolution of the flywheel was solved. Instead of relying on the atmosphere to push the piston down into the vacuum, he closed the cylinder at the top as well and invented a system of valves which allowed steam to act as the prime mover both up and down. Steam was admitted so that it forced the piston both up and down alternately, applying power to the piston rod. And with a 'head' of steam there was available a power far beyond any previously conceived. It was a force as smooth as it was regular, consistent with the motion of the crank and the valve rods which opened and closed valves alternately to inject steam and to exhaust it after the completion of each stroke.

The governor

The reciprocating double-acting engine was one of James Watt's greatest achievements. It was a vital step towards automation that led him to invent the 'governor'. This was a device whereby the steam admitted to the engine was governed in keeping with the speed and power required. Rotating balls on a vertical spindle were fixed to the rod which regulated the flow of steam to the cylinders. Increased speed of the engine resulted in centrifugal force widening the range of the governor balls which had the effect of throttling the steam inlet. This device was used for the whole of the steam era for stationary engines. It led to considerable fuel saving, and avoided the risk of an engine going out of control. Watt himself, however, was more pleased with his other invention to improve the double-acting engine. This was a system of 'parallel motion' which enabled a better connection to be made between the piston rod and the beam above.

By 1788 Boulton and Watt had embarked on the relatively large-scale production of double-acting engines. They varied in size according to need, to drive not only pumps, with greater efficiency than ever before, but also to power machinery of many types, including those for the vast new buildings being erected, which were to be dubbed in years to come the 'dark satanic mills' of the Midlands and North. By the time Watt's patent expired in 1800 Boulton and Watt had built about five hundred engines, most of which were of the double-acting type. These figures were however insignificant by comparison with the numbers built in the first half of the 19th century. Others, inspired by Watt's great invention, saw potentialities in steam that were well beyond his range of vision. Steam made Britain the most industrialised nation on earth, and for a time the wealthiest in the material sense. It also brought with it, unsuspectedly at the time, the most profound sociological changes in the life of the nation.

It would be giving a false impression to infer that James Watt was the only pioneer of his time concerned with steam power. His contribution was sufficiently outstanding in a historical sense to put his name on record as the most renowned. But without detracting from his achievements, it should be noted that he was a specialist in one type of steam engine, to provide power for industry, principally for mills and mining. It may well have been his success in partnership with Matthew Boulton that made him less expansive in his ideas as he grew older. He was for example convinced that high-pressure steam was quite unnecessary for efficiency, as if to suggest that his engines could not be improved upon, at least by a means which involved greater risks from explosion. There are no records of any of his engines exploding through faulty manufacture, for they were constructed massively and precisely to perform safely the work for which they were intended.

While it remains a matter of conjecture as to why Watt stuck rather rigidly to his own speciality, the fact of his success is clear enough. Watt was financially secure. This naturally made a vast difference to his outlook at a time when inventors were beginning to appear with novel but sometimes preposterous ideas for using the new-found source of power more widely.

One of these was William Murdock, another Scot and one of Watt's assistants. He made a model steam locomotive with a boiler heated by a spirit lamp but, perhaps dissuaded by his master, his idea never became a reality. Watt may well have believed that steam had no application other than for industry, because for transport an engine would have to be of much lighter construction, too light no doubt for the safe confinement and control of steam, and for the uneven tracks that passed for most roads in his day. For much the same reason he probably frowned on the use of steam for waterborne traffic; but nevertheless, by the time he died in 1819, others had to some extent succeeded in overcoming the main problems of steam-powered transport.

Crofton pumping station was built in 1809 to pump water to the summit of the Kennet & Avon Canal. The original Boulton and Watt engine was joined in 1812 by a second larger engine (being oiled in photograph). In 1846, the first was replaced by a Sims combined cylinder engine (foreground) with two pistons. Both the present engines can be seen, restored to working order by the Crofton Society, on special 'steam' days.

2

STATIONARY ENGINES

Low pressure– high running cost

The year 1800 marked the end of Boulton and Watt's patent and of their virtual monopoly of the condensing steam engine. Large numbers were in use by then but the market was still expanding, which could not yet be exploited by others. Matthew Murray of Leeds was at work producing engines of sound, exact construction on the Watt pattern and in time surpassed him for workmanship, especially by using improved material. But both Watt's and Murray's engines, ponderously reliable though they were, had reached the limit to which such low pressures could profitably develop. Pressures of 5 or 6 p.s.i. (pounds per square inch) had the merit of safety, but such engines were costly to install and their fuel consumption was still high in relation to their power.

The real reason for Watt's hostility to higher pressure is not on record, but it is safe to assume that in his success his inventiveness had become submerged in steady profits.

Trevithick and high pressure steam

The outstanding young engineer of the time, with no inhibitions whatever, was Richard Trevithick. His first high-pressure engine, departing from Watt's principles, had its vertical cylinder

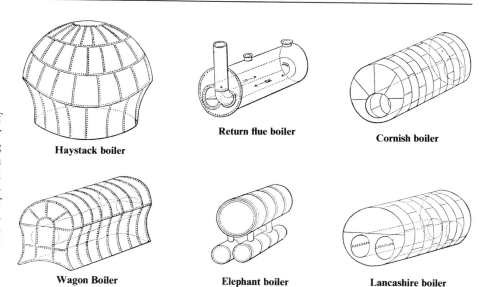

Haystack boiler **Return flue boiler** **Cornish boiler**

Wagon Boiler **Elephant boiler** **Lancashire boiler**

Boilers were made in many, varied designs (above), some so extraordinary they were even dangerous, such as the elephant boiler. The most common and most effective in industrial use was the Lancashire type. Below is the face plate of the No. 2 Lancashire boiler at Crofton pumping station.

sunk into a horizontal cylindrical boiler; it was installed for winding at Cook's Kitchen tin mine in Cornwall. He went on to use a cylindrical high-pressure boiler for a road engine in 1801. This met with some success, and similar boilers were used for self-contained semi-portable engines, for rolling iron plate and powering small mills. Misfortune came when the boiler

of one of those working at Greenwich exploded in 1803, but it was later proved that the calamity was not due to faulty boiler construction, as was put about at the time, but because the safety valves had been fastened down.

Trevithick's cylindrical boiler had suffered a set-back, yet it was the basis of what became the famous 'Cornish boiler' and a radical improvement on

those used by Watt and Murray. Their boilers were developed from the 'haystack' type employed for atmospheric engines, rounded in shape, with a dished bottom and the fire grate beneath. Watt's was called the 'wagon' type—like a 'haystack' cut in half and elongated, with straight sides and domed top. In both types the fire heat played on the boiler surfaces, but Watt's larger boilers had a central flue to provide extra heating surface. In contrast, Trevithick's boiler was cylindrical with a large central flue; hot gases were then led back along the boiler sides before being allowed to escape up the chimney.

This was the boiler, in hammered iron plate, which was installed for pumping in the Wheal Prosper mine at Gwithian, Cornwall, in 1812. It was so successful that this combination of Cornish boiler, beam engine, and pump became the forerunner of hundreds and was in general use, with further improvements in the course of time, throughout the tin-mining region. Many were built in Cornwall, with the Hayle firm of Harvey becoming prominent. Some engines outlasted the industry itself, and the last was overhauled and recreated for further use as late as 1924. A few have been preserved, and many of the tall engine houses can still be seen in Cornwall.

Trevithick himself was a temperamental genius. Soon after his successes both in Cornwall and with his railway engine he surprisingly sailed off to South America—and obscurity. Many years later he came back to Cornwall, where he died in poverty in 1833.

The main reason why beam engines had such a record for longevity was that the working parts were in perfect equilibrium, with the vertical cylinder directly under one end of the beam and the pump under the other. The slow steady thrust on each rod caused minimal wear, even on those connected to a crank and flywheel, as many were. These factors, however, together with their overall size, limited their use for all but the larger concerns in industry, and smaller works and factories were calling out for smaller, faster-working engines.

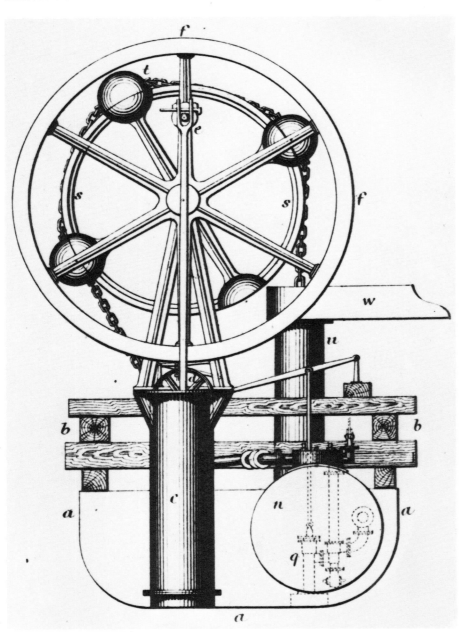

Trevithick's chain and ball pumping engine showed his ingenuity, but in overcoming some of the disabilities of smooth running by this means, other faults appeared, to hinder further development on these lines.

New designs

In 1807 Henry Maudslay patented the 'table' engine to cater for this demand. The beam was discarded, but the vertical cylinder was retained, with an arrangement of return connecting rods for the crankshaft drive. This much smaller engine was quite capable of driving factory and workshop machinery by means of lineshafting fitted with pulleys and belts where needed. An off-shoot of Maudslay's model had by this time been patented by Phineas Crowther of Newcastle as a winding engine for pit-head work in the surrounding coalfields. His too was a vertical engine with the crankshaft above the cylinder, and it became the standard type for winding, until much later when James Nasmyth reversed the cylinder position so that it was above the crankshaft.

Although the first direct-acting horizontal stationary engine was produced in 1801, the design found little favour until Taylor and Martineau in 1825 began building them as mill engines. Even then, they met with a limited demand because the weight of the piston wore the underside of the cylinder, making the bore oval. This fault however proved to be more imaginary than real, and very soon it was observed that both railway and marine engines with horizontal cylinders were not wearing unduly.

These basic forms of the stationary engine had been produced before 1850, and if not all were developed to the limits of their capacity for economic and efficient power by that date, those which were built later included some magnificent examples which were so eminently in keeping with the Victorian era of flamboyant inventiveness.

The engine house as the seat of power was an integral part of a new mill or factory. Some engines indeed required to be 'house built' and strategically placed with walls and floors specially constructed to take the weight and absorb the thrust. Such was the importance of these steam engines to production, that engineers, both as

The table engine was developed by Henry Maudslay in 1807 as a compact workshop power unit. It was easily operated and proved lasting. The single vertical cylinder was mounted on a table-like platform over the crankshaft. This model of Maudslay's engine can be seen in the Science Museum, London.

19

suppliers and tenders of engines, were in a special category in relation to the management of the concern. This was not surprising, because the output of the factory or mill and its profitability, as well as the livelihood of a large workforce, depended very much on those whose job it was to keep the engines running.

Social effects

The sociological effects of the Industrial Revolution, centred on the steam engine, were profound. Some of these have already been mentioned, including the drift of population from rural to urban life. Steam-powered mills and factories demanded and attracted labour and such labour had to be housed near places of work. So there came to be built the row upon row of back-to-back terraced houses in the shadow of the 'dark satanic mills' and their smoke-belching chimneys. All this has been well documented, but apart from the strangled life-style of the mass of workers, the child labour and other evils, there was scant regard paid to elementary hygiene. Domestic water supply and sewage disposal were woefully neglected until recurring outbreaks of cholera during the first half of the 19th century emphasised a serious omission on the part of the developers.

Steam was used to remedy a hazardous situation which its introduction in the first place had brought about. The authorities tackled the problem of inadequate and often polluted water supplies, both to existing large population centres such as London, and the North, using wells or reservoirs for clean water. Pumps of many kinds, all steam-powered, were installed, both for raising water and for sewage disposal. Their use made possible a healthier workforce, whose individual expectancy of life in 1850 had averaged little more than 40 years, for babies who survived their first year.

The demand for labour, due partly to the short life-span of workpeople and partly to the competition offered by the widespread employment of domestic servants, railway navvies and those needed for pipe-laying and reservoir building, in addition to house and factory building, could all be traced to the introduction of the steam engine. The paradox is that the steam engine was first employed as a means of saving labour. It was not until after

Left: Classic styles creating an impressive atmosphere of power at Blists Hill.

Below: The Beamish colliery winding engine (1855) had a vertical single cylinder which dispensed with the more usual beam as the winding drum was placed directly above the cylinder. It did however necessitate the unusually tall engine house.

the mid-century that some kind of balance began to take place, whereby steam became more of a servant so that many of those who worked could enjoy a greater freedom to travel for pleasure, behind the steam engines of the railways.

It is probably true to say that George Stephenson's success in building railway locomotives was largely due to the pioneering work done by Trevithick. Higher pressures had become safe and effective, with more strongly-built boilers; the 50 p.s.i. at which most Trevithick engines worked, was also that of the *Rocket*. By the same means of experiment and learning from others—higher pressures became slowly more acceptable to the more open-minded boiler makers.

The first compound engines

The 1830s was a period of many an experiment, both in working economies and the design of more efficient engines. One of the most important developments was that of compounding. This came out of experiments by Jonathan Hornblower, who as early as 1781 had turned Watt's condenser into a separate cylinder, in which steam could be used a second time before being condensed. Although it was not a success as a means of gaining extra power, due to lack of pressure, it paved the way in 1804 for Arthur Woolf to use higher pressure steam in a second cylinder. This was at Meux's brewery in London, and having learned by trial and error more about the expansive properties of steam, he gained a limited success as a builder of compound engines, once the twin cylinders had

Semi-portable engines were used where a permanent installation was not necessary but the work was likely to be of long duration. This highly efficient compound condensing engine was built in 1915 by Robey & Co. and is still in use at Hollycombe House, Hants.

been correctly proportioned. The principle of compounding is to allow high-pressure steam into one cylinder, and then to use it again to power a larger one at a lower pressure.

Generally the larger installations at work by 1840 were still of low-pressure engines. Having once invested heavily, owners were loath to make expensive changes. Few of the early engines worked at more than 10 p.s.i. or ran at more than 25 r.p.m. (revolutions per minute) because neither engine nor boiler were constructed strongly enough for speed, or for the high pressures which compounding required to be effective.

William McNaught hit on the idea of adding a small high-pressure cylinder on the crank side of the beam at a point where undue stress on the beam would be avoided. He then introduced boilers with higher pressure, so that his engines worked as compound by using both cylinders to give an increase in power and economy. McNaught had concentrated on the Cornish beam engine; later his new machines were compounds with cylinders side by side, and the system then spread for use on engines of other types. It worked especially well for stationary engines, because it enabled steam to be fully expanded and to give up all its force.

Compounding made for more economic working, but it also involved engines having more complicated valve systems. The 1840s saw the beginning of a period when engine types of proved reliability came in for maximum development in terms of power and capacity. The Cornish boiler was standard for large installations, and the newer Lancashire boiler, with its dual flues and tubes, proved to be a useful variation; with subsequent improvements it came to be preferred to the Cornish type. Installing their boilers, engineers became architects as well, with custom-built boiler and engine houses. Inside these lofty and sometimes ornate buildings they built engines to the goddess steam of awesome beauty and complexity, giving vent to the Victorian age's genius for artistic yet functional craftsmanship. The crudities of the

18th-century engine-house however had given way to architectural sophistication, as from bare branch to foliage. Very few of these superb examples of engineering art exist today. Some buildings may have outlasted their enormous engines because they were still capable of holding the more compact high-speed units—steam, diesel or electric—which progress demanded should replace them. Such replacements mostly came well after 1900, even though the original engines were far from being worn out.

It was mainly the public utility companies and authorities who could house their engines in splendour. Many Victorian installations were relatively plain. Engines installed for land drainage worked in purely functional houses—because the drainage authorities depended on what farmers could pay.

Draining the Fens

As a boy, in the Fens of Cambridgeshire, I spent many an hour watching the local pumping engines at work, fascinated by the slow silent movement of piston, beam, cranks and flywheel, which gave power to the scoop paddle wheels outside, lifting water from dyke to river level at flood time. Fen and marshland drainage had relied for nearly two centuries on windmills with paddles. Those with a lift of only a few feet often became ineffective (apart from the vagaries of the wind) since the peaty soils shrank after their release from water. A lowered drainage level from this cause could scarcely be met other than by installing more windmills—at a cost beyond the re-

sources of most farmers. The advent of steam was therefore a godsend to large areas of low-lying land, liable to drown. As a tribute, one engine house in the Fens near Littleport carries an inscription:

The Fens have oft times been by water drown'd
Science a remedy in water has found
The powers of steam she said shall be employ'd
And the destroyer by itself destroyed.

Two beam engines, one installed in 1819 and the other in 1830 in this drainage area of 26,000 acres, took over from eighty windmills with much greater effect. They began with paddle scoops of 43 feet in diameter, but as the improved drainage made the land shrink, they were later to increase to 50 feet. Such Fen pumping engines have been preserved at Stretham near Ely,

and Pode Hole near Spalding. But these are small in comparison to such wondrous monsters as those at Kew Bridge Pumping Station, which happily have also been preserved.

Although by 1850 Britain was producing, both for internal and export sales, far more engines than any other nation, others were becoming increasingly active. Not that foreign competition was considered a serious threat when British products were so far ahead. But competition there was, if only on the part of individual engineers with open inventive minds, and it was in America that George Corliss brought out a novel valve system which gave much better speed control, where not more than 80–100 r.p.m. was required. After seeing one exhibited at the great Paris Exhibition of 1867, several British firms began to make Corliss-valve engines, and they

were widely used in industry until well after 1900.

The Corliss-valve engine was only one of many horizontal stationaries in use for factories. Such engines were also capable of driving centrifugal pumps which were coming in for both drainage and for water supplies where no great output was required.

Centrifugal pumps, especially of the Gwynne type, gave a considerable boost to British engineers in the second half of the 19th century. Gwynne became contractors for dock drainage and irrigation installations, both at home and abroad. Generally simple horizontal or vertical engines were used, with the pumps connected directly to the crankshaft. One large irrigation contract was carried out near Ferrara in Italy and drained 200 square miles of swamp.

Drainage works undertaken in Holland enabled over 40 million gallons of water a day to be pumped, while for the Middle Level in the English Fens, Gwynne pumps raised water 11 feet into the tidal Ouse at the rate of 2 million gallons a day with steam as power. Worthington-Simpson was another famous name in this field.

For such vital work, duplication was very necessary. The breakdown of an engine could be disastrous, so it was the rule for practically all drainage works to have at least two engines, and three or more boilers. These generally worked alternately to maintain a reliable output, but in times of flood two could be brought into service.

Another large firm specialising in steam pumps was Easton, Amos and Henderson. They adopted the Appold centrifugal pump for land drainage, and evolved a patent design of engine and pump combined over a well-head. An example built in 1870 has recently been re-erected at Bressingham Steam Museum. Their range of products widened to include marine engines and, later on, steam generating plant for electricity.

A cleanly designed and well laid-out tandem compound condensing engine by William Philip of Kirkcaldy, with the flywheel sheeted over for clarity when being photographed.

Mill engines developed

As an indication of the great variety of stationary engine types developed up to 1900, Mr. George Watkins' book *The Stationary Steam Engine* contains 100 illustrations and describes 52 types. His later books cover an even wider field and are of great value to those interested in this fascinating aspect of the steam age. Volume I of *The Steam Engine in Industry* lists, describes and illustrates a further 100 engines for water supply, sewage disposal, land drainage, gas and electricity supply, docks, tunnels and use in ships. He also lists over 50 firms who built the engines described. Mr. Watkins has also published two similar books on mill engines.

Quoting Mr. Watkins' earlier book, the cross compound horizontal engine should be mentioned here as becoming the standard type for the textile mills of Lancashire and Yorkshire, in the prosperous days when every mill was powered by steam. This engine was in fact made in so many sizes that it could serve almost every industry. Robeys of Lincoln built them small enough to rate a mere 12 h.p., whilst Hicks Hargreaves went up to 4,000 h.p. As compounds, the smaller high-pressure cylinder was laid on a separate bed from the low, which was twice its diameter; each had its own

The interior of an underground boiler house for a colliery winding engine at Bargoed, South Wales.

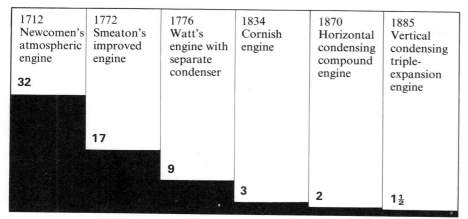

1712 Newcomen's atmospheric engine	1772 Smeaton's improved engine	1776 Watt's engine with separate condenser	1834 Cornish engine	1870 Horizontal condensing compound engine	1885 Vertical condensing triple-expansion engine
32	17	9	3	2	1½

Pounds of coal per horsepower per hour

valve gear and was coupled to its own crank. One or more condensers were below floor level. One of the largest and probably the last cross compound was built in 1914 for the Ace Mill at Chadderton. It had cylinders of 31 and 62 inches bore, a 5 foot stroke, and a central grooved flywheel of 25 feet diameter which weighed 65 tons, and was served by four Lancashire boilers providing steam.

Compounding was one of the means by which fuel economies were made. In the low-pressure era, of Newcomen and Watt, steam had virtually no expansive power, for once the piston movement was served, there was nothing for the steam to do but to condense back to water. But with high pressures, it could still be condensed and returned to the boiler after giving power to two or more cylinders. Triple expansion as a term indicates three cylinders, an engine type which became increasingly used, especially for marine engines which were of course bedded down as stationaries. Even four cylinders on this principle were not unknown, but such engines had to be very compact to conserve the maximum steam pressure possible as the steam passed from one cylinder to the next. Triple expansion was made possible by using cylinders side by side on vertical engines; but for horizontal engines the tandem pattern was often employed by which compounding added power to a single piston rod driven by multiple cylinders and pistons.

Most stationary engines were condensing, by various devices, because this too was a means of fuel economy. The water from condensed steam, returned to the boiler warm or even hot, took less fuel to evaporate into steam again than if it was cold. Some engines had feed-water heaters fitted for this purpose, using heat which otherwise would have been wasted.

The above comparisons for pumping engines show the coal consumption per horse power per hour as proof of progress in fuel economy.

High-speed engines

From about 1880 the vertical condensing triple-expansion engine was in increasing demand for engines to drive electric dynamos. Although for a time this purpose was served by belt drive—from a large flywheel to a small dynamo pulley, to gain the necessary high r.p.m. from low-speed horizontal engines—progress showed the need for direct drive from high-speed engines. The result was the production of totally enclosed vertical engines having two or three cylinders supplied with high-pressure steam. To avoid undue stress, these had a relatively short stroke, and the pistons were, as in the internal combustion engine, activated by steam on one side only of the

piston—a return to the single-acting principle.

The pioneer of this type of engine, with splash lubrication, was Peter Willans, and for a few years after his death at the age of 41 in 1892, large numbers were built till they were rivalled by an improved engine introduced by Bellis and Morcom. They not only went back to double-acting pistons, but used a system of forced lubrication to all moving parts and bearings, including the eccentric rods for the piston valves. Triple expansion halved their steam requirement, and as they were built in several sizes up to 2,900 h.p. they became formidable rivals to the slower working, more traditional types of engines.

The totally enclosed engine bore no visible comparison with its predecessors with exposed moving parts. Its power too, as a high-speed unit, was quite disproportionate to the small space it occupied. One other new type was evolved at about the same time as the Bellis and Morcom. It was the 'Uniflow', working on a principle on which experiments had been made as early as 1827 by Jacob Perkins. His invention made use of steam at the phenomenal pressure of 1,400 p.s.i. on a single-acting cylinder, with exhaust outlets uncovered by the piston at the end of the stroke. In 1881 Leonard Todd went one better with a double-acting engine on somewhat similar lines, but neither inventor met with final success. It was left to a German, Professor Stampf of Charlottenburg, finally to remedy previous constructional faults and introduce the engine anew in 1908. As an economical and compact triple expansion unit, it met with considerable success and over the next 20 years Robeys of Lincoln were among several British firms to build it under licence.

Overleaf: These 75 kilowatt turbine generators at Forth Banks power station are representative of the first generation of turbines built by Charles Parsons. High pressure steam is supplied via the curved pipes on the right, passes through the turbine and exhausts through the large pipe below the turbine housing. The generator driven from the turbine shaft is in the centre left.

Bellis and Morcom triple-expansion engine once used to generate electricity at Llay Hall Colliery, Wrexham. This type of high-speed engine was widely used to generate electricity before the advent of steam turbines.

The steam turbine

The last development in the use of steam for power was that of the turbine. The idea of a direct rotating engine powered by steam was born in the minds of the early pioneers, but it scarcely went beyond dreams for almost a century. Then in 1884 came the real thing, the Parsons turbine and generator to meet the increasing popularity of electric lighting. Charles Parsons, a son of the 3rd Earl of Rosse, was a versatile inventor, but his name remains celebrated for the steam turbine, in spite of his contemporaries working in this field.

To say simply that the turbine was a means of using high-velocity steam as a jet directly onto blades rotating a shaft, takes no account of the many obstacles encountered before trouble-free efficiency was reached. The expansive qualities of steam within the cylinder of a turbine undergo changes which called for many a modification of design. Metal erosion was one of the problems which had to be overcome. It is the velocity of the steam rather than the pressure which gives the power,

and the positioning of steam nozzles, blades and condensing apparatus is of vital importance for maximum power and minimum wastage of steam.

Steam in turbines exerts its greatest power by means of stages, from one bladed rotor to the next, with up to 35 stages in some cases, before the exhaust steam passes to another low-pressure turbine, or into a condenser. One great advantage of turbines over piston engines is that of smooth running at speed. With an even flow of steam there is not that uneven torque, for which piston engines need the provision of secure bedplates. Lubrication is confined to the rotor shaft bearings instead of a multiplicity of moving parts, and some of the exhaust steam if required can be used for heating. Turbines were built for special requirements, of which electricity generating was only one. For centrifugal pumps, gas supply boosters, blowers for iron and steel works and for many other industries, and for shipping, turbines became even more widely used after about 1905.

Tramways and textile mills

This is not to infer that the enclosed reciprocating engines were discarded. Willans, and Bellis and Morcom engines were giving good service, and catered well for the needs of many factories and a variety of public services. Cities often made use of a battery of such engines for their electric tramways. The Birmingham tramways, for example, had enough Bellis and Morcom engines to provide a total of 25,000 h.p. This firm built nearly 10,000 engines all told, of their enclosed forced-lubrication type, ranging up to 2,900 h.p. in the largest units.

The demand for electricity soon became so great that stationary engines of many types were employed, including the more traditional open types with a flywheel drive. Although British manufacturers were mostly able to meet this demand, some imports were made. The generating station for the Mersey Tunnel Railway had three huge vertical engines of 1,650 h.p. each, 27 feet high, with generators 20 feet in diameter, supplied by Westinghouse from America. These were served by nine Sterling boilers with mechanical stokers, to provide 160 p.s.i. to the engines working at 85 r.p.m. This was probably the last large installation of open-type reciprocating engines in Britain, and ran successfully for about forty years.

The patterns into which stationary engines evolved were based almost entirely on the specific primary needs of their users. A type built for one purpose could well be found suitable for another, with the ever-widening demand for steam power. But always there was scope for modification; in the 1840 to 1880 period especially, local requirements were often met by local engineers. This applied especially to such areas as South East Lancashire and the West Riding of Yorkshire, where cotton and wool were basic industries. From George Watkins' book *The Textile Mill Engine* it can be seen that over fifty engine builders were situated in that area. A number of boiler makers also catered for local demand.

A frequent practice was to have two engines connected to a crank-driven shaft at right angles to the stroke, with a massive flywheel in the centre, which often stood 30 feet high and weighed up to 100 tons. The broad rim of the flywheel was grooved to take perhaps sixty stout cotton ropes, for driving (or turning) the intricate system of pulleys and shafting in the mill above where several work-floors resounded to their whirring clatter as further shafts in turn drove the rows of textile machines. In some cases the first drive from the flywheel was transferred by ropes to another large pulley strategically placed. This acted as a distributor, with sufficient ropes at differing angles and lengths to power master pulleys on each floor above. Ropes were found to be cheaper and more reliable than belts for textile mills, where if a single rope broke, there remained others to ensure an uninterrupted drive. The sounds and scenes above were in marked contrast to the smooth, almost silent, running of the great engines below, with only an engineman or two in attendance, keeping them oiled and adjusted, or adding perfection to their splendid gleam of paint and polish.

The boiler house

The boiler house stood nearby topped by its tall chimney. Here the stokers (known as 'fireheaters') had little respite, with two or more boilers to feed, each having two firehole flues. Boilers were bricked in, so that only the face was seen in the wall. On this face were water and steam gauges, and steam pumps chugging away, feeding the boilers with water. The capacity of the boilers was always more than adequate because of their need for periodic servicing and scouring and to supply extra steam for overloaded engines, as they often were when trade was booming.

After 1900, many builders of stationary engines up and down the country closed down for lack of new orders, as turbines, and then electric and diesel power units, came in. But some boiler makers carried on, because steam engines already installed were outlasting their original boilers, and Board of Trade regulations on safety were becoming tighter. Annual reports by inspectors could not be ignored; and if the annual inspection revealed metal wastage, either pressures had to be reduced, or a new boiler had to be installed, if the old one was condemned. Although cases are known of a boiler lasting in service for over fifty years, half that period was the more likely life-span. The cost of boilers varied of course with their size and diameter, but a Lancashire boiler of 1890, 8 feet in diameter and 24 feet long, would then cost about £500.

This brief description of steam power for the textile industries cannot take account of all the variations on the general theme. In the broader spectrum covering other industries, there were even more variations. It would need a very large volume indeed to cover them all. Large concerns often had subsidiary steam engines as well as the mighty power centre, for pumping and for boosting; and some even had a small one to set a large one in motion, to move a single piston off dead centre. The method of starting less massive engines was to have holes in the rim of the flywheel, in which bars could be inserted for levering it into the correct position for the first piston stroke.

Very few industries in the early part of this century had no use for steam power. And because certain basic types of engine were adaptable for a variety of purposes, and because they had such long working lives, there was a considerable market for second-hand units. As an example, one engine built by Guest and Craven Ltd. about 1880 was used in a works near London until 1913, when it made way for something larger and more modern. It was then bought by a sawmill at Boxmoor, Hertfordshire, and consumed waste timber material for fuel. By 1969 it was replaced by electricity, and was bought for re-erection as an exhibit at the Bressingham Museum, where it now stands, restored and in working order. The total weight of this engine is about 30 tons.

As the restoration, transport and re-installation of an engine on a new site costs far more than its scrap value, it is not surprising that very few of the larger stationary engines have been preserved, when many weighed 100 tons or more. Most steam installations were made redundant before 1960; many had given way to diesel or electricity before 1940. Interest in this aspect of industrial archaeology had scarcely begun before practically all the old stationaries had been cut up on site for scrap. Happily there are a few exceptions which have been saved for posterity, in national or municipal museums, or where a band of preservationists has been able to ensure the retention of engines as relics on their original sites. But a few still stand where they were originally installed, forlorn and unseen except by special permission.

In this artist's impression of the Naval Review at Spithead in 1858, the use of steam power is as an auxiliary to wind. The Admiralty were sceptical for many years, one reason being that of fire risk in wooden-hulled ships, the design of which had scarcely changed for 50 years. The success of Cunard and Brunel using iron-plated vessels finally persuaded the Navy to follow suit, but the change-over to steam took many years to complete.

3

MARINE ENGINES

British and French pioneers

The first attempts to use steam power for navigation were made when James Watt was still a baby. In 1737 Newcomen's atmospheric engines were well-established for mining and this was the year in which Jonathan Hulls of Chipping Campden put his idea into practice. His plan was to use the power of steam for towing ships into and out of harbours and ports, where sails were least effective. The difficulty of moving large ships had been apparent for long enough, but Hulls soon found that the Newcomen engine was not very adaptable. His boat was built at Evesham on the river Avon, but no details exist as to how the stern paddle was driven, nor how he managed to place a weighty Newcomen-type engine in a wooden hull. Old artists' impressions have however survived, showing his steam-boat towing a Navy ship of the line, even though it is unlikely that it ever left the spot on which it was built on the Avon. Belated credit was given to Hulls' attempt, and a portrait of him hung in a stateroom of the *Queen Mary* nearly two centuries later.

Steam for waterborne vessels can be taken as the first of the branches from the main trunk in the simile of steam as a tree. Hulls was well ahead of his time in his ideas but to a large extent the link between marine and land-based engines has always been close. Both rank as stationary engines, in the sense that they remain, whether working or not, bedded down to the structures on which they were installed. This section is therefore devoted to ways in which the development of the stationary engine was varied to suit its watery environment.

Jonathan Hulls' failure was scarcely to his discredit, when one imagines how primitive and ponderous the Newcomen-type engines were. Had he been given sufficient backing, he might well have succeeded, but it would have needed a much larger and sturdier hull in which to place an engine than was possible for him to build at Evesham. But it had to be only a matter of time before others grappled with the problem. It is rather surprising that two Frenchmen made the next attempt, contemporaries of Cugnot and his steam road vehicle. Unlike Cugnot, Comte d'Auxiron and Chevalier d'Eollenai, two artillery officers, had the backing of higher authority, and they decided to use the Newcomen basic design for the engine. Their vessel was built on the Isle des Cygnes on the Seine, and after its launching in 1772, a brick foundation was built in the hull. The boiler and engine were hoisted into position and all was well at the end of the day. But when the workers returned next morning, the boat had sunk to the bottom.

The ignoble end of this venture did not deter others. Steam power, new in France, appealed to many. Jacques Perier, a leading engineer, having failed with a small low-powered steam-boat, made a steam fire-engine beside the Seine which people flocked to see in operation. The young Marquis de Jouffray was among the spectators and decided to build a steam-boat on the river Doubs near Besançon. Having studied how waterfowl propelled themselves, he centred a series of paddles on each side of his 40-foot boat powered by a two-cylinder engine, working on the Newcomen principle. But this too was a failure.

His next effort, with d'Eollenai's assistance, was based at Lyons, and he reverted to using paddle wheels. Having learned of James Watt's recent invention of the double-acting engine, he copied it, placing it on a horizontal plane. It operated a ratchet system for driving the paddles. Jouffray gave the vessel the name of *Pyroscaphe*, and when it steamed, in July 1783, it became the first vessel ever to move against a current under its own power. His success was the subject of weighty consideration by the Commission des Savants, but his hopes of forming a company were finally thwarted. It was not until the French revolution had passed that he was able to try again; but by then others had forged too far ahead for success to come for his ratchet-drive boat.

Success in Scotland

During the years of Jouffray's trials and errors, there was no significant activity in the same field of development across the Channel. But up in Scotland William Symington and Patrick Miller had joined forces to build a steam-boat. Symington was a practical engineer and Miller a man both of means and of ideas. His first small steam-boat was successfully tried out in 1785 on Miller's estate at Dalswinton in Dumfries-shire. From this experiment came Miller's notion of a vessel with twin or triple hulls, with rotating paddles between them. He employed thirty men to drive them by means of a capstan, and it was to

The Charlotte Dundas was built as a single paddle-wheel tugboat in 1802 for the Forth and Clyde Canal Co. On her first trial she towed two loaded sloops of 70 tons each and transported them 19½ miles in six hours, against a head wind. Unfortunately the canal company decided her wash was eroding the banks and she was taken out of service.

replace the waste of manpower that he commissioned Symington, who though only 24 had already been granted a patent for an improved form of atmospheric steam engine, to design a power plant. Symington's engine, having a separate condenser, was in fact an infringement on Watt's patent, which in that year, 1788, had another 12 years to run.

Miller's capstan-drive twin-hulled boat had been tried out on the Firth of Forth, but the steam-powered trial with a smaller version took place on Miller's Dalswinton Lake. Spectators included the steam engineer Alexander Nasmyth and Robert Burns, who was one of Miller's tenants. Although the little boat achieved about five miles per hour, Miller was not satisfied with its rather complicated drive mechanism of chains, drum and pulleys.

A second trial with a larger boat and engine designed by Symington was made late in 1789 on the Forth-Clyde canal, but still the method of driving the paddles proved faulty.

In desperation Symington approached James Watt through a mutual friend, and in supplying details of his engine inadvertently revealed that

Watt's own patent was being infringed. Having already gone to the courts several times to protect his interests, and having no sympathy whatever for any other use of steam power than his own, Watt issued a stern warning which Miller could not ignore. Symington at the time had no other type of engine to offer and Miller abandoned all experiments with steam. This left Symington without a financial backer, and for a few years he too had to seek other outlets for his ingenuity.

The Charlotte Dundas

At last, in 1800, Watt's stranglehold on development based on his patents came to an end and Symington immediately took advantage of it. In the following year he took out a patent for a new design for driving a paddle wheel, and ordered a new ship, 56 feet long, with a beam of 18 feet, to be built at Grangemouth by Alexander Hurt. It was a tugboat designed for the

important Forth-Clyde Canal and was named *Charlotte Dundas*, after the daughter of Lord Dundas, a director of the canal company. This was just the opportunity Symington had been waiting for and if the boat was a success it would be a boon to the canal operators.

Using the best features of the Watt engine, he placed the 10 h.p. double-action single cylinder of 22 inch diameter on the port side of the deck, and the boiler on the starboard to equalise the weight. The condenser was fitted below deck along with an air-pump operated from a bell crank attached to the engine's crosshead.

This steam engine did not differ greatly from Watt's standard model but Symington now had had more experience in overcoming the problems of the drive, and this time he solved it simply by using a guided piston rod, with its connecting rod linked directly to a crank attached to the shaft of the single stern-mounted paddle wheel. This arrangement was so simple and effective that it became universally adopted as the drive for all subsequent paddle-wheel steamers, whether they were single stern-wheelers, or the side-wheel paddlers which became standard in Britain for over a century.

As a steam-boat the *Charlotte Dundas* was a success. It towed two barges a distance of 19½ miles against a strong head wind in six hours. But just when Symington appeared all set for a splendid career, misfortune struck. The Duke of Bridgewater, who had been so prominent in the development of the canal system, died suddenly in 1803. The order for eight tugboats similar to the *Charlotte Dundas* for canal use, which the Duke had recently placed, had to be cancelled. At about the same time the Forth-Clyde Canal Company became alarmed at the damage to their canal banks from the wash of the vessel's paddles, and decided to take it out of service. The *Charlotte Dundas* languished in a canal creek for fifty years and was finally broken up in 1861. Symington lost heart, and he died a disappointed man in 1831.

Developments in America

The reason why so little development of marine engines took place in England during the Miller-Symington period in Scotland is not easy to understand. As the leading maritime nation, it is surprising that no-one attempted to use steam for larger ships, but one can imagine that the notion would have appeared preposterous to such devotees of sail as Nelson, and the directors of the East India Company. Long-distance voyaging with a 'fire' engine assisting sail in wooden ships could scarcely have made a great appeal. But steam did appeal to the Americans along the Atlantic coast, with its great rivers and estuaries where waterborne traffic had every advantage and where a road system was virtually non-existent compared with that in England and France. Whatever the reasons for lack of development in England, there was ample incentive for the New Englanders and others down the coast to go in for steam navigation.

Robert Fulton's name has often been paired with that of George Stephenson as being the respective progenitors of the steam-boat and the railway locomotive. But both men had the good fortune as well as the sagacity to make full use of the experience of others who pioneered before them. This was especially true of Robert Fulton, who began a steam-boat service on the Hudson River in 1807 with what was later known as the *Clermont*. Ever since 1785 other Americans had been experimenting with steam navigation. John Fitch and James Rumsey had made considerable advances, even if real success eluded them in their separate endeavours. Although both had made attempts to adapt Watt's principles they were handicapped by lack of skills in the manufacture of components. Rumsey's ideas included the possibility of using a forced water-jet under the surface as a means of propulsion, while Fitch tried out a steam-operated series of paddles, six-

a-side, based on the way in which Indians paddled their canoes. In 1790 Fitch advertised a passenger service, using a steam-boat of a more conventional paddle design, between Philadelphia and Trenton, New Jersey. But for lack of custom it was withdrawn after one summer season.

Other names of pioneers were Nicolas Roosevelt, Samuel Morey, John Stevens and Robert Livingston, who was Fulton's principal backer. As well as having the benefit of their experiences, he also avoided the setbacks and disappointments of such pioneers as Rumsey and Fitch by studying developments in Europe, including those undertaken by Symington. He was influenced by Trevithick's originality, and found that, with James Watt having retired, his two sons were much more forthcoming and informative.

Fulton's success was therefore the result of making full use of what represented the most up-to-date steam techniques which could be used for his own purpose. And because Boulton and Watt's beam engines were of proven reliability, he had one shipped over from England for his new vessel on the Hudson River. The *Clermont* afforded a river service 90 miles up to Albany and with its cabins and its ornamentation became very popular. From then onwards, he and other Americans became self-sufficient in both the design and the manufacture of steamers, in what soon became a flourishing maritime industry in America.

Any comparison between the advances achieved by the Americans and the British pioneers should take account of one other factor: apart from the knowledge and equipment exported. Since Britain was at war with France for much of the 1800–1815 period. This served to drain their resources; but as a young nation America was well endowed with incentive and inspiration, and the spasmodic hostilities between the old country and the new in 1812–1814 were no deterrent to American inventiveness. James Watt's views, opposing the use of high-pressure steam, were not set

aside for a long time, however. Americans were content to adapt his type of engine working at under 5 p.s.i. for their steam-boats.

Higher boiler pressure

Richard Trevithick was the leading rebel in favour of higher pressure, and in 1806 an engine of his design working at 40 p.s.i. was installed in a dredging vessel for work on the East Indian Dock on the Thames. Such pressure was unheard of before that time, nor was it exceeded for marine vessels for many years to come, in spite of Trevithick's dredger being used successfully until about 1816. He had, by the way, done away with a separate condenser for this engine and replaced it, because of the high pressure in the boiler, with a water feed pump worked from the motion of the engine. The low-pressure Watt boilers relied on gravity feed from the water supply tank. This was only one of the improvements Trevithick made to remedy the inadequacies of marine boilers and engines before he became a specialist in railway locomotives.

Matthew Murray was another engineer to break out from the restrictions of the Watt engine, after the latter's patent lapsed. His Leeds foundry turned out some first-class work, but he was too far inland to bring marine engines into his orbit to any extent. One boat was however fitted out on a local canal with a steam engine, which ran a river service for a few years from 1813 between Yarmouth and Norwich. A boiler explosion in 1817 brought an abrupt end both to the boat and to the lives of several persons.

The London firm of Woolff and Edwards were better placed for the slowly developing outlets for marine engineering, but for some years the new Woolff compound engine was considered to be of too high a pressure for safety on a waterborne vessel. His patent of 1810 was of great importance, for it was to make use for the first time of the expansive qualities of steam. The unfortunate Jonathan Hornblower had known of it thirty years before, but came up against Watt's monopolising patent and subsequent litigation went against him.

The Watt principle was to condense exhaust steam by cold water in his separate condenser, but Hornblower saw this as wasteful, since once-used exhaust steam of sufficient remaining pressure could be used again. But he took out no patent and when Woolff did so his higher boiler pressure enabled a second, larger low-pressure cylinder to give extra power output to the engine.

Henry Maudslay's factory was close to that of Woolff and Edwards at Lambeth and for a time he con-

centrated on industrial engines, using much improved machine tools, including a screw-cutting lathe and a slide rest. Later, as Maudslay, Sons and Field, the firm became famous as marine engine builders, with Joshua Field as the boiler specialist of great and long-standing renown. But this was in the period when, with England so often at war, and the demand for stationary engines for mining and industry wellnigh insatiable, serious interest in marine engines was lacking. Symington had faded out and only his fellow Scot, Henry Bell, persisted in spite of having no financial backing. Bell knew Symington and how his *Charlotte Dundas* had performed. He had also met and exchanged ideas with Robert Fulton before the latter returned to America to build the *Clermont* and remained in correspondence with him.

Henry Bell and the Comet

Bell was spurned by the British Admiralty when he tried to interest them in steam propulsion for the Royal Navy, with plans based on his own hampered experiments. The Lords of the Admiralty gave him a hearing, but finally concluded that there was no future for steam at sea.

It was the first but not the last time they reached this decision, before they had to admit that there was a future after all.

Back once again on his own slender resources and no less determined to prove his faith in steam, Henry Bell was eventually able to place an order in

1811 for a small vessel with the Port Glasgow shipbuilders of John Wood & Son. He named it the *Comet*, after the sight of Donati's celestial voyager earlier that year. The boiler was ordered from John Napier & Sons' workshop in Glasgow, to cost £27. David Napier, then only 22 years old and destined for fame later in life, installed the boiler in brickwork, with Bell's own design of engine made by John Robertson, also of Glasgow, at a cost of £145. Its one cylinder, of 12½ inches diameter and a stroke of only 16 inches, was adequate for a boat only 51 feet long and of 15 feet beam, including the side paddles, driven by a spur wheel from an overhanging crankshaft which also carried a 6 foot flywheel as stabiliser.

This engine, an important relic, can be seen at the Science Museum in London. At the time the ship first took to the waters of the Clyde, it was expected by some to blow up. After seven years plying between Glasgow and Helensburgh, it was tried out on more open sea and wrecked on a rocky shore a year later. But Bell had already a larger vessel, the *Margery*, built in 1814. The following year it went to sea, assisted by a sail fixed to the 30 foot tall chimney. This idea of Bell's, used also on the *Comet*, was followed by other later builders. After one season plying between London and Gravesend, the *Margery* became the first cross-channel steamer from Newhaven to Le Havre.

Bell's success spurred Henry Maudslay into belated action. His boat was of 50 tons and had a 10 h.p. bell crank engine; but its London–Richmond run abruptly ended when the boiler burst in 1817 near Westminster Bridge.

Passenger services by steam

Doubts as to the value and safety of steam-powered boats may have remained in the minds of those who preferred sail, but in spite of mishaps the new power of the age had caught on as the greatest invention of all time. The derisory epithet of 'butterfly boats', was given to paddle steamers by some; but all the same steamer services began from Greenock to Belfast, and Holyhead to Dublin, and in 1821 the *Rob Roy* of 90 tons inaugurated the Dover–Calais run.

The obvious risk of fire with a boiler aboard a wooden ship was a very real one. As early as 1817 the *Regent*—the first sizeable Thames-built ship—caught fire off Whitstable on its run to Margate, and although the 50 souls aboard were rescued by shore boats, the hull was demolished. This was by no means an isolated case, since both cinders from the furnace and sparks from the chimney were a hazard.

Fire risk was in the mind of Aaron Manby, an ironmaster at Horseley, near Tipton, when he laid the keel of an iron-hulled vessel in 1821. Also in this unorthodox venture was Charles Napier, who later became Admiral Sir Charles Napier. The rivetted plates were ¼ inch thick, and two oscillating cylinders produced 30 h.p. to drive the two 12 foot diameter paddles, giving a speed of 7 knots. The *Aaron Manby* was not only the first iron-plate ship but was virtually the first cargo steamer; she began a direct London–Paris service up the Seine in 1822.

The name Napier was becoming well-known on the Clyde, where shipbuilding was a fast-growing industry. David Napier had installed the *Comet's* engine for Bell, and in 1818 began experimenting with model ships in a special tank, realising that steam paddle ships required a shape of hull and construction different to that needed for sail. He was responsible for the *Rob Roy*, which began the

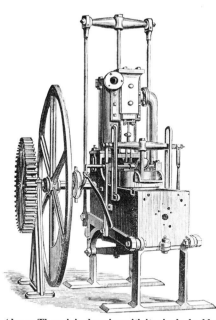

Above: The original engine with its single double-acting cylinder, which Henry Bell designed for the Comet.

Left: The Comet, built in 1812 by Henry Bell, was one of the first successful steam powered boats. She plied for seven years between Glasgow and Helensburgh and although she was eventually wrecked in the Firth of Clyde her engine was salvaged and can be seen in the Science Museum, London.

Dover–Calais service, and built the 150-ton *Robert Bruce* for the Liverpool–Glasgow run, followed by the *Superb* and *Eclipse* of 240 tons, powered by a 35 h.p. engine for each paddle. Another Napier, Robert, had established a high reputation as a leading Clydeside shipbuilder, while on Thames-side another man whose son was to become more famous still was engaged on valuable pioneering work. This was Marc Brunel, an emigré Frenchman, whose son Isambard became a legend for brilliance and versatility. Marc took out several patents, including one for a mechanical stoker, but this last was ahead of its time. He also developed a condenser to recycle fresh water, because sea water left a dangerous encrustation of salt in boilers, a problem with which the new seagoing steamers were confronted.

The Savannah

The year 1819 is historic because it marks the first Atlantic crossing by a ship fitted with steam engines. But the bare fact implies more credit than is due to the paddle schooner *Savannah* and its American owners. It was built for coastal work, and had a single jet-cooled condensing engine with a cylinder of 40 inches diameter and a 5 foot stroke, working as an auxiliary to sail at barely 1 p.s.i. to give a speed of only 4 knots. The *Savannah* was remarkable for having folding paddles; but her owners found custom lacking, and decided to sell the ship in Europe.

With 75 tons of coal and 25 loads of wood on board, but no other cargo or passengers, she set sail for Liverpool. The journey took 27½ days, and although she ran under steam for only 85 hours, her fuel was exhausted before reaching Ireland. No English buyer was interested, and the *Savannah* sailed on to the Baltic and to Russia without finding a buyer; and back she went to America entirely under sail, to be finally auctioned.

The record of the British-built *Rising Star* would probably rank as an epic if it were fully known. This was the first paddle-steamer warship, built on Thames-side in 1820, powered by a 70 h.p. twin-cylinder engine, with two funnels, three masts and twenty gunports. She sailed from Gravesend for Valparaiso via Cape Horn, a voyage which with a stop for repairs took six months. But although it was said she could attain 12 knots, it is not known to what extent steam was used, for as with all the early steamers she was rigged for sail as well.

Engine failure was less of a problem in the early days at sea than that of marrying successfully the dual elements of fire and water in a seagoing vessel. The engines used were the simple and mostly reliable but ponderous beam type; though boiler making had made strides by the 1820s with a better knowledge of metallurgy. Speeds under steam were still generally low, under 10 knots, but coal consumption was high—several tons a day—and there was no space to carry sufficient for long voyages.

For this reason alone, steam was used only when wind for the sails failed. It was not thought necessary to carry water as well, with a limitless supply to pump from, but salt, as Marc Brunel had realised, led to problems—a good example occurred in a ship of 426 tons built by Dukes at Dover in 1825 given the name of *Calpe* and sold to a Dutch firm. It was renamed *Curacao* and set off in 1827 to the South American port of that name, a distance of 4,000 miles. But the engines had to be stopped several times to clean off salt encrustation, and as coal was consumed at the rate of 5 tons per day, the lessened weight raised the water line and made the paddles less effective.

Boilers and salt water

Even more difficult was the voyage to India of the *Enterprise* in 1825. This too was British built, and sailed from Falmouth to Calcutta in 113 days, of which only 64 were under steam because of salt deposits. The coal bunkers were of iron, so that as they emptied they could take on sea water as ballast. To reduce the effects of brine, the boiler was frequently 'blown down' by drawing the fire and emptying the boiler while still under pressure. But de-scaling the hard salty deposit with hand tools caused trouble. The captain and engineer disagreed, one being afraid that hammering or chiselling it off might damage the copper, while the other was more concerned with getting the ship under steam again.

It was the need for such servicing that led builders to install more than one boiler. With a Canadian-built ship, partly owned by Samuel Cunard—another name to become famous—a west–east crossing of the Atlantic was made in 1831, almost entirely under steam. But each boiler had to be desalted every fourth day and the voyage took 28 days. Leaky boilers were another problem in the early days, especially before they had been 'run in' with use. A dodge which persisted throughout the remaining age of steam was to add oatmeal to the water, which on swelling would find its way into leaky rivetted plates or stay-bolts and plug a leak. But where copper was used, a 'weep', as a tiny leak was called, could be stopped by the use of a special tool and a hammer by a skilled boiler-smith or engineer.

The first warship

Mention has already been made of the reluctance of the Admiralty to use steam. The Navy was finally, in 1819, persuaded to try it for towing ships of the line—harking back to the efforts of Jonathan Hulls long before. This followed a previous trial on the suggestion of Sir Joseph Banks, when a Watt engine was fitted to a boat so small as to risk it sinking under the weight. Then, backed by John Rennie and Marc Brunel, a Thames steamer was hired to tow the warship *Hastings* for several miles against the incoming tide. After this performance the Admiralty ordered a steam tug for harbour duty, and then came *H.M.S. Comet*, to be launched at Deptford in 1822. She was of only 238 tons—but was to become the first British steam warship.

Two years later a second ship, *H.M.S. Lightning*, also Deptford built, with twin-cylinder Maudslay engines, was in action against the Barbary Coast pirates. Preserved in the London Science Museum there is a report by one of the *Lightning's* engineers which makes interesting reading, of how repairs at sea were made, and on her performance generally. Although his ship became a veteran, by remaining in service until 1872 with her original engines, during that time no less than four sets of boilers had to be fitted, due to salt encrustation and other stresses.

There was no rush to replace sail with steam in the Navy. Indeed, records show that such a slow conversion was intentional. The Nelson tradition of 'Hearts of Oak' battleships of the line was very strong and it lasted till well past the mid-century. In 1837 the Navy list included only 27 steamers, used mainly as auxiliaries to the main fleet; and an appointment as captain of a steamer carried no prestige whatever. Some steamers acted as despatch and mail packets for the Navy at sea, once it was realised how much faster they were than any sailing ship. One result of having a small section of the fleet propelled by steam was a shore establishment where maintenance work was done and experiments could be made. From this came the invention of the Kingston valve which made 'blowing down' much safer and reduced the frequency of boilers having to be scraped.

Coaling stations

Another outcome of the increasing use of steam generally was the setting up of coaling stations on regular routes. In due course they became worldwide. Specially built 'colliers' carried shiploads of coal, to be offloaded at the stations by native labourers with baskets, and loaded back again into the bunkers of ships needing fuel replenishment. This need for coal acted to some extent as a deterrent to any very rapid switch from sail to steam, and for a long time steamers were often obliged to revert to sail, either to save fuel or because the bunkers were empty. To refill them at a coaling station was also time-consuming, and when the *Bernice* voyaged from Falmouth to Bombay via the Cape in 1837, 25 of the 88 days she took were spent on coaling at ports en route.

Ships were at that time still being fitted with low-pressure engines, often working at under 5 p.s.i. Fuel consumption was inordinately high in relation to power and speed—one reason why the Navy was against any widespread adoption of steam. They argued that a battle could be lost, or a blockade become a farce, if the ships engaged ran out of coal. When the Royal Yacht Squadron for senior naval officers was formed in 1829, it was decreed that membership must exclude anyone owning a steam-powered vessel of any kind. It was not until 1856 that the rule was relaxed. But Sir John Ross, the explorer, wrote a treatise on the advantages of steam in 1837. He advocated higher pressures and the use of water-tube boilers. But years elapsed before any notice was taken of him or of the forward-looking book in much the same vein written by Commander Robert Otway, R.N., in 1834.

The Admiralty was not entirely to blame for its hostility to steam, until such time as less ponderous steam engines became available. Maudslays hoped objections would be overcome when they produced their new 'Siamese' engine, so called because each pair of duplex single-acting cylinders was placed directly under the drive shaft of the paddle wheel. This made for a much more compact layout, and was patented in 1839. In 1843, this type of engine was used for one of the earliest screw-driven ships, *H.M.S. Rattler*.

Brunel and the Great Western

The 1830s were undoubtedly the years in which steam gained its first real hold, even if the eventual eclipse of sail was foreseen by few if any of the pioneers. It was a decade when commercial interests flourished as never before, with the formation of such shipping concerns as the General Steam Navigation Co., the Peninsular and Oriental, and others—while the railway companies had embarked on steam packet services to Ireland and the Continent. By 1835 Isambard Kingdom Brunel persuaded the Great Western Railway Company to form a subsidiary, the Great Western Steamship Company. He was then engaged to take the railway to Bristol; but he had in fact set his sights on New York, using Bristol Avonmouth as the port of departure. Backed by his friend Claxton, managing director of the new steamship company, work began at Bristol on a ship to be named The *Great Western* for the transatlantic service. It was launched in 1837, having a hull 236 feet long and a beam of nearly 60 feet over the paddles. The engine—with two cylinders, each driving one 28 foot paddle wheel but capable of being coupled together—was a side-lever type built by Maudslays. The cylinders, of $73\frac{1}{2}$ inch diameter with a 7 foot stroke, gave 450 h.p. at 15 strokes per minute, but the pressure was only 5 p.s.i.

All possible refinements had been installed in the belief that Atlantic crossings were a profitable enterprise and in the knowledge that other companies were of the same opinion. The British and American Company was a close rival. Having its own *British Queen* still on the stocks, it hired *Sirius*, a 700-ton cross-channel steamer, to thwart Brunel's *Great Western*. *Sirius* left Cork with forty passengers and 450 tons of coal in April 1838, three days ahead of the date the *Great Western* was due to leave Avonmouth.

But only 3½ hours after the *Sirius* arrived in New York harbour, the *Great Western* steamed in to claim the first official record for the Atlantic crossing, at 15 days 10½ hours. Competition for the Blue Riband, which lasted effectively until the jet aircraft age, had begun.

The first Cunarders

It was now the proven success of steam power at sea that brought Samuel Cunard into the picture. The Admiralty put out a tender for a mail service. Cunard left his business and shipping interests in Nova Scotia, came to England, and secured the contract. With finance to find for the necessary ships, Cunard formed a company which later was to bear his name alone. He placed his orders in Glasgow, where Robert Napier and John Wood were the leading builders. The first of four new ships, each of 1,150 tons, was the *Britannia*, whose speed was up to 10 knots, and by 1841 all four ships were in service to the satisfaction of owners and passengers alike.

Cunard's ships were in the lead for many years. The *Persia* was the fastest ship, holding the Blue Riband from 1856 to 1862. The Great Western Company failed to compete with Cunard and in 1846 dropped out of the race for supremacy. His main rival was Edward Collins, who, backed by the American government in 1849, founded a new line. The first of four new ships, the *Atlantic* of 2,845 tons, clipped 12 hours from Cunard's record. But the *Arctic* was rammed in a fog when in sight of land in 1854, and amongst the 233 passengers were Collins' wife, son and daughter, who were not included in the eighty that were saved. Collins refused to despair, even if Cunard had regained the Blue Riband with the *Persia*. Collins' new *Adriatic* had however a brief spell of glory, not only in speed, but in running costs; but then his company collapsed, due partly to the oncoming American Civil War.

The Great Britain

Brunel's *Great Western* venture had been hampered to a large extent by lack of finance. It had been proved that full success on the Atlantic service could not be achieved by just one ship. A fleet of at least four was needed, and with finances very low, the *Great Western* was sold to the Royal Mail Line.

But Brunel had plans for a ship larger and more powerful than this, using screw propulsion. She was the *Great Britain* and her iron keel was laid at Bristol in 1839. The design was of great longitudinal strength, incorporating Brunel's own bridge building principles, with bulkhead compartments. Due mainly to financial setbacks she was not ready for service until 1846, but after being launched at Bristol was fitted out in the Thames, attracting a stream of sightseers as the largest and most advanced ship to date. But for all Brunel's genius, the *Great Britain* did not pay—mishaps occurred, from a broken propeller, to being run aground and stuck fast off Northern Ireland for nearly a year.

Then the Great Western Company gave up and this remarkable ship was sold. For several years it gave excellent service on the Australian run, but in 1886 was storm-damaged and eventually beached on the Falkland Islands. How, in recent years, the *Great Britain* was towed back to England to become a floating museum at Bristol is an epic in itself.

The Great Eastern

The story of Brunel's greatest achievement in shipbuilding has often been told, and only bare details need be given here. It was born in Brunel's mind as a ship for the growing trade with Australia. His belief was that it had to be large enough to carry all the coal, estimated at over 10,000 tons, for the outward and return voyage. But not even he, as the most forward-looking designer, could visualise steam as dispensing with the need or added advantage of carrying sails as well. So it was that the new ship was designed to be of 692 feet length, of iron construction, and the keel was laid at Millwall on the Thames. Its first name

Preceding page: Launching of the Great Britain at Bristol in 1837 amid scenes of great jubilation. It was 236 ft. long and marked the beginning of the era of sumptuously appointed passenger liners for the Atlantic crossing.

Above: The Clydestream boatworks' Vulcan Foundry with busy riveters. The portable forge in the foreground kept up the supply of red-hot rivets necessary for watertight plating.

was aptly *Leviathan* for no ship of any such size had ever been conceived before. It was to be six times the size of any ship previously constructed and was to have sails, paddles and a rear screw propeller.

Six double-ended water tube boilers served four horizontal direct-action cylinders to produce nearly 5,000 indicated h.p. at 25 p.s.i. These powered the screw. The paddle engines, with four oscillating cylinders of 6 feet 2 inches diameter with a 14 foot stroke, were supplied by four more boilers at 24 p.s.i. Tremendous engineering difficulties had to be met to fulfill the demands for such huge components as were required. The screw itself was 25 feet in diameter, and the paddle wheels 60 feet. It is interesting to note that Brunel had discussions with James Watt and Company before

placing the order for the screw engines with the firm whose founder would scarcely have imagined such a project. They weighed 836 tons.

The trials and tribulations of a project so far ahead of its time took its toll not only of those responsible for its cost, but of its designer. The ship, renamed the *Great Eastern*, was launched on 1858 at Millwall, not without mishap and the loss of one life; and in 1859 Brunel himself died suddenly, from a stroke and kidney disease—a genius who had burned himself out. The *Great Eastern* was not a success as a passenger ship, but later gave several years of good service laying ocean cables far and wide. When this activity came to an end she was used as a floating fair and exhibition on the Mersey, finally to be broken up in 1888. In retrospect the great ship may

have fallen short of Brunel's expectations; but his ideas on design and construction were of great value to future shipbuilders, especially when, forty years or so later, the great passenger liners became the last word in this splendid epoch of development.

British supremacy

Long before the advent of steam navigation, Britain was the leading maritime nation in the world. But when steam came to be used widely, even if only as an auxiliary to sail, it put Britain even farther ahead. As the mills, factories and engineering works produced more goods with the aid of

Left: Human figures are dwarfed by the huge machinery of the paddle engines in this contemporary engraving of the Great Eastern. Hidden below this deck were the boilers, while the massive twin cylinders and crankshaft are seen on the right.

Above: The screw engines of the Great Eastern were of twin cylinders with piston rods direct on to the propeller shaft, from both sides. These ran with a shorter stroke at much higher speeds than for the paddle engines. The man at the spoked wheel on top is controlling speed by manipulating the entry of steam to the cylinder.

Overleaf: A contemporary sketch in The Illustrated London News, 14 November 1857, of the first attempt to launch the Great Eastern. It shows the arrangements on the river side of the ship, and the positions of the barges. Brunel planned two inclined ways, each 120 ft. wide and 120 ft. apart, running beneath her for 300 ft. from the riverbank at an inclination of 1 in 12.

Left: The distinctive shapes of the lofty engine houses can still be seen in Cornwall, though almost all of the tin mines they served are now derelict. A few have been preserved. The engines were of the beam type, used for keeping the mines clear of water, as well as for raising the ore. The example is near Redruth, the principle Cornish mining town.

Below: The interior of an old engine house at Shaw, Lancashire. This served a cotton mill for many years. As a compound steam passed from the smaller cylinder on the left to the larger one on the right, both thus contributing to reciprocal motion on the crankshaft, a single flywheel seen at the far end of the building.

Right: The magnificent Cornish engine, now at Kew Bridge Pumping Station, is the largest beam engine still in steam in the world. Once used to drain Cornish tin and copper mines at the rate of 472 gallons per stroke, this engine was built in 1846 by Sandys, Carne & Vivian of Copperhouse Foundry, Hayle, Cornwall. The cylinder diameter is 90 inches and the beam weight 35 tons.

steam power, so the steam-driven merchant navy expanded to boost export trade to less favoured, less industrial countries. The Great Exhibition of 1851 served to proclaim the supremacy of Britain as the workshop for the world.

The mid-century was also a period of colonial expansion, with England usually a jump ahead of her main rival, France. Even where such countries as Spain already had large overseas possessions, they were industrially backward and the door was wide open to British exports. It was not surprising that a great upsurge in shipbuilding also took place, not only for the British export-import trade, but for new ships ordered by foreign buyers. And if some foreigners were inclined to be jealous, and others were inclined to resist the imposition of the Pax Britannica, there was the great British Navy always ready to enforce it, and guard the nation's interest.

Although in 1860 the number of steamships, with a growing proportion built of iron instead of wood, was steadily increasing, they were still in a minority, due to the vast increase in overseas trade and the number of sailing ships still needed for it. This was the heyday of the tea clippers, to be followed by that of the grain ships, and in 1860 there was still only one steamship to five under sail; it was another twenty years before parity was reached.

Those who manned the sailing ships were steeped in the techniques of sail, based on centuries of experience. The new steam men had no such advantage, nor had they much benefit from the scanty research into the properties and inherent dangers of this mighty power. There was no organised research into engineering until after the mid-century. Nearly all the firms engaged in shipbuilding began and continued with the application of steam on an *ad hoc* basis, and made progress by experiment, trial and error. And errors were sometimes fatal. A boiler explosion could sink a ship; and those that did acted as a brake on the development of higher steam pressure, which in turn would have made steamships more economic.

Research and technology

The Institute of Naval Architects was formed in 1860, and was followed four years later by the Royal School of Naval Architecture and Marine Engineering in London. In Glasgow, William Thomson, later Lord Kelvin, and Professor Rankin had been at work for a few years, so that building on the work of such pioneers as Carnot, Rumford, and Davy, the mid-century researchers were making authoritative information available to the engineers and craftsmen who could then rely much less on trial and error. This new knowledge spanned all aspects of engineering and science from metallurgy to thermodynamics. On a humbler yet equally important level, Joseph Whitworth was improving and standardising nuts, bolts and screws.

Compounding—the use of exhaust steam from a high-pressure cylinder to power a second, lower-pressure cylinder, took hold in earnest during the 1860s. The new P. & O. ship *Mooltan* of 1861 was fitted with John Elder's patent engine, which showed a fuel saving of over 30%. By 1866 the company had ten such vessels, which gave a decided fillip not only to compounding for smoother and more economic running, but to the acceptance of the higher pressures which compounding required. Superheating (see Chapters 4 and 12) was another improvement but brought the disadvantage of greater cylinder wear from the dryness of steam so treated. Teething troubles occurred with other newly introduced auxiliary equipment, which acted as a brake against its more widespread use until the necessary modifications were made.

Elder's success with compounding led to the Admiralty holding trials in 1865, as they had previously to test screw propulsion. A race took place, with the compound-engine ship being 120 miles nearer to the finish at Madeira than those with the single-expansion engines, although all three ran out of coal at about the same time.

This and other trials eventually confirmed Lord Kelvin's and Rankin's advocacy of higher pressures, and by the 1870s new Navy ships were running at 70 p.s.i., with 74 r.p.m. on the propeller shaft, giving a speed of nearly 15 knots.

Steel hulls and greater power

The first steel-hulled ships in the Royal Navy came off the stocks in 1876–78. They were the *Iris* and the *Mercury*, and were remarkable for having duplicate screws and duplicate sets of engines, with a total of 8 cylinders. They produced 7,735 h.p. at 62 p.s.i., and gave a top speed of $18\frac{1}{2}$ knots. The twin-screw ships had shown their advantages during the American Civil War, which brought orders from the Confederates for fast blockade-runners. This had led to the practice of having separate engines for each shaft, and to a more economic use of engine-room space, as one of the effects of compounding. The duplex cylinders of each engine were more compact in relation to the power they produced, with their direct drive onto the propeller shaft.

It was the widespread adoption of compounding in the 1870s and 1880s which hastened the steamship's predominance over sail. There were other factors, such as the opening of the Suez Canal in 1869. The trade route to India and the Far East had been via the Cape of Good Hope, which was arduous and costly to fuel-carrying steamers, but favourable to sailing ships, Suez was a much shorter route, but not one which sailing ships could easily use. Now compound-engined steamships could carry less coal and more cargo, needing no more than two stops at coaling stations on their way via the Canal to the East.

By 1860 iron-plated ships were gain-

Three steamers taking on passengers at Broomielaw, Glasgow in 1885. In the foreground is the Lochgoil steamer Chancellor, built in 1880. Immediately behind her is the paddle steamer Vivid and in the distance Eagle, both these built by Buchanan in 1864.

ing over those built from wood. But after a few years they were found to suffer badly from corrosion and fouling. Experiments then went ahead to produce steel more cheaply, since steel plate cost about five times as much as iron. The firm of Siemens, having found the secret of making high-tensile steel, were able to fill the specifications laid down by the Admiralty for the *Iris* and *Mercury* in 1876. And by 1879 Dennys, the Dumbarton shipbuilders, were able to prove that steel for both merchant ships and warships was far ahead of iron for strength and durability, thereby incidentally reducing the displacement weight of a vessel.

The 1870s and 1880s were also years in which experimenters in design and propulsion had their fling, as if to probe all possible variations on the established theme. Apart from having the first warship to be armour-plated with steel, the Russians went in for circular warships. These were so unwieldy that they became a laughing-stock in naval circles. Henry Bessemer, who was overcredited for his work on steel-making, designed a cross-channel steamer with its saloon amidships, to

Below: The Great Eastern was Brunel's last achievement, by far the largest ship ever built, when launched in 1859. Brunel's death at the early age of 53, took place before The Great Eastern began her first voyage. It was fitted with engines for both paddles and screw propulsion, as well as sails, but never fulfilled its designer's hopes and was beset with mishaps. It was however, used extensively for laying marine cables after its failure as a liner.

Above right: A typical steam launch for private pleasure. Victoria is seen here going through Marsh Lock, near Henley on Thames.

Below right: Sleek paddle steamers such as Waverley were widely used for short coastal voyages, mainly for passengers. They were especially important along the west coast of Scotland, serving the islands and mainland ports of call, but many were in service for day trippers. That from London to Margate was very popular, and paddle steamers were also standard for many years for routes to the Continent. In most cases, passengers could gaze down at the fascinating engines at work amidships, but the boilers and the firemen who fed them with coal were out of sight.

be capable of countering the rolling effect of the waves on passengers by remaining on an even horizontal plane regardless of how the hull behaved. This was a failure, but a reversion to twin-hulled ships for the same service was more successful. Nevertheless, the Bessemer ships gave way after ten years to conventional paddle steamers capable of higher speeds.

Other types of ship developed during this period were icebreakers, train ferries, and oil tankers. Ruthven's idea of waterjet propulsion was taken up on trial by the Admiralty. A comparison was made of the performance of one standard screw-driven vessel, and one fitted with a 150 h.p. steam engine driving a large centrifugal pump. This sent powerful jets of water taken from the sea back under the surface through openings along each side and the stern. The idea had first been used by the American pioneer Rumsey, but though feasible enough, exhaustive trials proved the superior merits of the screw method. Hydraulic propulsion was better in theory than in practice. By 1880, designers, engine and boiler makers and shipbuilders concentrated on getting greater efficiency out of existing principles.

The water–tube boiler

As long as steam pressures remained low for marine engines, the conventional box-shaped boiler was more or less standard. In these, flues and fireholes had likewise been flat-sided; but gradually, as pressures above 35 p.s.i. were required, the longer cylindrical boiler with its fire-tubes giving a greater heating surface came into use. The railways had been using them very successfully for many years,

The steam coaster SS Robin, built in 1880, by R. Thomson on the Thames, being restored on the Medway. She has a length of 143 ft., and is 23 ft. in beam, of 336 tons. She is coal-fired, with a Gourlay Bros. triple expansion engine. For over seventy years she had a succession of Spanish owners under the name Maria before being rescued by the Maritime Trust to be berthed at their historic ship collection at St Katharine's by the Tower.

but the fear of explosion at sea had been largely responsible for keeping marine pressures low. There had been advocates of water-tube boilers, but they were scarcely heeded. Thomas Cochrane was one of them, for he had used them as early as 1844. His faith was rewarded much later in having his name attached to his own boiler design, for it was water-tube, rather than fire-tube, boilers which were to become finally accepted by the Navy, as being more suitable for its more arduous service.

Such reversals of policy often came about because earlier designs, once discarded, were revived years later when their faults had been remedied. The water-tube boiler had been used on the cargo ship *Thetis* as early as 1858, along with other experimental equipment. It gave the then very high pressure of 115 p.s.i., with very low coal consumption. But success did not last long, owing to the rapid corrosion of the iron from which it was made. Working with more durable materials available twenty years later, Loftus Perkins made an experimental boiler to produce no less than 500 p.s.i. after subjecting both tubes and boiler shell to prior testing at enormous pressure.

But these too were ahead of their time, because no pump was then capable of sustaining a supply of feed water.

The British Admiralty played a large part in the development of this period. Having standing committees of experts in the field of design for its ships and their equipment, and having become wedded to both steam and steel, the Admiralty could lay down constructional standards, and the leading firms were able to benefit from official research. Marine engineering as well as shipbuilding had become big business, kept safely under the wing, in a sense, of the mighty British

SS Raven was built in 1871 by T. B. Seath for the Furness Railway Co. to operate on Lake Windermere. She is the oldest vessel with original machinery on Lloyd's Register of yachts. Her rivetted iron hull is 71 ft. 10 in. long and 14 ft. 9 in. in beam and her coal-fired vertical cross-tube boiler supplies a single cylinder engine. Abandoned and sunk in the 1950s, she has now been taken up and restored by the Windermere Steamboat Museum.

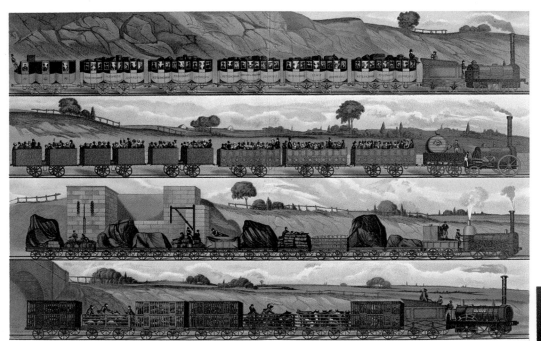

Below: A close view of the motion of the most famous of all British express locomotives, No. 4472 Flying Scotsman. It was built at the Great Northern works at Doncaster under Sir Nigel Gresley, then recognised as one of the topmost designers of the period between the two world wars. Flying Scotsman was purchased from British Rail by Alan Pegler and used for steam specials both in Britain and North America, but it was brought back from America as a rescue project and is now at Carnforth, still privately owned and is still used for special steam hauled excursions.

Above: A contemporary print showing the four different types of rolling stock in 1831 on the Liverpool and Manchester Railway. It is interesting to note the resemblance in the coachwork of the first class carriages to that of the horsedrawn highway coaches of the period.

Below: Class 115 No. 673 is a fine example of Midland Railway practice from 1870–1900. Other companies also used the large single driving wheel, of which the 'Stirling Single' of the Great Northern is perhaps best known. The 4-2-2 wheel arrangement was widely adopted for express locomotives, but the Midland policy was to double head rather than go in for larger 4-4-0s and 4-4-2s or 4-6-0s with which other companies met the need for greater power for heavier trains towards the end of the century.

Right: No. 70013 Oliver Cromwell was the last locomotive to be overhauled at Crewe works. This was in 1967/8 and after a few runs, was used for the final one under British Rail in August 1968, from Manchester to Carlisle. It then travelled through the night to Norwich, having been assigned to a permanent home at the Bressingham Live Steam Museum. It is the only active Class 7 B.R. Standard express locomotive, until No. 70000 Brittannia is also restored.

These passenger carrying river steamers were especially popular on the river Thames and were in regular service up to World War II. Their lengths and beam were restricted to that of the locks through which they had to pass.

Navy. The demand was not only for cargo and passenger ships, but for launches, ferries and tugboats. The Royal Navy, too, ordered a variety of vessels ranging from the new ironclad battleships and cruisers down to gunboats, and, by 1875, torpedo boats,

along with all sorts of auxiliary craft. Foreign governments were also placing orders for warships of various kinds to boost the importance of British shipyards and engineering works, and adding impetus to the arms race. The proliferation of the speedy torpedo boat led to the introduction of a special ship capable of countering its menace. This was the origin of the torpedo boat destroyer, bringing in another line of development of steam power in which speed was the vital factor and providing an example of one warlike invention calling for another as a defence against it.

Triple-expansion

With compounding accepted as a principle, so there appeared variations and extensions of it, which had been discarded years before because they were then impossible to apply. In 1881 Alexander Kirk, a man with wide knowledge and experience, was allowed to design a triple-expansion engine for a contract Robert Napier

had been given for a ship to serve the Australian trade. Its three cylinders were inverted, driving three cranks set at 120 degrees to each other on one shaft. Steam at 125 p.s.i. entered the smallest cylinder of 30 inches in diameter, then went into the second of 45 inches, and was finally exhausted from the third of 70 inches diameter, giving 1,800 h.p. This arrangement was so successful from the first, that within five years triple-expansion engines were in use in just over one hundred ships, either newly constructed or conversions. They set the general pattern for the thousands of what became known as 'tramp steamers' in service up to and beyond World War II.

Triple expansion, depending on higher pressures than any previously employed, gave greater power with a reduced fuel consumption. It also made even larger ships an attractive economic proposition, by stepping up boiler pressures and cylinder diameters even further. By 1888 transatlantic liners were built with 20,000 h.p. engines having cylinders up to 113 inches in diameter, and the Blue Riband went to *City of Paris* for a crossing of only six days. The Royal Navy was for once able to take advantage of Kirk's com-

mercially inspired enterprise, and triple expansion was adopted for all its larger ships. By 1898 *H.M.S. Diadem* took to the high seas powered by engines at the peak pressure of 300 p.s.i. which meant that the third cylinder, though taking the lowest pressure of steam, was in fact making its power contribution at a higher pressure than any engine in general use only twenty years earlier which had taken steam direct from its boiler.

The use of higher pressure was resulting in records being broken in almost every application of steam power, especially at sea. Passenger

Below: The agricultural traction engine built by Ransomes, Sims & Jeffries is powering a Ransome threshing drum. Threshing corn was the most frequent task for such engines, but such is the present nostalgia for steam that at some engine rallies they are brought back into use purely for display—as in this picture.

Right: This lightweight Mann's tractor of 1920 came too late to fend off the oncoming paraffin tractor. As tractors they were quite versatile but still needed firm ground on which to work effectively, as is shown hauling a plough over stubble. The contemporary Garrett 'Farmers Friend' steam tractors were in production for only a few years.

ships broke records for size—over 20,000 tons—and for speed—nearly 20 knots; while in the Royal Navy, 30 knots were attained before the close of the century. Unsuspected problems arose which had to be overcome, especially with ancillary equipment. Steam power was used for steering gear on many ships, as well as for capstans and donkey engines on deck, and gun turrets on warships. Pumps and condensers, which now recycled fresh water, were apt to become contaminated with oil. High speeds endangered crankshaft bearings, and it was also found that if drive shafts turned too fast, screw propellers lost thrust through the phenomenon of cavitation.

Triple expansion was not the ultimate in the development of the compound reciprocating piston en-gine. Quadruple expansion had to follow in the quest for maximum power. From about 1846 to 1907 this was used on a number of large ships, the last being the liner *Asturian* with two sets of four-cylinder engines whose cylinders ranged from 27 inches up to 79 inches in diameter. Such ships had to be built where yards had access to deep water. Thus shipbuilding went north, away from Thames-side where Brunel had such difficulty in launching his *Great Eastern*. Clydeside became the most favoured site, with Belfast, Birkenhead, Barrow and Tyneside also accounting for the immense volume of orders for shipping that came to Britain. As early as 1883, a book by W. H. Maws stated that of the 138 steamships then in service of over 4,000 tons, regardless of their ownership, only ten had been built in foreign yards.

Auxiliary equipment

The unsuitability of salty sea water for boilers could not be overcome by any other means than its evaporation and condensation as distilled water to make it acceptable. It was many years before a fully satisfactory method of doing this was found, and although boilers and supply tanks could be filled before leaving port, losses in the earlier condensing processes were inevitable. The trials and errors of the past were to some extent overcome by Alexander Kirk, and to a greater degree by Caird and Rayner, and James Weir later came up with notable improvements, both for marine distillation plant and the necessary feed pumps for high-

pressure boilers. His firm produced a wide range of equipment. The firm of Brotherhood filled the need for air-compressors; and with the advent of electric lighting came the steam-driven dynamo. As an extreme example of the complexity of auxiliary equipment the battleships *Thunderer*, *Inflexible* and *Dreadnought* each carried no less than 39 auxiliary steam engines for various purposes. Some of these were not especially designed for marine service, but were standard products of firms who were already supplying land-based industries, such as Bellis and Morcom with their steam-powered electricity generators.

The reciprocating engine reached its zenith for marine and industrial use with the enclosed, high-speed oil-bath type as produced by Bellis and Morcom. This and others have already been mentioned in the chapter on stationary engines. To emphasise the kinship existing between these and marine engines, the need both on land and sea for high-speed steam power was finally met by the introduction of the turbine. In principle, the turbine was not new. Hero of Alexandria had been aware of it in St. Paul's time on earth, and it had appeared again during the Renaissance. Watt and Trevithick had been aware of the power of steam jets playing on vanes to promote a revolving motion, but the less advanced technology of their time prevented this idea's practical application.

The 143 ton Lydia Eva is the last survivor of the great fleet of east coast herring drifters. After the depression hit fishing she spent thirty years as a Naval auxiliary. In 1972 she was acquired for restoration by the Maritime Trust and can be seen at St. Katharine's by the Tower. She is coal-fired and has a triple expansion engine driving a single propeller.

This model from the Science Museum is based on the engines of H.M.S. Duncan (1900). The engine is of the inverted vertical triple expansion type, and if we number the cylinders (with the domed centre covers) from left to right, the steam is admitted first to the high pressure cylinder (3), exhausts to the intermediate cylinder (2) where it does more work at its reduced pressure and is then exhausted to the low pressure cylinders (1 and 4) where what remains of its power is used before being finally exhausted to the condenser where it is converted back into hot water for further use in the boiler.

Parsons and the turbine

The development of the steam turbine, with the success attending that designed by Charles Parsons, is mentioned in the chapter on stationary engines. His first turbine worked on Hero's principle of the rotating hollow sphere. This was in 1884, and successful trials led to turbo-generators being installed in both warships and power stations to fulfill the rapidly increasing demand for electric light. Parsons formed several separate companies based near Newcastle, one of which specialised in marine steam turbines. Research experiments continued into the 1890s, and before Parsons was satisfied seven different turbines were made and tried out in a total of 31 trials at sea. His specially-built vessel for these trials was the *Turbinia*—she displaced only 45 tons but she served a vital purpose.

By 1897 Parsons was satisfied, and now he wanted to make a sea trial into a demonstration. What better opportunity could he have than to take the *Turbinia*, fitted with his latest turbine, to the Naval Review on the occasion of the Queen's Diamond Jubilee? There, to the astonishment of all, he steered her between the long lines of warships and at one time reached a speed of $34\frac{1}{2}$ knots. It was an unauthorised and dramatic display, especially when the picket boat despatched to put a stop to it was nearly sunk by the *Turbinia's* wash.

Parsons' invention could not now be ignored, and in spite of opposition he was invited to present his case to the Institute of Naval Architects. Largely as a result of this, two new destroyers were fitted with his turbines, driving four shafts with two propellers to each, and launched in 1899. Speeds of up to 37 knots were reached, but both vessels had a short life, which was due more to faulty hull designing, in relation to the stresses from high speed, and to bad luck, rather than to any failure of Parsons' turbines.

The Dreadnoughts and the great liners

For a time, the Admiralty held back from using turbines, but a momentous decision was reached when the *Dreadnought* was ordered to counter the growing threat from the German navy. She was the largest-ever British battleship, and ten turbines were installed in her taking steam at 250 p.s.i. She was launched in 1906 and from then on, until the end of steam, turbines became standard for all naval ships. When their first teething troubles had been remedied, turbines proved to be more reliable, having fewer moving parts than piston engines, as well as being more economic and capable of higher speeds.

The era of the great liners had arrived, and the main operators were quick to switch over to turbines. The 1907 *Mauretania* gained fame with turbines which developed 70,000 h.p., supplied by 25 boilers. As competition increased between British and foreign shipping lines, so did the search for the ultimate in speed, comfort and capacity. The ships included such names as the *Aquitania*, the ill-fated *Titanic* and the greatest of all, the *Queen Mary* and the *Queen Elizabeth*. These and most other new passenger ships were powered by steam turbines, though with many modifications, and with a switch from coal to oil as fuel, which preceded the later change from steam to diesel engines. The last great liner to be built with steam turbines was the *Queen Elizabeth II*, launched in 1967 and happily still in service.

The remarkable advance made in steam turbine propulsion between 1887 and 1907 shown by the 45 ton Turbinia alongside the great liner Mauretania.

Coal and oil

The switch from coal to oil as fuel for steamships was a slow, spasmodic process. The first trials with oil took place well back in the 19th century, but at the time coal was cheaper, and oil presented a fire hazard which did not apply to coal. As the century advanced the exploitation of oil resources reduced its price, but coaling stations had become widespread. It was not until about 1900 that the Admiralty showed interest in oil as fuel, as its calorific value was higher than that of coal, enabling ships to remain at sea for longer periods and to travel longer distances without refuelling. Better storage bunkers aboard ship, and burner equipment, led to the first warships being oil-fired about 1908. And as always, the larger shipping lines took advantage of the Naval Research Department's findings.

But this was only a limited development. There was too little oil storage capacity at the ports for the Navy to convert many of its ships to oil firing and in 1914 the majority were still relying on Welsh steam coal. But hostilities with Germany soon brought oil into focus again, not only because of the limitations of coal firing, but because a coal-burning fleet could be located long before the ships themselves were visible, from the blur of smoke on the horizon.

The battleship *Orion* was typical of many units of the Grand Fleet in the First World War. They were often known simply by their class name of *Dreadnought*, having a top speed of 21 knots. But to produce even 19 knots, sixteen of the *Orion*'s eighteen boilers had to be fired, and a day's steaming consumed 350 tons of coal. The full tonnage carried was 3,000 and, because stock was never allowed to fall below 750 tons, the ship was restricted in its range. To replenish at sea from a collier could be a slow and hazardous process, out of keeping with the mobility and readiness for instant action demanded in wartime.

Oil and turbines came into use more or less at the same period, slowly and

An impressive bird's eye view of the most famous of all the giant Atlantic liners, Cunard's Queen Mary, at Southampton Ocean Terminal.

not very surely, until finally their heat and power properties could be fully exploited as a result of research, experiment and trials over many years. The use of superheated steam took a somewhat similar course of development, for it held dangers as well as advantages, depending on the type of engine for which it was used. In theory, dried and hotted-up steam was more powerful than 'saturated', straight from the boiler. In some circumstances, superheating made for appreciable fuel economies, but it could also make complications, demanding

stronger pipework and more sophisticated equipment, the cost and care of which were found sometimes to offset any gains. Neither the application of higher pressures nor of higher temperatures was a simple matter. Nor indeed was steam quite the infinitely-adaptable means of marine power that some pioneers had imagined, as those who tried using it for submarines discovered; though a few steam-powered submarines were actually built and used for a time.

All the same, the saga of steam power is nowhere better illustrated than in its use for marine propulsion. It takes in a whole era covering two centuries—from Jonathan Hulls' first efforts to the final developments of the high-speed turbine.

Richard Trevithick brought his engine Catch Me Who Can to London as a 'Steam Circus', hoping to popularise his invention by charging 1/- per person per trip. This was in 1808 and took place in a field which later became part of Euston Square. Only the intrepid, willing to risk travelling at 12 m.p.h. dare ride in the open coach. After a few weeks' running at no profit, the circus was abandoned when the engine fell over as a result of a fractured track.

4

RAILWAY LOCOMOTIVES

Coal from the pit-head

If James Watt settled into the groove of his own success, building low-pressure stationary engines, there were several budding engineers of his time whose vision of the potentialities of steam power was anything but cramped. Watt's contemporaries were concerned chiefly with a wider use of steam at higher pressures. These were seen to be necessary for transport engines, but the idea of specially constructed railway roadways hardly occurred to them, although several private tramways existed for horsedrawn trucks to ease the transport of coal from the pit-heads. 'Common roads' such as they were in the late 18th century offered scope enough for improvement as a means of easing transport problems for both goods and passengers. To use these for railways would have appeared as outlandish as to consider entirely new routes especially for railways, an idea likely to meet massive opposition from landowners.

The first locomotive

Boulton and Watt's assistant, William Murdoch (unlike his master) was unconvinced that high-pressure steam had no future, and showed his belief and ingenuity in a model, which still exists, and a copy of which can be seen in the Science Museum, London. Watt would have nothing to do with it, but before long Trevithick's ideas on loco-motion led to the building of an engine at Coalbrookdale to his design, to run on a tramway. He used a horizontal boiler in which the cylinder was immersed. The firebox heat travelled through the boiler and back again, still inside the boiler, to the chimney. The double-acting piston with its long stroke of 4 feet 6 inches revolved a large flywheel which was tooth-geared to the pair of driving wheels.

This, said to be the first railway engine ever built, appeared in 1802, and in 1804 another, obviating some of its predecessor's faults, was made for the Pen-y-Daren Ironworks in South Wales. This ran well enough, but proved too heavy for the rails, which in those days were of angle iron, with one edge acting as a flange for the plain unflanged wheels of the locomotive. It was believed right from the first that the question of adhesion—of the grip of iron upon iron, of driving wheel rims on rails—would be a difficult one. Existing tramways for collieries were made for horsedrawn coal tubs and stone blocks were used to carry the rails, leaving the space between for horses' hooves.

Trevithick's second engine proved that adhesion was a matter of having adequate weight on the rails, but such a weight was more than the existing rails could stand.

For all its fragile appearance, Murdock's simple model built in 1784 was said to have worked well using a much higher boiler pressure than Watt had advocated.

Hedley's Puffing Billy of 1813 with its spidery cranks and beams was both novel and successful for use in the north-east coalfields.

The problem of adhesion

After a lapse of a few years, there was a rack railway laid at Middleton Colliery near Leeds. Matthew Murray and John Blenkinsop, using a patent taken out in 1811 by the latter, set about building two engines to run on the rack system—with cogged driving wheels fitting into the toothed rack railway. The engines had two vertical cylinders immersed within the boiler, with pistons connected to cranks set at right angles so that one of them was always ready to exert power. The second, or main, shaft carried a toothed gear wheel on each side of the engine acting as the 'driver' between two unflanged weight-carrying wheels.

Above: A coalfield scene, typical of the earliest days of steam locomotion, depicting Hetton Colliery near Newcastle.

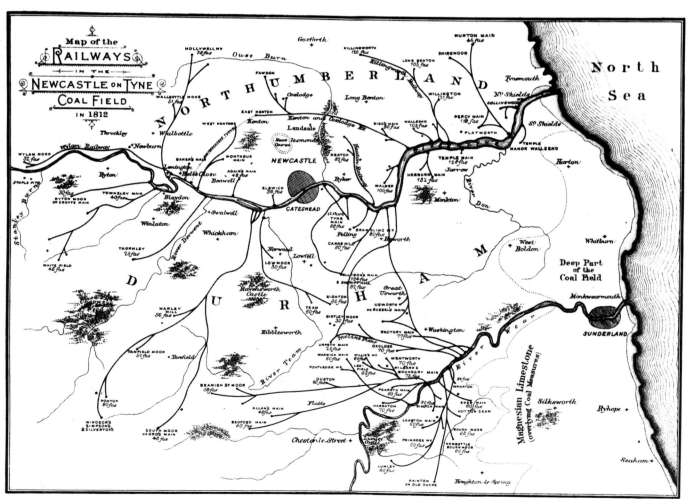

These were the two first commercially successful railway engines, but the rack system itself was much less so. The scene then shifted to the Tyneside coalfields. At Wylam, where smooth rail tracks using horse power was already in use, William Hedley had been experimenting with the adhesion problem using a test carriage crank-propelled by men, and had proved Trevithick's contention that rack rails were not needed for reliable traction.

Hedley's first engine failed because it had only one cylinder, which could only transmit power to one side by means of cogs. Another engine soon followed having two cylinders and a beam action above, whose long connecting rods suggested the name *Grasshopper*. Hedley's name for it was *Puffing Billy* and it can be seen in the Science Museum at South Kensington; his next engine named *Wylam*

Dilly is now in the Royal Scottish Museum, Edinburgh. Both Hedley's engines were built originally as four-wheelers, but they broke so many rails that, to spread the weight, the number of wheels was doubled, with each one cogged to the driving gear-wheels. They embodied two more of Trevithick's early suggestions, of having a return flue to give extra heating surface, and a narrow chimney up which the exhaust steam could be directed to increase the draught to the fire.

The early railway engines were regarded with wonderment, awe or distaste, but nevertheless people flocked to see them, and to be carried by them when they could afford the fare. This shows the opening of the Stockton & Darlington Railway in 1825.

George Stephenson's first engine

By this time, 1814, George Stephenson had also begun engine building at the nearby Killingworth Colliery, but until he too adopted Hedley's improvements of the return flue and narrow chimney, his efforts were largely unsuccessful. But he made progress by abandoning the geared drive in favour of direct coupling from the overhead beams to the driving wheels. His *Blücher* (named after the Prussian marshal, a doughty ally of the Duke of Wellington) had only four wheels. It was reckoned to be the fourteenth locomotive built in England, but others were soon to follow, for Stephenson had built three more by

J. R. Brown

1816, all with improved features. They had flanged wheels, and vertical cylinders immersed in the boiler, above each axle, with connecting rods direct to the wheels; while the draught was improved by a smaller exhaust pipe leading into the tall chimney. On one, a chain and sprockets connected the drive to both axles.

Steam power in this early period was by no means welcomed and accepted by all as the great leap forward. There were detractors who saw no future in machines liable to break down, or to damage rails over which horses could pull coal tubs with comparative ease at a speed which was quite adequate. Horses could be relied upon, said some, but the new-fangled engines could not. Such opposition did nothing to quench the faith and enthusiasm of those who strove to harness steam for transport, even if they were almost entirely concerned with moving coal from the pit-head.

There were collieries on both sides of the Tyne, and there were others besides Hedley and Stephenson attempting to produce iron horses. William Brunton was one of these, but his engines emulated horse power to the extent of having pusher legs instead of wheeled drive. The legs, as extensions of the piston rod, pushed the engine forward from behind; but although two such engines were built and put to work, at Rainton and Newbottle, both were said to have failed by 1815 from burst boilers. W. E. Chapman of the Hetton Colliery tried another method. His engine pulled itself along with a chain laid along the track which was wound round a drum.

The Stockton and Darlington railway

The life story of George Stephenson is also virtually that of the early history of the railway locomotive. He found it a small, crude and very imperfect machine—but when he died in 1848 at the age of 67 it was a reliable basic type on which, for the next hundred years, others were able to make their own various refinements and improvements, largely concerned with greater speed, power and economy. By profession, Stephenson was a mining engineer. His versatility extended to inventing, simultaneously with Humphrey Davy, a safety lamp for miners. By 1822 the Stockton and Darlington Railway Company was formed and Stephenson was invited to survey it and to provide motive power for it—although it is probably nearer the truth to say that he persuaded the directors to invite him.

This line was to be the real testing ground, as far as steam versus horsepower was concerned, since there were sceptics still as to whether steam would prevail, even among the directors of the new railway. By 1823 Stephenson had built 14 engines for various pit lines—out of a total of 28 produced up to that time. 1823 was the year in which George and his son Robert set up their own works at Forth Street in Newcastle, and there in 1825 they built the first locomotive for the Stockton and Darlington, which really fired public imagination. At last steam power was no longer hidden away on colliery tramways—it was working on a public railway for all to see.

A vast crowd turned out on 27th September 1825 to witness the passing of the first train, behind the new engine named just *Locomotion*. It had taken all the persuasion of the line's manager, Timothy Hackworth, who had been Hedley's assistant, to overcome the final opposition of the horse faction amongst the directors. Stephenson was dour but confident, and with only 50 lb. pressure of steam, his engine hauled 450 passengers as well as 90 tons of freight at 12 m.p.h.. *Locomotion* weighed just under 7 tons, but it embodied improvements which gave it extra power, including a direct drive to each of the four wheels, which for the first time were coupled by a rod on each side to achieve maximum adhesion.

Locomotion became No. 1 on the Stockton and Darlington, and al-though many replacement parts have been made, it still stands as it has done for years in Darlington North Road Station Museum. Its last run was at the centenary celebrations of 1925, but, thanks to a band of enthusiasts led by Michael Satow, a replica was built which took part in the S. & D. 150th anniversary cavalcade of live steam in September 1975. *Locomotion*, however, with its wierd array of beams and cranks, bore little comparison with the engines which only a few years later came much closer to the more or less standard design of the 19th century.

Another engineer closely connected with these north-country developments, Timothy Hackworth, built an engine himself in 1827, using the boiler of the Stockton and Darlington's No. 5 which, with its four cylinders, had proved unsuccessful. The *Royal George* had six driving wheels, the now conventional return-flue boiler and two vertical cylinders. It had several other improvements, including steam force pumps for the pre-heated boiler feed water, and a spring-controlled safety valve instead of the primitive weight-loaded valve. Its performance in hauling a 50-ton load over an up-and-down gradient at an average speed of 11 m.p.h. was noted by two visiting engineers named Rastrick and Walker. They reported their observations to the directors of the newly formed Liverpool and Manchester Railway and this led to the famous Rainhill Trials of 1829 being held.

The Rainhill Trials

The section of track selected by the Liverpool and Manchester Railway Company was near the village of Rainhill outside Liverpool. The qualifications for entry were that engines should cost less than £550, weigh under 6 tons, and make twenty runs back and forth, each of $1\frac{1}{2}$ miles. Hackworth, who had followed the *Royal George* with several others for the Stockton and Darlington

Railway, incorporating further improvements, entered his *Sans Pareil*, a four-wheeled engine with direct drive from the piston rods. It failed to complete the prescribed number of runs due to a cracked cylinder and a faulty water pump, though it had exceeded 20 m.p.h. at times.

George and Robert Stephenson entered the *Rocket*, with its inclined cylinders above the rear wheels. It reached 24 m.p.h., during the twenty runs over the course, hauling 9½ tons, and was finally declared the winner. It is worth noting some brief details of the other contestants. One of these was Brandreth's *Cyclopede*—which was disqualified, for it was horse-powered, the poor animal being yoked to the frame and having to propel the vehicle on the treadmill principle. *Novelty* was the name given to Braithwaite and Ericsson's entry, weighing only 2¾ tons. It had a pot boiler over the rear axle, and a curious vertical fire grate, which allowed heat to pass through 36 feet of coiled tubes. Bellows were used for a forced draught; but if the drive on to a cranked axle was on the right lines, the engine put up a very poor performance, as did another machine, the *Perseverance* from Burstall and Hill. This too weighed a mere 2¾ tons, with a vertical boiler centred between the two axles.

The *Rocket* however, became not only the winner, but the model adopted for the other locomotives built for the new railway. Examples of both the older 'Grasshopper' and the newer 'Rocket' types of this period are preserved. One of the former is the 11-ton *Agenoria* built in 1829 by Foster and Rastrick of Stourbridge. It must have been fairly reliable, for it worked on a colliery railway at Kinswinford till 1864 and can be seen at the National Railway Museum at York. The *Invicta* stood for many years in the open at Canterbury. This was built in 1830 by

The Rainhill Trials of 1829, showing Stephenson's victorious Rocket triumphantly ahead of two of its rivals, for which it was awarded the £500 prize.

Stephenson for the Canterbury and Whitstable Railway where it ran for a few years. Unlike the *Rocket*, its outside inclined cylinders were behind the chimney.

The *Rocket* still looked decidedly primitive, showing few signs of the shape of things to come in locomotive design. Stephenson's success, rewarded with the £500 prize, was however due more to new inside features than to any visible on the outside. His was the first engine to have a multi-tube boiler. The 25 copper tubes each of 3 inches diameter, through which the hot gases from the fire were drawn, made available a far increased heating surface compared with that of a return-flue boiler. The blast pipe automatically increased the draught to the fire, by concentrating exhaust steam through a reduced aperture at the base of the chimney.

These two features set the pattern for practically all future steam locomotives. Apart from having its cylinders refitted to a less acute angle than is seen on the original now in the Science Museum, to avoid a tendency to lift the rear wheels, the *Rocket* needed little modification and the Stephensons were now ready to forge ahead confident of continued success. The *Rocket's* boiler was only 5 feet long, and their next design extended it to make greater use of the inner tubes.

Above: The Great Western had finally to give in over the battle of the gauges, and by 1890 its tracks were those of Stephenson's standard 4 ft. 8½ in. The change caused practically all Great Western broad gauge locomotives to be scrapped and here at Swindon they were assembled awaiting destruction.

Left: The Great Western's North Star of 1837 showed significant developments over those in the Rainhill Trials. It had outside frames and the inside motion was connected to the cranked axle of the 7 ft. driving wheels.

Right: Aveling & Porter, although better known for their road engines, built a large number of gear drive shunting engines for industrial railway systems. These were in fact conventional compound traction engines mounted on railway frames and wheels. This is the common type, 0-4-0, but there were some 2-2-0s whose resemblance to the traction engine was even more marked.

in the Municipal Museum in Newcastle.

The 1840s saw not only the beginning of the 'railway mania' but of the 'battle of the gauges'. The origin of what became known as the 'standard gauge' of 4 feet 8½ inches is obscure. Probably Stephenson built engines to this seemingly odd measurement because tracks of this gauge were already laid. Anyway it was the one he chose, and as he was a powerful pioneer, others followed suit, including the designers of almost every railway projected during this decade. Stephenson even chose 4 feet 8½ inches as the diameter of the *Rocket's* driving wheels.

The broad gauge – and Brunel

While most of the promoters of the many new lines being laid were content to follow George Stephenson's lead in setting a standard gauge, there was a young man appointed as engineer to the new Great Western Railway in 1835 who believed this was too narrow. Isambard Kingdom Brunel was convinced that a broader gauge would

This appeared in 1830 and was named the *Planet*. In outward appearance it was well on the way to what became for so long the accepted locomotive shape. The whole assembly was now built within a frame, to take the longer boiler—and the previous outside inclined cylinders were now placed inside the frame beneath the smokebox to be connected to the cranked axle of the rear driving wheels. The *Planet*, unfortunately, was not preserved, unlike the last 'Grasshopper' type built by the Stephensons—now under the name Robert Stephenson & Co. This was made for the Hollingworth wagon railway in 1830, where it ran until it was rebuilt in 1867. After a further spell at work it was placed on a pedestal as long ago as 1896; it is now

make for more stable and therefore faster running, and had decided that 7 feet was the ideal. He was a man of great and varied talents and a determined individualist. He had an 1837 Stephenson engine, built for export to Russia for a 6 foot gauge, converted to his 7 foot standard by his locomotive superintendent Daniel Gooch, and named it *North Star*. It was a great success and, after being reboilered in 1857, continued to run until 1871. Although the original was scrapped in 1906, a replica of this historic locomotive, a 2-2-2 with a 7 foot centre driving wheel, was built for the Great Western Railway Museum, Swindon.

There are a very creditable number of early locomotives preserved, but some of the more noteworthy are missing; the existence of replicas of a few of them is some consolation to the enthusiast. The most outstanding omission, now never likely to be rem-

edied by a replica, is that of one of Gooch's larger Great Western broad-gauge locomotives, such as the *Lord of the Isles*.

Some important developments in the field of economy, efficiency and safety came in the 1830s. Stephenson's *Planet* and *North Star* were fitted with a steam dome on top of the boiler, and with few exceptions this remained a feature until the end of the steam era. Its function was to act as a collecting vessel at the highest point of a boiler, where steam would be at its hottest and driest, to be taken direct from there to the cylinders.

Another early feature was the use of strips of wood as lagging to avoid loss of heat from the boiler. These close-set strips, laid lengthways and clamped by metal bands, continued to be used for most of the century, though from about 1840 onwards the strips were covered in a sheet-iron casing as well.

Placing the cylinders

The angled cylinders and motion were soon dispensed with, because the up-and-down lift of the piston was felt on the springs. A more natural position for the cylinders, now placed side by side, was under the smokebox, the pistons being horizontally connected to a cranked driving axle. Stephenson's 'link motion', by which the valves allowing steam into and out of the cylinders were operated, worked by rods connected to eccentrics on the cranked driving axle, and fitted in neatly with this arrangement.

Problems however were encountered due to lack of room between the axles where only two were employed, especially as it was believed that a low centre of gravity was vital

Cornwall was built by Richard Trevithick's son Francis in 1847 at Crewe. It was originally a 2-2-2 with the boiler beneath the driving axle to obtain what was then believed a necessary low centre of gravity—made possible with an 8 ft. 6 in. pair of driving wheels and outside cylinders. In 1858 it was rebuilt with the boiler in the orthodox position, and now remains in preservation at York.

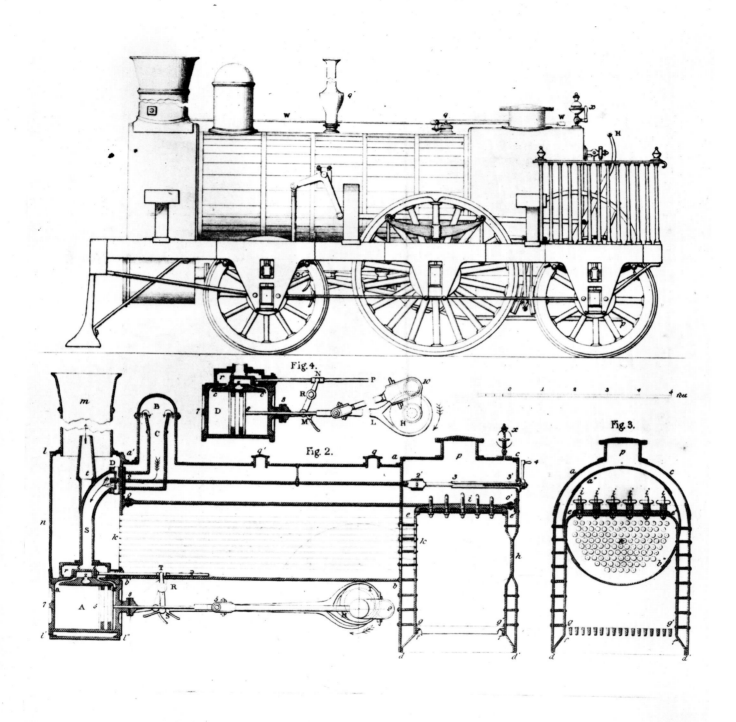

These diagrams are taken from an early instruction book, dated 1846, illustrating how steam was made and pressured in the boiler and its direction and passage through the cylinders, to be expelled finally through the blast pipe.

for safety, and the boiler and firebox were the heaviest parts of the engines. To some extent the trouble was overcome by a 2-2-2 wheel arrangement. This placed the front axle clear of moving parts, and the rear axle farther back to allow for a larger pair of driving wheels on a cranked axle, at the most convenient point in the centre. This was the design of the *North Star* and it was a pattern setter for the future. Timothy Hackworth had however continued to develop his own design of colliery engine, and a late example was built in 1839 as a coupled six-wheeler. This locomotive had inclined cylinders projecting above and beyond the rear wheels, with long connecting rods to the front pair of drivers. It was named *Derwent* and now stands in the Darlington Museum.

The Railway Juggernaut. This contemporary caricature reflects the attitude of some people to the steam powered railways. The devil behind the chimney is no doubt fostering the greed for money on the part of those who saw and worshipped the new source of wealth.

The first trunk lines

The first railway companies were formed to make transport easier over fairly short distances, as being most likely to attract profitable traffic. As such lines proliferated, it was soon realised that links between them, and longer lines, were desirable. The Great Western Railway was formed in 1835 with a trunk-and-branch system in mind, but the Grand Junction, an amalgamation of small companies between the Midlands and Lancashire, was the first trunk line to be operational, in 1837. The existence of three main lines led to the appointment of engineer-designers of locomotives to run on them. Daniel Gooch on the Great Western was outstanding. In 1838 Edward Bury became Locomotive Superintendent, and a rival to Stephenson, on the Grand Junction (Birmingham to Warrington). This later became the London and North Western, after amalgamation with Robert Stephenson's London and Birmingham.

Bury's designs were distinctive; most of them were 0-4-0s with bar frames, inside cylinders and outside coupling rods. The *Lion* of 1838 (built for the Liverpool and Manchester) was an early example, with its copper firebox, domed well above boiler level to become the steam chest. It was light, simple and low-pressured at only 50 p.s.i.; after 80 years' service of one kind or another it was restored to its original condition and used for special occasions such as the Liverpool and Manchester's centenary and for the film 'The Titfield Thunderbolt'. Another Bury engine, built in 1848 but with only one pair of driving wheels, is preserved at Cork Station in Eire; while *Coppernob*, built in 1846 with 110 p.s.i., is safely housed in the National Railway Museum.

Higher boiler pressures, along with greater weight and sounder construction, were the outcome of a steadily improving technology. In turn, speeds were increasing, a consequence of the greater diameters of driving wheels, and the magical mile a minute was in sight. Along with this went heavier and more varied loads for industry and commerce; while for passengers railway travel at previously unheard-of speeds was gaining in popularity, even if the third class had to travel in open trucks until Gladstone's Bill of 1846 made the covering of these trucks compulsory. Queen Victoria's lifelong addiction to railway travel began in 1842 and her first trip was itself a fine advertisement, setting the seal of respectability on the new mode of transport.

Although by 1840 there were a number of firms in business as locomotive builders, the first of the railway companies to inaugurate its own works was the Grand Junction. A Cheshire village was selected which was soon to become a sizeable and later a world-famous railway town making locomotives and rolling stock. It is worth noting that the parish was Church Coppenhall, and the name Crewe was taken from the 'Crewe Arms' public house adjacent to the site of the new works. A similar town was founded at Swindon for the Great Western.

Above: This little engine, Prince, ran on the Festiniog Railway for nearly 120 years. A George England & Co. 0-4-0 engine, she was built in 1863 to the narrow gauge of 1 ft. 11½ in.
Below: No. 316 Gwynneth and No. 994 George Sholto being renovated at Bressingham. These diminutive but powerful outside-framed 0-4-0 saddle tanks were built for the Hunslet slate quarries narrow gauge railways.

for over 50 years, finally to rest at York.

Columbine was followed in 1847 by a larger engine with 8 foot 6 inch driving wheels, named *Cornwall* after the county of its designer Francis Trevithick, son of the pioneer Richard. During its life, until its retirement in 1927, it was subjected to much rebuilding. It began as a 2-2-2, changed to a 4-2-2, and was rebuilt in 1858 back to a 2-2-2 with a boiler mounted higher above the axle. Designers were by that time learning by trial and error that high boilers were safer than low, especially at high speed. Another factor contributing to the rebuilding was the greater diameter of boiler fitted. *Cornwall* is now preserved.

Two interesting designs of the 1840s have sadly not been preserved. The *Jenny Lind* of the Midland Railway, named after the 'Swedish Nightingale' soprano, was so called because it was such a good-looking engine, having several refinements to give an otherwise fairly conventional 2-2-2 a very pleasing appearance. It worked at the then high boiler pressure of 120 p.s.i.

Crewe and its early locomotives

The first engine to leave the Crewe works in 1845 marked another advance in design. This was *Columbine* with single driving wheels of 6 feet diameter, driven by slightly inclined outside cylinders and inside valve gear. The tall ungainly chimney of the early locomotives had given way to one which, with ornamented wheel splashers and a curved casing over the cylinders, made a far more graceful outline. *Columbine's* cab may have been a later addition, for in the 1840s protection for enginemen was considered a luxury, and only a few engines had a windshield with peepholes for protection against wind and smoke. It was not until the 1860s that cabs were fitted, and these at first gave scant cover for the crew. *Columbine* weighed 18 tons and worked

The Crampton engines

The other design was that of a locomotive designed by T. R. Crampton and built by the firm of Tulk & Ley for the London and North Western in 1848. He was probably influenced by Norris, an American who had supplied engines for the Gloucester–Birmingham line. He believed that the driving wheels should be well to the rear to gain maximum adhesion, and support for his theory came when Norris engines were successfully used as rear-pushing 'bankers' on the Lickey incline outside Birmingham. Crampton went further by placing a pair of 8 foot single-drivers just behind the firebox, with pairs of smaller carrying wheels under the very long low boiler, where weight was less concentrated. This strange-looking engine, weighing 55 tons with its tender, was by far the heaviest engine so far built in England. For several years the two Crampton engines named *Liverpool* and *London* gave good service on the easy gradients south of Birmingham.

In the 1850s steam technology expanded in all directions—for industry and for the proliferating railway system. This euphoric mid-century period—despite the disaster of the Crimean War—excited the imagination of engineers and designers and induced the capitalists and captains of industry to use steam for every conceivable purpose. A booming export business thrived, and locomotive builders were ready to design and deliver engines to their customers' requirements at home and abroad. 'Made in Britain' became the hallmark of reliability all over the world, especially for things mechanical.

For industry and for branch lines, the tank engine was in increasing demand during the 1850s. For public railways the tanks were mostly on each side of the boiler, and the absence of a tender made them more economical for short runs; since they could run equally well backwards they had no need of turntables. Tank engine variations mainly for industry were the 'saddle', 'well' and 'pannier' designs (the names describe the shape or position of the tanks) all of which, unlike tender locomotives, had the weight of the water tanks available for added adhesion.

On the main lines the 'battle of the gauges' became a contest between the Great Western at 7 feet and the rest at the 'standard' 4 feet 8½ inches. But soon after 1850 an extraordinary range of gauges began to emerge for industry and transport at home and overseas, with a dozen or more widths of track, from 1 foot 3 inches to 7 feet. The London and North Western, for example, built as late as 1865 the *Pet* of only 18 inch gauge for use in their works, but well before this date factories and quarries were using a variety of narrow-gauged steamers. Their range led to designs and modifications which proved the versatility both of designing engineers and the application of steam power.

David Jones 'big goods' were the first 4-6-0 tender engines in the British Isles. Built to Jones' design by Sharp Stewart & Co. in 1894 for the Highland Railway, No 103 remained in service until 1934 when she was withdrawn by the L.M.S. In 1959 she was restored to running condition and spent several years hauling special trains. She is now permanently housed in the Glasgow Museum of Transport in the yellow livery originally applied to Highland locomotives.

Compounding

The year 1850 also saw the introduction of more economic use of steam in locomotives, though it was not a new invention. This was compounding, which meant that exhaust steam from a high-pressure cylinder was used for a second stroke in another, before being ejected through the blast pipe into the smokebox and up the chimney. The invention of the exhaust blast pipe had led to higher pressures from hotter fires. It occurred to Nicholson that if steam at say 120 p.s.i. as it entered a cylinder came out again at perhaps more than half that pressure, it held a force capable of being used instead of being allowed to go to waste up the chimney. Of necessity, the secondary low-pressure cylinder had to be of larger diameter, to contain a greater volume of steam at a lower pressure; but with its piston coupled to the motion it would increase the engine's power and result in economies in fuel and water.

Compounding was first tried on the Great Eastern Railway, but was not immediately taken up by other designers as a major advance. Many of them thought that the powerful thrust given to a piston by high-pressure steam gave sufficient torque to the crankshaft, without the complications of additional low-pressure cylinders and their separate valve gear. In theory, however, compounding gave an advantage both for smooth running and economy, and some railway engineers persisted in trying to perfect its application. F. W. Webb of the London and North Western was one of these, and tried various modifications for twenty years. And although the 4-4-0 Midland Compounds were very successful, they did not appear until much later. They were still being built in 1930; yet in general, compounding never reached the necessary perfection in Britain to make it a standard railway locomotive practice. It was however used much more in stationary and road engines.

The great expansion of railway engine building during the 1850s and 60s was also to meet a demand for

The Great Western 32XX class, built in 1938, were actually rebuilds of two earlier classes, 'Duke' and 'Bulldog'. They soon required the name 'Dukedogs'. No. 3217 incorporates parts of No. 3258 The Lizard (1895) and the frames of No. 3245 (1906). She was withdrawn in 1960 and became the Earl of Berkeley. She is now preserved on the Bluebell Railway, Sussex.

cheap, small engines for use by small companies on short lines, for industry and even for country estates. These lines were also a market for engines discarded by the larger companies, which were now going in for heavier and more powerful types, for both express and goods trains, since engines built twenty years previously were often quite capable of further service. Dealers and hirers catered for this demand, and J. W. Boulton had sidings with a large selection of second-hand engines on offer, for sale or for hire. He was also reputed to have converted traction engines to rail working, while later on, Aveling and Porter, who were specialists in agricultural engines, built some railway engines of traditional road design, with boiler and top motion, and a flywheel geared down to drive flanged wheels for rail use. Two of these are in preservation, one being on view in the York Museum.

By 1870 a pattern of design was established which persisted well into the 20th century with no basic changes.

A further feature of the period was for the larger companies to build their own locomotives, following the example of the L. & N.W.R. and Great Western, at Crewe and Swindon respectively. Derby, Doncaster and Darlington became important railway towns while the independent locomotive-building firms concentrated more on export and industry.

Firms such as Avonside and Peckett (of Bristol), Barclay of Kilmarnock, Beyer-Peacock of Manchester, Stephenson of Newcastle, Bagnall of Stafford, Kerr Stuart of Stoke, and several firms in and around Leeds began producing engines for this expanding market. Most of these were 0-4-0s and 0-6-0s in various gauges, built in vast numbers as reliable and purely functional iron horses. Here and there a new or unorthodox type appeared, such as Sturrock's Great Northern 0-6-0 heavy goods engine of 1863, on which the tender wheels were also steam driven. This arrangement, though not too successful then, was used later in America.

Built in 1918, G.W.R. Churchward No. 2857 is an example of the first class of 2-8-0 heavy freight engines to be built for a British railway. Regarded by many as the finest of all heavy freight locomotives, the 28XXs did superb work on the many coal train runs on the G.W.R. No. 2857 is being restored by the 2857 Society for service on the Severn Valley Railway.

The heyday of steam

The fifty years from 1870 to 1920 can be regarded as the heyday of steam. It was a vital factor in the life of the nation. Steam was the supreme means of power, and not until after 1920 was the internal combustion engine seen as a serious rival, at least for transport on land or sea. Takeovers and amalgamations had in no way lessened the rivalry between the leading companies. Some set such high standards of efficiency that their prestige, enhanced by the splendid liveries of their passenger engines as well as their performance, became a matter of pride which

filtered down from top to bottom among those who ran them. Not for nothing were the rank and file of employees known and referred to as 'Railway Servants', and the Chief Mechanical Engineer of a line was treated with respectful awe. He was more often than not the designer of new locomotives and the final arbiter on rules affecting their performance. And although the railways were taken for granted as a national asset by the British people, they made a substantial contribution to the overall national pride so evident during this period.

The main emphasis in the continuing development of steam on the railways after 1870 centred on increased power and performance. Greater

heating surface by means of more but smaller boiler tubes achieved greater sustained power—higher boiler pressures alone were of little value without them. The year 1870 was a landmark. Patrick Stirling put the Great Northern Railway well ahead in speed and performance with his single-driver 4-2-2. It was a handsome engine, and the 8 foot driving wheels were powered by outside cylinders and inside valve gear with boiler pressure at 140 p.s.i. At $38\frac{1}{2}$ tons it was lighter than some tank and freight engines of the period, but F. W. Webb, of the L.N.W.R., the G.N.R.'s great rival, who had met with only qualified success with his compounds, followed up with the even lighter 'Precedent' class of 2-4-0s. Both Webb's No. 790 *Hardwicke* and Stirling's No. 1 are preserved at the National Railway Museum at York.

Hardwicke differed little in form from many other passenger engines produced over the next 25 years. It had inside cylinders—a feature common to most 2-4-0s and to the singles, whether 2-2-2 or 4-2-2. In all cases, whether cylinders were placed inside or outside, the valve gear was inside the frame.

Some further degree of standardisation came when the typical 0-6-0 goods engines carried the same boiler and frame as did the passenger locomotives, whether built 2-4-0, 2-2-2, or 0-4-2. The latter wheel arrangement is seen in *Gladstone* which is preserved at York. By increasing the size of the boiler, adequate sustained power could be obtained for the greater speeds and heavier loads this period demanded. The larger diameter of boilers also contributed to a higher centre of gravity. At York too can be seen an example of the pretty little 'Brighton Terrier' class, of the London Brighton and South Coast Railway, 0-6-0 tank engines which were from 1872 onwards regarded as maids-of-all-work for the next fifty years on suburban and branch lines south of London. They weighed only 28 tons, and of the fifty built, no less than ten are in preservation at various museums and steam centres.

Driver and fireman

Boiler pressures rose slowly. By the 1880s more consideration for the crew was being given by locomotive designers, who provided larger cab cover. On tank engines, a cab was naturally more complete; but now, in an age when operatives' comfort and safety have become of almost paramount importance, one can but marvel at the hardihood of crews driving express trains in all weathers with the minimal protection from the elements that the older engines provided. And it was not only weather some crews had to endure. In tunnels smoke could be almost overpowering. There were steam engines at work on the Metropolitan Railway in London which had underground lines operational by 1870, and they continued in service for many years until electricity took over from steam. The Metropolitan No. 26, a 4-4-0 tank with cab, built in 1864, was in service till 1948, though it was on surface work only well before that

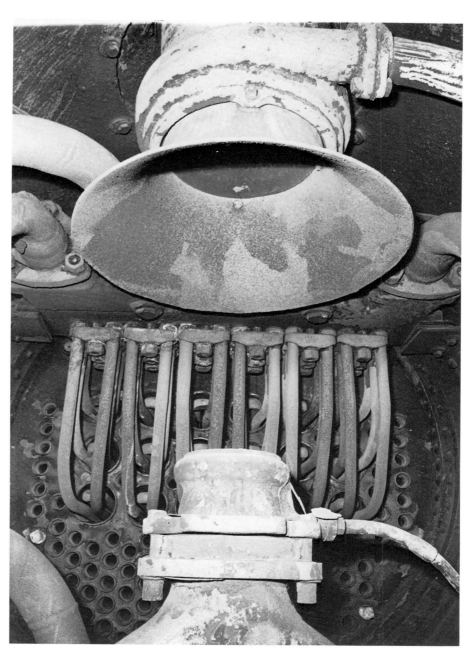

Inside the smokebox of L.M.S. 4-6-2 tank locomotive of 1934, No. 2500, of 3 cylinders. The boiler tube plate holds over 100 small tubes of about 2 in. diameter. A number of larger tubes are flues, which also lead direct to the firebox, but in them are multiples of small element tubes through which steam comes from the boiler to be dried and pressured more before entering the cylinder via the header. The pipes on either side of the bell-shaped exhaust aperture lead down to the cylinder outside and steam, having activated the pistons, is discharged from the (bottom centre) blast pipe, with its small blower pipes.

date. The 'District' and the North London, as well as the Great Eastern, the Great Northern and the L.N.W.R., also had suburban services running in tunnels and deep bricklined cuttings, and the grimy deposits from smoke on these is still to be seen. Most tunnels had smoke ventilation shafts to the surface at intervals, but the spaces between must have been grim for drivers and firemen, even if coal smoke then was a less objectionable intake than diesel fumes are now.

Speeds by 1870 had easily passed the magical mile-a-minute, even though averages for long journeys were less than this. Speedometers were considered useless until much later, mainly because wheelslip would give false readings. Drivers gauged their speeds by checking lineside objects against a pocket watch for both speed and timing, and late running had always to be explained at journey's end. Although not a common practice, it was not unusual on some lines for crews to have an engine for their more or less exclusive use.

Crew training took on a regular and practically unalterable pattern. The apprentices began with cleaning engines on shed, and later were allowed to light fires and raise steam ready for crews to take over. Servicing was under strict supervision, and rules on periodic tube sweeping, boiler cleaning, and greasing were strict. Fines could be imposed— as deductions from wages for any shortcomings and misdemeanours. This was the hard, disciplined way up the first rungs of the ladder, and the peak of ambition would be to become a driver on express trains. It could take ten or more years to become a qualified fireman on such trains, but first aspirants—and there was never a shortage—had first to fire shunters, then goods trains and branch line engines. Having become a fully-fledged fireman, the next step was to be an acting driver, able to take charge as driver in an emergency. Many men had to wait years in this grade until the death or retirement of a senior driver allowed the upper rungs of what was an elite craftsman's profession to be reached.

Apprentices taken into locomotive works were in a different category. It was their job to learn all there was to

Above: Built in 1909 by Robert Stephenson, this London, Tilbury & Southern Railway 4-4-2 No. 80 Thundersley is one of the final enlarged versions of 'Atlantic' tank engines designed by Whitelegg for the tightly-timed trains on the sharply curved and graded lines out of Fenchurch Street, London. Thundersley is now restored and in running order at Bressingham.

Right: One of a class of 192 engines built by the Midland Railway to Sir Henry Fowler's 1911 design, Class 4F No. 43924 was built at Derby in 1920. She is a prime example of the classic British 0-6-0 freight engine; simple, rugged, built to last and capable of sustained hard work.

know about steam and how its power was utilised, as well as all related aspects of mechanics. In due course they were expected to sit for examinations under the auspices of the Locomotive Section of the Institute of Mechanical Engineers. Those who passed were eligible for appointments which included Locomotive Shed Masters, graded according to the importance of a given shed within a system, while the apex of a wide-based staff pyramid was the plum but exacting post of Chief Mechanical Engineer.

And it was open to ambitious men to apply for higher positions with a company other than the one which gave them their early training.

One of the new and larger express locomotives of the 1890s was the 50-ton North Eastern 4-4-0, which took part with honours in the 1895 races to Scotland. One of the first 4-6-0s appeared on the Highland Railway in 1894, the engine without tender weighing 56 tons. Then came Ivatt's 1898 4-4-2 'Atlantic' for the Great Northern on the London–York run, weighing 60 tons. It was the first of its type, and was followed in 1902 by a larger and re-boilered version, at nearly 70 tons. The Midland Railway preferred for a long time to use smaller engines double-headed for express trains, but in 1902 brought out a 3-cylinder compound with 200 lb. pressure. The Great Western 4-4-0 'City' class also had 200 lb. pressure, and the *City of Truro* was claimed to have touched 100 m.p.h.

Superheating

These last two engines were super-heated, a practice which became practically general on all larger locomotives, both passenger and goods, for the remainder of the era.

There had been proof enough that the greater the heat and dryness of steam, the greater its force. The multi-tube boiler had a large number of small tubes—a hundred or more of about 2 inch diameter which ran from end to end of the boiler. They occupied about two-thirds of the water space in the boiler barrel, and the space above the tubes was used for evaporation of the boiling water. But the steam was not fully dry by the time it reached the dome or main pipe leading to the cylinders. Superheating dried it still further, by making it pass through a system of smaller tubes in direct contact with the intensely hot gases emerg-

ing from the firebox. Steam from the boiler passed through the header in the smokebox and was then passed back through the elements inside the flues, to return to the header superheated.

Newly designed goods engines also came in for superheating. The Great Eastern 0-6-0 of 1901—later classed as T.17—weighing only 45 tons at 180 p.s.i., was the first of 90 very successful locomotives built by James Holden, and was reckoned to be the most powerful 0-6-0 of its time. It was however eclipsed for power by the Churchward 1903 Great Western 2-8-0, a much heavier engine of 75 tons, superheated and having a boiler pressure of 225 lb. This class of which 167 were built, worked until the last days of steam. Churchward, one of the giants among designers, also brought out the famous 'Star' class, with four cylinders, and some heavy express tank engines. He introduced a system of interchangeable standard-sized boilers,

The Walschaerts valve gear (and the Belpaire firebox) came from Belgium, and became more widely adopted than any other valve gear both in the U.K. and abroad. This ingeniously simple invention operates as an attachment to the big end bearing on the driving wheel so that the down rod outside the crosshead controls entry and emission of steam to the valves situated in a smaller cylinder above the main one.

above requirements and its weight restricted it to the London–Bristol run. It was eventually reboiled, converted to a 4-6-0, and renamed *Viscount Churchill*. Curiously enough, Gresley's first Pacifics were in production when the *Great Bear* was rebuilt; but while other companies built 4-6-2s, the Great Western never again attempted to do so.

Increased power and improved performance had become a vital factor. So much trial and error in the past gradually led to a more scientific approach to speed, efficiency and economy of running. Although 'horse power' had been adopted in the early days as a means of assessing the pull of a locomotive, it had become a merely nominal rating. Comparison with horses became unrealistic for machines which were far more swift, yet could stall if their wheels slipped when starting off on wet rails. Sand boxes were of course used to lessen wheel slip; but accurate tests only became possible through the use of a dyna-

one of the practices which gained the Great Western enormous prestige during his reign as Chief Mechanical Engineer from 1902 to 1921.

Decapod and Great Bear

Both Holden and Churchward were responsible for new designs which proved to be short-lived wonders of the steam age. The first was Holden's *Decapod* 0-10-0, a massive small-wheeled tank engine built at Stratford Works which had a tractive effort and acceleration far greater than any other heavy-duty locomotive of its period. It proved too heavy for any existing track to enable it to be widely used, and was scrapped after a short time. Churchward built the *Great Bear* in 1908, and this too proved to be ahead of its time. It was the first British 4-6-2 'Pacific', and although it remained unique for 14 years, its power capacity was well

mometer car. Churchward used one for test runs in 1903, an advance on previous attempts made on the L.N.W.R. The car, staffed by specially trained operators, provided records not only of speed but of the actual power exerted—known as tractive effort—for a known fuel and water consumption. Tractive effort was the measure of the drawbar pull against a spring, and calculated in pounds. For example, the Midland Compound mentioned earlier was rated at 21,840 lb. Tractive effort of the G.W.R. 'City' Class was 17,790 lb., while that of the Great Eastern 0-6-0 J.17 was 24,340 lb.

Although steel for fireboxes was commonly used by makers of industrial locomotives, the main line railways used copper for preference. Its properties of being more malleable, as well as more durable and resistant to forming scale, made it worth the extra cost where high efficiency and low maintenance was vital. Railway locomotives tended to become more com-

plicated in having equipment not deemed necessary for the slower-moving, short-run industrial engines. Oil feed, especially to the cylinders, demanded an automatic action to avoid wear and tear which could be disastrous on long runs. Cylinder oil, incidentally, was thicker and heavier than other lubricating oil. An ample oil supply for bearings and axle-boxes was equally important—a 'hot box' could stop an express train. Worsted was used in 'stuffing' boxes filled with oil, while a slow-acting drip along threaded wool took oil to parts in constant need of slight lubrication.

Steam brakes on the engines and continuous vacuum brakes on the passenger coaches were all under the control of the crew on the footplate, but they added to the need for ever more sophisticated equipment, as well as skill and vigilance on the part of the crews.

It is very noticeable how over the years locomotives gradually became taller and chimneys shorter. The expla-

nation is simple enough; that trial and error proved that a higher centre of gravity made for greater safety, especially at speed, and of necessity chimneys had to be shorter to clear tunnels and bridges. Another factor was that with the larger boiler well clear of the wheels, axles and motion, there was easier access to them for maintenance. The introduction of the Pacific 4-6-2 wheel arrangement allowed the driving wheels to be well placed for adhesion, and the rear wheels—or 'pony truck'—allowed more room for a larger firebox.

Flying Scotsman has become the most famous of all express locomotives. As the first of Gresley's Pacifics it also took the name of the train which ran daily at 10 a.m. from London to Edinburgh. In spite of its long chequered career since it was built in 1923, it is still in service for B.R. steam specials, but is now privately owned. The 4-6-2 wheel arrangement allowed a larger firebox to be fitted.

Continental innovations

Some of the improvements to locomotive boilers have been noted, with the emphasis almost entirely on maximum heating surface obtainable. There was a good deal of interchange between foreign and British designers—on the whole the continental engineers came up with the new ideas. In this period the de Glehn compounds came out in France, and the Great Western was not above trying some out in service. The Belgians came out with several innovations which were taken up in England. One of these was the Belpaire firebox, which became quite widely used. Its outline was roughly shaped like an inverted letter U, wider at the top than at the bottom, to give a humped appearance just in front of the cab, with more space above the fire for combustion, and above the water-line for steaming.

Fireboxes of all but the smallest locomotives were fitted with brick arches. These were constructed with firebricks arching over and away from the base of the boiler tube-plate towards the firehole door, of a size and shape according to the grate area. The idea was to draw the hot gases, swan-neck fashion, over the firebrick arch so as to improve combustion, before entering the tubes and flues.

Contemporary with the first Pacifics was the introduction of the Walschaerts valve gear, also from Belgium. This gear, operating a piston valve, brought all the motion outside, with the piston valve in what appears to be a separate cylinder above and twinned to the main power cylinder. The outstanding example of this practice, with its large firebox, high boiler and squat chimney, burst upon the locomotive scene in 1922, designed by Nigel Gresley and built at Doncaster. It was named *Great Northern*, and the third in the batch, No. 1472 (now 4472) carried the name *Flying Scotsman*, to become the most famous locomotive since the *Rocket*, nearly a century earlier.

The 1923 grouping

The period when British steam achieved its greatest glory had begun, even if its death knell had also sounded unheard, with mass production of the motor car fast beginning. The year 1923 began with the amalgamation of practically all the existing railway companies into four groups. It was a logical step, making for more rational and economic working, at a time when post-war depression was seen as a threat to profitability. But if a decline had in fact begun, it did not affect competition between the four groups: the Great Western Railway; the London, Midland & Scottish Railway; the

London and North-Eastern Railway; and the Southern Railway. They all competed for supremacy in motive power. When the mergers took place in 1923 there were nearly 20,000 miles of active railways providing both goods and passenger service, with a total of over 18,000 locomotives. Once the ravages of war, in terms of depleted manpower and run-down rolling stock, had been overcome, the pre-war standard of efficiency and cleanliness was largely restored. The railway hierarchy was headed by a high-powered General Manager, but the Chief Mechanical Engineer frequently came in for a knighthood as an indication of his importance.

Gresley improved on the *Flying Scotsman* by fitting a higher-pressured boiler of 225 p.s.i. to the *Enterprise*,

and one of his later streamlined A4 Pacifics of the mid-1930s, the *Mallard* achieved the world record speed for steam of 126 m.p.h. Collett of the Great Western following Churchward's earlier 4-6-0s, came out with the splendid 'Castle' class, also in 1923 with two outside cylinders and two inside, using Stephenson link valve gear. No less than 161 'Castles' were built, but in 1927 the larger 'King' class appeared and was even more successful, though still only a 4-6-0. Examples of both classes have been preserved, along with later but smaller editions of engines with a distinctive Great Western stamp.

The smallest of the four groups, the Southern, sometimes lacking in prestige, was under R. E. L. Maunsell as C.M.E. In 1925 he introduced the two-cylinder 'King Arthur' class, built by outside contractors, and the larger 4-6-0 named 'Lord Nelson' built at the S.R. Eastleigh works; but only fifteen more of the latter were built. His most successful design was the 'Schools' 4-4-0, of which fifty were built. For the much larger L.M.S. system, which at one time was the world's largest single employer, Sir Henry Fowler was C.M.E. from 1925 to 1932. He had been for several years C.M.E. with the Midland Railway, the second largest system to be amalgamated with the L.N.W.R. to form the L.M.S. After some frustrating disagreements with his board, he came out with the *Royal Scot* in 1927, in a vain effort to keep up with Gresley on the L.N.E.R. in spite of it being a very powerful 4-6-0 with three cylinders. Sir William Stanier

In 1933, Stanier introduced the first two of his 'Princess Royal' Pacifics for working on the West Coast main line between London and Glasgow. They were relatively massive 4 cylinder engines with 250 p.s.i. boiler pressure, 6 ft. 6 in. diameter wheels and a tender-less weight of $104\frac{1}{2}$ tons each. These two engines went through a long test period before a further batch of 10 was constructed in 1935. No. 6203, Princess Margaret Rose, is one of the 1935 batch and after withdrawal in the 1960s was purchased by Messrs Butlins and displayed at Pwllheli. She is now at the Midland Railway Centre, Butterley, Derbyshire. One of the original pair of engines, No. 6201, Princess Elizabeth, is now actively based at Ashchurch, Gloucestershire.

took over in 1932, and became famous for the several other classes he was able to build, including the first L.M.S. Pacifics in 1933, the big 'Duchesses' of 1938, and the 4-6-0 'Black Fives' of which twelve have been preserved.

In the Beyer-Garratt locomotive, the boiler is articulated between two power bogies. This allows an excessively long rigid wheel base, enabling the locomotive to negotiate sharp curves easily. William Francis, works No. 6841, was built in 1937. She is now at Bressingham Steam Museum and is the only standard gauge Garratt left in this country.

Gresley and Stanier

As an introduction, this book can scarcely do justice to what might be termed the golden age of steam on the railways of Britain, nor to such outstanding designers as Churchward, Collett, Gresley, Stanier and to the latecoming Bulleid of the Southern Railway. Nor is it appropriate to make comparisons between them. Collett, following in Churchward's footsteps on the Great Western, enhanced a tradition which could scarcely be criticised for producing thoroughbred locomotives, making use of every technical advance consistent with reliability. Stanier came to take over the L.M.S. in 1932 when the long struggle to integrate three distinctive railway companies into one system had scarcely succeeded as far as motive power was concerned under Fowler. Stanier's achievements in design for power and reliability have sometimes been credited to his Great Western background. Gresley, on the other hand, was an individualist restlessly experimenting

throughout his career until it ended in 1941 with his sudden death.

These two, Stanier and Gresley, stand out as the giants of the period. Even if their rivalry as engineers to the two largest systems lasted only nine years, this was an historic era, and their story is well told in the centenary tribute to them published by H.M.S.O. This fully illustrated book, written by two well-informed staff members of the National Railway Museum at York, is strongly recommended to those wishing to read how the British steam locomotive achieved its greatest glory.

But there is another side to the story. It concerns not only the rivalry between Gresley and Stanier, but how both men as individualists backed their own beliefs, and, one could almost add, their obsessions. Of the two, Gresley was the more outstanding innovator, but paradoxically he clung to certain ideas and principles, such as the superiority of three cylinders over two or four, and the virtues of his conjugated valve gear to work the third (inside) cylinder. Both men were searching for a breakthrough, in the belief that steam had a greater power

potential if the century-old Stephenson layout could be developed into something new.

To meet the needs of the times, some radical change had to come. Gresley, after two years' intensive work, brought out the hush-hush No. 10,000 in 1930. It had a Yarrow water-tube boiler with a pressure of no less than 450 p.s.i. and was a four-cylinder

compound. Although it must be said that locomotive engineers in other countries were also working on similar lines, aiming at maximum efficiency with very high steam pressures to enable compounding to be fully effective, No. 10,000 was hailed as a breakthrough. The hush-hush building period gave way to maximum publicity as it took to the rails, but after extensive trials the engine showed neither appreciable fuel savings nor the hoped-for power performance, and was quietly withdrawn, later to be converted to a conventional design.

Fuel consumption had always been an important factor. Gresley, in a famous paper delivered to the Institute of Mechanical Engineers in 1931, had made cogent claims for the value of

Stephenson and Hawthorn's 0-4-0 crane tank Millfield at work in the Doxford shipyard, Sunderland. When the yard closed in 1971, there were five crane engines still in service of which four have been preserved. Power for slewing and raising the jib is provided by a donkey engine mounted in front of the crane turret. Millfield still works for her keep at Bressingham, assisting in standard gauge track-laying and maintenance, and moving heavy equipment.

high pressures, as a means of extracting the greatest power from coal. He also stated that the British railways in total were consuming coal at an annual cost of £12 million, or one quarter of the gross total of locomotive running costs. At the then cost of coal, this would amount to a use each year of at least 8,000,000 tons!

In 1938 one of Gresley's pupils, Oliver Bulleid, was appointed C.M.E. to the Southern Railway. There was a need for more steam power, to supplement the electrification programme which had taken place on shorter and commuter routes. Longer hauls had been somewhat neglected. Bulleid came up first with the fine 'Merchant Navy' Pacifics and the smaller 'West Country' 4-6-2s which embraced some of his own ideas as well as Gresley's.

But he also had the dubious distinction of taking innovation too far with the 'Leader' class engine, whose prototype proved to be an expensive failure. He built the remarkably ugly, if quite successful, 'Austerity' 0-6-0 freight engines. By comparison the wartime 'Austerities' designed by R. A. Riddles were good-looking, for all their being 2-8-0 and 2-10-0 freight engines with squat little chimneys.

Locomotives in World War II

No more tribute has been paid than was justly due to the role played by steam on the railways during the dark days of 1939–45. Although many older engines, some already over fifty years old, were retained in service, thanks largely to Gresley and Stanier the heavy building programme of locomotives in the 1930s made an invaluable contribution to the war effort. This applied especially to the classes of mixed-traffic engines such as Stanier's 4-6-0 'Black Fives' and Gresley's 2-6-2 V2s. The most successful express Pacifics, the A4s of the L.N.E.R. and the 'Duchesses' of the L.M.S., also had a fine record, and all of these classes are represented in preservation.

For all his refinements, which included a steam-operated coal pusher at the rear of the tender, Stanier overlooked or failed to include two useful features which were used on contemporary designs. One was a master valve in the cab, which in case of trouble would cut off steam from all face plate controls. The other was that of a drop-grate mechanism for the fire. Lack of these was acutely felt when, after the *Duchess of Sutherland* had been restored and put in steam at Bressingham, valve failures necessitated the fire having to be hurriedly shovelled out through the cab, to avoid danger from loss of water. A master valve would have prevented the back-flow of steam through the injector overflow and so made the fire safe to leave undrawn and burning.

The H.M.S.O. book *Gresley & Stanier* mentioned earlier gives descriptions of experimental locomotives constructed and projected which demonstrated the fertility of their minds towards the fullest exploitation of steam. If it had not been for the war, Gresley's untimely death, and the upsurge of diesel power, even the failures might have led to steam retaining its supremacy, through the use of improved valve gear, superheating, blast pipes, streamlining and such in-

A group of women cleaning L.M.S. engines in the round house during the Second World War. This involved cleaning springs, wheels, brake gear, valve gears and coupling rods, thus enabling the short-staffed engine fitters to do their work more easily and more quickly.

An example of the Patriot class, after the name of No. 45500, the first of 52 built between 1930 and 1934 on the L.M.S. system.

ventions as the Giesl ejector and the Crosti boiler. The last were foreign inventions—as was the not entirely successful Caprotti valve gear.

Gresley's Beyer–Garratt

Stanier was also intrigued by the idea that steam on the rail had greater potentiality if exploited by other means than that of the Stephenson piston/cylinder method. He built one turbine-powered 4-6-2, but the circumstances of the time put a brake on using steam turbines successfully in a locomotive. Time and funds for what would have been a long and expensive process of development were not then available.

Sad to relate, two of the most powerful locomotives ever built in Britain, one for freight and the other for passenger running, were not preserved. The former was Gresley's Beyer-Garratt, built by Beyer-Peacock of Manchester on the very successful

articulated principle still being used in Africa. The Garratt had two separate sets of coupled wheels, with four cylinders and valve gears. Each set of wheels carried a 'tender', and the boiler on a separate frame was suspended on pivots between them. The rear tender carried both coal and water, while the front one carried water only. Articulation was made possible by means of flexible steam pipes from the boiler. The only example preserved of this distinctive design is at Bressingham, but it is relatively small, having an 0-4-0 + 0-4-0 wheel arrangement.

Gresley's 2-8-0 + 0-8-2 Garratt had a tractive effort of no less than 72,849 lb. (compared with the 34,440 lb. of the L.M.S. 2-8-0 standard freight loco) and weighed over 200 tons as against the 72 tons of the 2-8-0. The most powerful passenger engine at the time of its introduction in 1934 by Gresley was the P2, a 2-8-2 named *Cock o' the North*. Only four others followed, and though successful for their designated purpose in Scotland, these five locomotives were later rebuilt by Gresley's successor Edward Thompson as very undistinguished Pacifics.

Nationalisation

Although a large number of engines had been built during the war years, both for the railways and vital industries, many were sent overseas as replacements for engines destroyed in the wartime ravages of overseas railways. With peace and a Labour government came the demand for nationalisation of the railways, which brought with it the requirement for standardisation of motive power.

Dozens of types and classes among the 18,000 or more locomotives then running were to be made gradually redundant, as new designs were specified by the Railway Executive under the overall authority of the British Transport Commission, set up in 1947. R. A. Riddles, with A. C. Bond and E. S. Cox, were the triumvirate appointed to carry out the task, but controversy arose on whether to continue with steam as the source of power, or to switch to either diesel or electric propulsion, or to both, at this crucial stage. The cost factor, in terms of capital outlay, cast the die in favour of steam, in spite of the growing belief that its days were numbered.

One of the first acts of the Railway Executive was to inaugurate a system of trials, whereby the best locomotives of the four pre-war companies were interchanged, with teams of technicians to record their respective performances. But what seemed in principle a very sensible idea failed in practice because so many variables emerged, and relatively little useful data was gained on which to base future standard designs which would embody the best features of all. It was found, for example, that the skill of the drivers could greatly affect performance calculations, as did the quality of the coal available.

Meanwhile, between 1945 and 1948, the existing railway workshops continued to build their respective pre-nationalisation designs in considerable numbers. This production had to be maintained, if only to keep the work-force employed until the new standard

designs were available, and this was not to be until 1950. Despite the lack of reliable data after the interchange trials, it was decided to go ahead with twelve new standard designs.

The British Railways designs

The first of the new British Railways standard locomotives took to the rails early in 1951, but it was not until 1954 that all twelve types were seen. And it was quite noticeable that some classes bore a strong resemblance to existing L.M.S. types. There were strictly speaking only nine classes, because there were tank versions of the Class 2,

3 and 4 tender engines. These were designed for light hauls and short runs. Class 5 was for mixed traffic, and the 29 built in 1951 showed no great external variations on the already numerous L.M.S. 'Black Fives'. The Class 6 was a Pacific designed especially for Scottish routes; two were built in 1951, and eight in 1952, with no more following after that date.

The greatest impact came with the appearance of 25 Class-7 4-6-2s which took the class name 'Britannia' from that of the first to appear in 1951. This was an entirely new design for an express passenger locomotive, and apart from a few teething troubles, proved to be very successful. It was a simple two-cylinder engine, relatively easy to service, and it could sustain a long spell in constant use. The improvement to passenger timetables in East Anglia, where some of the first of them worked, was quite spectacular. Although they had lost something of the sheer sleek lines of the British

tradition, they were nonetheless both imposing and majestic.

It was in 1954 that the goods version came out, as a Class 9 2-10-0. The wheel arrangement was the only vital difference from the Class 7 'Britannias'. This too was very successful, and despite its small wheels was capable of quite high speeds. Class 9 had the distinction of being the most numerous of the new range with a total of 251 built. No. 9220 was the last steam locomotive to be built for British Railways and was appropriately named *Evening Star*—one of two of the class which have been preserved. Two 'Britannias', of which 55 were built, are also preserved, and Classes 2, 3, 4 and 5 are well represented up and down the country.

Although 999 standard locomotives were built between 1950 and 1960, the programme was ruthlessly axed during experiments with such innovations as the Caprotti valve gear, the Crosti boiler and the Giesl ejectors.

Southern Railway No. 35029 Clan Line is one of Bulleid's revolutionary 'Merchant Navy' class Pacifics, the first of which was built in 1941. In spite of it being wartime, novel features included streamlined overall casing, giving them a nickname of 'spam cans', and chain driven valve gear working in an oil bath. They were rebuilt in the 1950s to become one of the most handsome engines to run in this country.

The diesel threat

It was seen by all concerned with steam on the railways that diesel and electric power were becoming ever more competitive. A Class 8 Pacific, designed for greater power than Class 7, had been tried out in 1954, carrying the number 71000 and the name *Duke of Gloucester*. No more were built, for despite the use of Caprotti valve gear and three cylinders, with a greater heating surface and tractive effort, performance was indifferent. Initial building and running costs on trials were high, and there were misgivings as to the wisdom of building ever larger engines to compete with diesels, which by now had largely taken over from steam in the U.S.A. During the 1950s quite a large number of small diesels for shunting had been built, and these doubtless gave some proof that low axle loads and greater adhesion from multiple driving wheels was a pointer to the way ahead.

Any new steam locomotive design could scarcely avoid some extra axle weight. With the Britannias it was 20 tons per driving axle. To build engines with great tractive effort, capable of sustained high speeds over heavy gradients, would have meant going in for 4-8-4s, with three, four or maybe more cylinders. Weights would have been too great for many existing tracks and the prospect was seen to be fraught with dangers. Such engines had been built in the U.S.A., but even they were now on the way out in favour of diesels. André Chapelon, the famous French designer, had produced some remarkably powerful high-speed locomotives, and was convinced that steam on his lines still had a future. But

British designers, restricted as they were by Government directives, remained hesitant; and when one of those directives was that steam was to be phased out, the total demise of steam became a reality. The stupid haste with which this was carried out under Beeching has been sufficient to call down on him a widespread and justifiable opprobrium.

The 'Beeching Axe'

The drastic and seemingly ruthless application of the 'Beeching Axe' is a sad story. It began in 1955, with a much publicised Modernisation Plan prepared by the B.T.C. under its chairman Sir Brian Robertson, and energetically continued under his successor Dr. R. Beeching who came from I.C.I. in 1961. It was as though the railway top brass became suddenly ashamed of its own image. Steam was seen as antiquated and out of keeping with modern times, with diesel and electric power in the ascendant. The Americans had again set the pattern for Britain to emulate, and diesel locomotives were hastily procured for main line working, despite their capital cost being up to four times greater than steam engines of similar power. The first diesels gave trouble—but the die was cast and the Plan went ahead, including the closure of many routes whose tracks were hastily torn up and sold for scrap.

Steam locomotives were relegated to lesser duties, and large numbers, once they could be classed as redundant, were towed to breakers' yards to be cut up for scrap. Those remaining in dwindling service became steadily dirtier and more forlorn through sheer neglect, and this applied not only to older types, but to some of the new B.R. standard designs also. Vital repairs were of course made and most servicing regulations obeyed, but the element of pride in the motive power had vanished, from top to bottom of the railway hierarchy, with only a minority caring that the end of steam had come. One heard of instances where locomotives, newly overhauled, or in basically sound condition, were condemned for some relatively minor fault which could easily and quickly have been remedied.

All this neglect and hasty destruction affected not only the locomotives themselves, but the many railway workshops, where stores and equipment were to hand, along with the men skilled in steam engine lore. The shops were run down. Bonfires were made of thousands of patterns, new boiler tubes sold for scrap or for fencing posts, and machine tools and heavy equipment were sold off; while relic hunters whipped off name-plates and whistles from rows of engines standing discarded and forlorn on sidings up and down the country, awaiting their turn for execution under the breaker's acetylene torch.

Although there was ample reason for the railways of Britain to be modernised, the millions spent on the project failed to yield the expected return. The railways were making losses when the programme began in 1955, and continued to do so for a further twenty years. This was to some extent due to the switch from steam to diesel being over-hastily carried out; it would have been wiser to concentrate on improving the track for the higher speeds of which the more modern steam locomotives were capable. In some countries, notably Germany and France, the phasing out of steam was much more gradual, tending to avoid the introduction of diesels in favour of electrification as the more efficient and reliable source of power.

As it was, British Railways spent vast sums on diesels, while discarding all its steam potential. In August 1968, B.R. ran its last steam-hauled train as a swan-song trip from Liverpool to Carlisle, using a 'Black Five' 4-6-0 and the Class 7 Pacific No. 70013 *Oliver Cromwell*, the last of the steam locomotives to be overhauled at Crewe. At that time the large number of derelict locomotives was fast diminishing—but the enthusiasm for preservation was gaining momentum.

Nostalgia and preservation

It really began with the re-opening of the 'Bluebell Line' in Sussex, although there were a few narrow-gauge steam railways already catering for the nostalgia which the demise of steam had called into being. During the 1960s nostalgia had prompted individuals to form societies, mainly to preserve sections of discarded railway on which to run steam trains, manned mainly by volunteer helpers. Some locomotives were purchased direct from British Rail, but at Barry in South Wales Woodham Brothers had stockpiled nearly 300 engines of several types, instead of cutting them up for scrap, as had all the other scrap merchants who had been taking them in. They no doubt anticipated rising scrap metal prices rather than a demand for preservation, but the fact remains that well over one hundred engines were bought by enthusiasts for preservation.

Of those bought earlier, the *Flying Scotsman* acquired by Alan Pegler in 1965 ran a succession of special trips which not only filled the seats of the coaches it hauled, but attracted thousands to see the engine itself in stations and along its route as it passed. I witnessed this phenomenon from the footplate of this famous locomotive one rainy day in May 1969, following a trip it had made to Diss station for its passengers to come to the Bressingham Museum. At every crossing, station and vantage point along its route from Stowmarket to Cambridge, all were waving and cheering. The *Flying Scotsman* was soon afterwards taken to North America where it ran many thousands of miles, causing considerable excitement wherever it went, as had another famous engine, the *Royal Scot*, years before in 1933. There the latter had performed very favourably against much larger American engines, as told in a booklet published by the L.M.S.

entitled *The Triumph of the Royal Scot*, which has now been reprinted.

The *Royal Scot* is now at Bressingham on permanent loan from Messrs. Butlins, along with three other locomotives which formed part of a collection acquired by Sir Billy Butlin to be on static display at four of his holiday camps. Sir Billy had bought engines of his choice direct from British Rail in the early 1960s as another way of catering for steam nostalgia, but within ten years they were deteriorating in the salty seaside air and just in time were brought inland for restoration and preservation.

There was a period when British Rail would have nothing to do with steam locomotives on its tracks. It occurred after Alan Pegler's contract allowing him to run excursions with the *Flying Scotsman* had ended, in 1969. But by 1972, a change of attitude occurred. It was due in part to the silencing of those in high places who saw steam as an anachronism, in part to an acceptance that their former locomotives were a worthy national heritage, and because there was potential revenue in catering for steam nostalgia. Since then selected routes have seen well-patronised trains hauled almost entirely by steam locomotives which British Rail no longer owns.

The railway museums

On the credit side, it must be said that British Rail, nationalised in 1948, was fully aware of the need to preserve a range of locomotives as relics of the steam age, but many historic examples had already vanished by then.

When the decision came to abandon steam in 1955, the British Transport Commission, strongly influenced by growing public opinion, at last decided to save a variety of relics for posterity. Locomotives were of course given a high priority, and a Consultative Panel was set up to decide which examples should be retained.

John Scholes, who had shown great initiative as curator of the York City Museum, was appointed curator of a new railway museum at Clapham. Existing railway-owned museums at Swindon and York had no room to spare for more locomotives, and Clapham also had to accommodate rolling stock, as well as to become a storehouse for a wide range of other relics and archives which John Scholes collected. Many locomotives, once earmarked for preservation, had to be stored in out-of-the-way sheds, awaiting their turn to be smartened up for museum display.

Clapham became an interesting museum, but due to its location it failed to attract enough visitors to be self-supporting. It became in fact rather a burden to British Rail. After lengthy negotiations, responsibility for all railway relics passed to the Department of Education and Science, who in turn finally decided to build a large new museum at York. This was opened in 1975, but still there was insufficient space in which to display the total of sixty locomotives preserved. Under the 1968 Transport Act, British Rail became empowered to allow some of these to go to private museums, and the first transfer made was to the newly-built live steam museum at Bressingham. Since then allocations have been made to a few other sites on preserved railways, privately owned and run.

Most of the officially preserved locomotives have now been restored, but not many are in running condition, because at the start, preservation was on the principle of their being static exhibits. However, the intense interest in live steam, with its smells and sounds added to the visual appeal, has increased beyond all expectations. This has led not only to British Rail steam-hauled trips, but to more effort being made to restore engines fully to steam again, in spite of costs and difficulties that were unimaginable a few years ago before all repair equipment and spares were scrapped.

Far more locomotives have been saved by enthusiasts than are included on the official list, which was of necessity restricted to one representative each of certain outstanding classes. Apart from these, it is believed nearly one thousand engines have been rescued of both standard and narrow gauge, about half being industrial locomotives. They are owned both by private individuals and societies, many of which have not only a centre but also a stretch of line on which steam trains are run for the public to enjoy.

Introduced by Stanier for working the accelerated Anglo-Scottish expresses, the 8P class Pacifics were enlarged, improved versions of the earlier 'Princess' class. Duchess of Sutherland ran until 1963. She is now on permanent loan from Messrs. Butlins to Bressingham.

After a lapse of 11 years as the owner of a traction engine, the author bought this single crank compound Burrell in 1961, the first of many following as a museum collection at Bressingham where it is seen here at work. The cleat in the rear wheel enables the wheel to grip when going through mud. The larger second cylinder, as a compound, can be seen as a bulge below the excess steam blowing from the safety valve beside the governor, the revolving balls of which automatically control the inflow of steam to the high pressure cylinder.

5

STEAM FOR AGRICULTURE

The needs of agriculture

As the branches of a tree diverge from a single trunk, so the development and application of steam power branched out once certain basic principles had become established. Steam for transport followed close behind its use for mining and industry, and its application to boats and railways was a simple process when compared to that of its use in road-using vehicles. Those who attempted to meet the need for passenger transport on the roads were probably so concerned with overcoming the many obstacles they encountered, that the development of steam power for agriculture was largely neglected for much of the first half of the 19th century. In this period steam was very much an urban and industrial concern and the farming community was scarcely competent either to invent or adapt the new technology for the land, to lighten the work of men and horses. Prejudice against new-fangled notions was also more prevalent among the farming community.

The triple needs of agriculture were

of haulage and cultivation, and for such operations as threshing corn. Each called for a different type of engine. None of those made for passenger-carrying on the roads during the 1820s and 1830s was sturdy enough to haul farm commodities over farm tracks, even if a farmer were wealthy enough to purchase one. For cultivation or harvesting there was no choice but to stick to men and horses, and it was not until about 1860 that the problem of engine weight on soft ground began to be solved. Harvesting and threshing were the most labour-intensive of all farming operations and when machines began to replace the scythe and the flail, there were riots and rick burnings, and a sharp increase in the number of paupers in rural areas.

These three maker's engravings are of early portables by Ransomes of Ipswich, dated about 1850. All have very tall chimneys to increase draught and reduce risk of fire when threshing, cylinders over the firebox, and the flywheel positioned forward to link up with belt driven machinery.

The portable engine

There are no reliable records as to when steam was first used for threshing. Threshing machines appeared early in the 19th century but it was the standardisation of the horizontal tubular boiler on the railways during the early 1830s which indirectly opened the door to those engineers who were in touch with farming. These were the makers of ploughs and other implements, who often as not had expanded from modest smithies in market towns and villages. In studying the locomotive-type boiler, they saw no reason why its transmission could not be altered to drive a flywheel instead of a wheeled axle. They saw no reason either for keeping the cylinders beneath the boiler, as on a locomotive, when by transferring just one cylinder to a position on top, it could easily be connected to a flywheel as a prime mover able to drive machinery by means of a belt. The engine needed only to be fitted with four wheels and a swivelling axle in front to make it a portable power unit sufficiently light to be moved by a team of strong horses.

Once the door had opened, the demand for portable steam engines was sufficient to step up the supply. They were relatively cheap and reliable, costing little more than £100, and their simple mechanism called for no great skill to maintain it in good working order. Farmers possessing a portable engine were able to thresh corn at strategic points on the farm, instead of having to cart it all to a large barn where men with flails and winnows threshed by hand on the floor. Portable engines could also be used for stacking at harvest and haytime, by driving an elevator, and they could work grinding mills and saw benches.

A rapidly increasing urban population due to industrialisation led not only to a greater demand for food crops, especially of wheat for bread,

but to an upsurge of interest in farming techniques. In turn this gave rise to the formation of agricultural societies, and in 1839 the Royal Agricultural Society of England became established.

The Society's decision to hold competitive shows in different centres each year was a tremendous fillip to machinery and implement makers. This was one of the classic examples of how a basic discovery developed sideshoots which in the main were mutually beneficial. The spread of railways boosted attendance at agricultural shows, but the resultant improved prosperity of farmers, landowners and railway shareholders, brought but scanty help and sympathy for the poverty of farm workers, a social evil during the 1840s and 1850s due largely to the spread of machines.

The first self–propelled engine

The portable steam engine was the true progenitor of what became known loosely as the traction engine. For several years however, it was accepted simply as a power unit, incapable of using its power to move itself. Although most engines weighed no more than three or four tons, which horses could move quite easily on dry hard ground, it was a different matter where soft earth or muddy farmyards had to be negotiated. It may well have struck some owners as absurd that a machine of such potential horse-power should

actually built by the Leeds engineers, E. B. Wilson and Co., but it was faulted for being too lightly built, and too much like a railway engine with its two cylinders beneath the boiler.

Although it is curious to note how long it took to convert the horizontal-boilered portable to self-propulsion when so many locomotives were in use on the railways, one can but assume that cost was the main consideration. The simple portable was within reach of most sizeable farmers, but the extra mechanism for propulsion meant extra weight as well as about treble the purchase price. Against these and other hindering factors there was nevertheless no lack of incentive, generated both by the competitive spirit between a growing number of engine builders and by the prestigious awards offered at Agricultural Society shows, now an important factor in the improvement of farming techniques.

Left: A Fowler portable engine with winch, used experimentally from a barge for land adjoining a Fenland river.

Below: In 1871 Lord Dunmore tried out a new ploughing system by steam haulage, using a Thomson engine. In spite of the engine's broad wheels it still proved too heavy on soft or wet earth and in the end only the winch system with two engines solved the problem.

Traction on soft ground

It so happened that the first engines to be self-driven were not designed so much for threshing as for haulage and cultivation. James Boydell had seen that the greatest problem of traction lay in the driving wheels which carried the main weight of an engine over soft ground. Trials, following his first patent in 1846, of a revolutionary type of wheel led to improvements by 1855 which were taken up by a Birmingham engineer who fitted them to a portable. The Back/Boydell engine was chain driven, but enthusiasm centred on the Boydell wheels which were in effect track layers. Stout boards were so fixed to the rim of all the wheels that each one in turn spread the weight. To these wooden shoes iron grooves were fixed, into which ran a ridged iron strip on each wheel, to earn the description of an 'endless railway'. Within a year or two other builders adopted Boydell's patent—including Clayton and Shuttleworth, Garrett, Tuxford and Burrell. All four were go-ahead engine and machinery builders and Burrell designed an engine specially suitable for road haulage which put up a very good performance.

have to be hauled to work by horses, but it was not until 1842 that a serious attempt at self-propulsion was made.

The Ipswich firm of Ransome exhibited the first self-propelled engine at the 1842 Royal Show held at Bristol. It proved a failure, in spite of gaining a prize of £30. It had a vertical boiler on a platform and was designed to transport and drive a threshing machine, but although it created much interest it returned to Ipswich unsold. This and other attempts at mobility gradually focused on the need to return to basic principles, by adapting the already successful railway locomotive to make it capable of hauling and driving the new and evolving farm machines. Again it was Ransomes who at the Royal Show near Leeds in 1849 exhibited their 'Farmers' Engine'. It was

But such engines were beyond the pockets of farmers. Burrell's cost over £600, and Tuxford's machine—a three-wheeler weighing 12 tons—cost £1,000. Far more were exported than were used in England, where it was found that the harder roads wore out Boydell's 'flip-flaps' very quickly.

By 1862, the year of Boydell's death, his last engine had been made. Another inventor, William Bray, produced a haulage engine with wide, weight-spreading wheels having teeth which dropped down to bite into the road surface. As a tractor, it was lighter, more economical and more powerful than any previously invented; but though highly acclaimed, in more than one variation of the original, it disappeared from English roads within a very few years, as did the weird 'Steam Elephant' of 1859–60 built by James Taylor of Birkenhead.

Although all three of the above engines fall into the category of traction engines, they were in a sense too far ahead of their time to become the prototypes of a standard efficient design, and unfortunately none has been preserved.

Boydell's patent had been taken up by firms who were closely linked to farming interests. The true traction engine, which by the end of the century was widely used also for heavy haulage for industry, evolved from what became the standard agricultural engine. Its era was about to begin, and should be given due emphasis if for no other reason that so many examples have been saved as active relics.

Portables self-propelled

Portables remained as useful power units with very few modifications from the 1840s to the 1940s. The first to appear in a true self-propelled design appeared in 1858. Like the standard portable it had the crank and flywheel just behind the chimney and the cylinders above the firebox; it was propelled by a chain pitched from the crankshaft to a large sprocket or spur wheel on the inside of a rear driving wheel. This was of necessity a much larger, broader wheel than was fitted to a normal portable, with traction such a vital factor. The steering was not altered. Horses had always been used both to haul and steer portables; now they were needed only to perform the latter function, and it was observed at the time that there was no finer way of breaking a horse of bad habits than to put him to this task.

Thomas Aveling, however, farming on Romney Marsh, saw this as literally wasted horsepower, and, after one or two experiments in conjunction with Clayton and Shuttleworth, patented a steering gear worked by a man sitting in front of the engine. Not content with the saving thus made, Aveling boldly transposed the layout of cylinders and flywheel crankshaft so as to place the latter above the driving wheel, and so obtained a more direct vertical drive by a much shorter chain. This method was quickly adopted by other builders, but by 1861 Aveling had set up his own works at Rochester and had become one of the leading patentees among those builders now forging ahead on a firmer basis. The way ahead for traction engines proper was at last becoming clear. And this included road haulage in spite of heavy tolls on British roads, which, however, were offset by an increasing export market for engines of all types.

Above: Tuxford's traction engine, or 'steam horse', fitted with Boydell patent 'endless' wheels.

Below: Wall plaque to mark the site of Burrell's works at Thetford, Norfolk, depicting Boydell's patent tracked wheels on one of their engines.

THIS MEMORIAL COMMEMORATES THE FIRM OF CHARLES BURRELL & SONS LIMITED WHO CARRIED ON BUSINESS IN THESE PREMISES FROM 1770 TO 1930 THEY PRODUCED THE WORLD'S FIRST HEAVY-DUTY STEAM ROAD HAULAGE ENGINE IN 1856 FOLLOWED BY A GREAT VARIETY OF TRACTION & OTHER ENGINES & AGRICULTURAL MACHINES ERECTED BY PUBLIC SUBSCRIPTION IN 1957, BEING THE HUNDRED AND FIRST ANNIVERSARY OF THE ABOVE ENGINE LEAVING THESE WORKS

The standard chain engine arrangement with the cylinders over the firebox, crankshaft behind the chimney, front steering position and ventral water tank are clearly shown on the first of Charles Burrell's chain driven agricultural engines.

Standardisation

Patents did not of course apply to the design of an entire engine, but to its component parts. This meant that almost any minor improvement patented by one builder could be copied without fear of a lawsuit by making some slight modification—which might be in itself an improvement. So within a few years a high degree of standardisation was effected by the dozen or so principle builders. Success bred success, and rear-mounted crankshafts with cylinders forward were soon adopted as standard; and then followed gearing, instead of chain drive, onto the driving-wheel sprocket. Geared transmission involved additional shafting to carry further sprockets or gear wheels, each on a shaft cogging in with one below. With a hand-operated gear-change two and later three speeds became possible.

Manual front steering remained standard for a few years; the tiller first used gave way to a spoked wheel rather like one used for steering a ship. This wheel operated a rack and pinion to effect a turn. In 1870 Thomas Aveling brought out an engine with worm-driven chain steering operated from the driving position at the rear. This engine was fitted with a built-in tender, serving as water tank, coal bunker and footplate, and except for further refinements the traction engine in its final form had arrived. Of these refinements, Garrett of Leiston, Suffolk, first used compounding in 1879, followed by the important firm of Fowler in 1881. It made for a real economy, because steam having driven the piston of one cylinder passed at lower pressure to another cylinder next door and drove a second piston, so adding additional force to the motion.

Before 1880, steam pressures had risen considerably. Boilers were 'pressed' for steam up to 150 p.s.i.—often doubling the pressure usually employed for portables, if only because the self-propelled engines were at least double the weight and needed more power to move them. Compounding, however, never became a general practice, and single-cylinder engines continued to be built until the last days.

Springing was applied mainly to haulage engines, when the 1896 Road Act finally did away with the necessity of a red flag being carried ahead of a mechanical vehicle. Farm engines were already exempt from this stupidity, which had restricted road-using engines to 4 m.p.h.; they did not need springs. Another refinement was the provision of a differential to prevent the strain of wheel slip on tight turns, which was considered by most agriculturalists as an unnecessary expense. Driving wheels were fitted with heavy pins which, if drawn out, allowed a wheel to become freed from the drive, to make sharp turns quite negotiable, at the expense only of the time it took to find the hole for reconnection.

By 1880, the last of the front-steering and chain-drive traction engines had been made. None are in preservation as far as is known, although one replica has been built in recent years based on the designs of Savage of King's Lynn. A few engines now preserved were built before 1880, but nearly all the 2,000 more recent

Below: 1904 Burrell 'showman' road locomotive Black Prince after restoration from its dilapidated state shown on Page 131. It is an 8 N.H.P. double crank compound, weighing 16 tons, with three speeds and on springs. The high backed tender was for additional coal and the underslung belly tank enabled longer distances to be covered, without having to stop for water, at speeds of up to 8–10 m.p.h.

Right: Burrells of Thetford were the first to cater for the flamboyancy required for the 'Showman' and led the field throughout the period of its popularity. That shown is of the smaller type used by the elite of the fairground operators as an extra engine both for haulage from place to place, and for providing electric light. This was of 4 N.H.P., against the 8 N.H.P. of the larger version for the heavier 'rides' of 'gallopers', gondolas, etc.

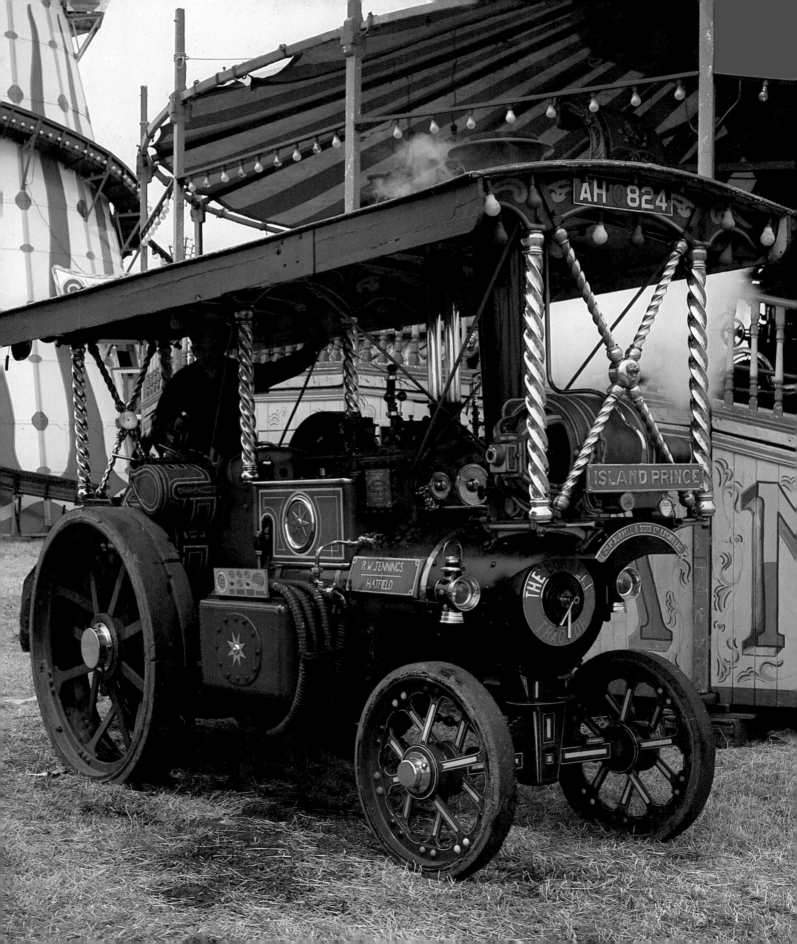

engines believed to be in active retirement, or still awaiting restoration, differ in minor detail only from standard, despite the variety of makers given in the list below:

Burrell, Thetford, Norfolk
Clayton & Shuttleworth, Lincoln
Robey, Lincoln
Foster, Lincoln
Marshall, Gainsborough
Aveling & Porter, Rochester
Ruston & Hornsby, Lincoln
Ransome, Ipswich
Foden, Sandbach
Davey Paxman, Chelmsford
Fowler, Leeds
McLaren, Leeds
Tuxford, Boston
Garrett, Leiston, Suffolk
Allchin, Northampton
Fowell, St. Ives, Hunts.
Tasker, Andover
Wantage Engine Co., Berkshire
Wallis & Stevens, Basingstoke
Brown & May, Devizes
Savage, Kings Lynn

There were several other lesser firms in the business, some of whom made only portable engines, often to go with implements and machinery they also produced. Most of the firms listed above also made other farm equipment, as well as road rollers, haulage and ploughing engines, and a few steam wagons. It is also noticeable that almost all the firms mentioned were located in or near the eastern arable farming districts of England. This gives emphasis to the effect of the restrictions on road transport for industry and the concentrated effort made to fill the needs of agriculture. Inventors and builders were coming out with ideas of applying steam to as many aspects of agriculture as possible. Steam trials sometimes ended in tribulation for those who had backed a failure, but this was no deterrent to others at a time when steam was seen as the answer to all power problems.

The view from the footplate of a Fowler ploughing engine. Inside the flywheel on the left is the vertical drive shaft with its bevelled pinion to drive the winch. Top centre is the steam chest, with safety valve and whistle above. The throttle rod is above the motion of piston rods and valve rods linked to the crankshaft with gear change mechanism.

Left: The White steam car was first built in America in about 1901, but production lasted only 10 years or so, during which time over 3,000 were sold. Prices were up to $5,000 for the largest model. The introduction of mass production methods for internal combustion motors became cheaper and steamers could not compete. This model had a prop shaft drive to a bevel geared axle and ran smoothly up to 35 m.p.h.

Below: One of the last Atkinson steam lorries to be built. Restored by Mr. Tom Varley of Gisburn, Lancs., it had a 6 ton capacity and was capable of about 20 m.p.h. This was brought back from Australia in a derelict condition by Mr. Varley and is the only survivor of the 500 built by Atkinson between 1916-1929.

Cultivation by machine

It is worth noting that while 1860 is often quoted retrospectively as marking the end of the Industrial Revolution, this date cannot be applied to

changes in agriculture. As an industry, it had far wider ramifications, and many variable factors. Mechanisation had indeed begun more than a century before, along with the improvement of husbandry techniques. But by the 1860s, especially after the American Civil War, cheap imported grain was beginning to threaten British agriculture, and the need for power to drive cultivating and harvesting

machines to compete with cheap imports became a vital necessity. Britain had become an industrial rather than an agrarian nation, and the population to be fed had doubled since 1810.

The first half of the 19th century had seen many attempts to design engines specifically for work on the land, even before the portable was introduced. Tindall in 1814 designed a weird contraption with what could be described as pushing legs instead of wheels, since it was realised then that traction was a major problem. David Gordon in 1824 with a somewhat similar machine also failed, and a

Above: Wheeled cultivator working between 2 Fowler's ploughing engines.

Left: Ploughing competition in Rutland.

Above right: Crosskill's steam cultivator, a rotary digging machine invented by Robert Romaine.

Right: The Darby 'Digger', having no wheels or tracks, literally 'walked' on its digger legs, which were activated by a very complex system of crankshafts, eccentrics and con-rods.

steam-raising unit both adequate and reliable was lacking. John Heathcoat of Tiverton in 1837 invented the first tracklayer as a means of ploughing, having an engine placed between four enormous wheels on which broad canvas mats were stretched, designed to keep the wheels on the surface. This 30-ton monster had a winch amidships which, placed in the centre of a field, drew ploughs back and forth at right angles by cables fixed to anchors. It created widespread interest as a machine capable of ploughing peat moss areas. After trials on Chat Moss, more were carried out on Lochar Moss near Dumfries, but after two days' work there it mysteriously disappeared overnight and was never seen again. It had cost Heathcoat £12,000 to develop.

It is not difficult to understand the strong inclination there was for agricultural engineers to press on with the invention of a steam engine capable of replacing teams of horses for ploughing and cultivation. At least a dozen machines were tried out by different engineers between 1837 and 1857, as Victorian ingenuity blossomed. The virtues of cable-hauled implements—as opposed to direct traction—and the strengths of various implements—the plough, the tined cultivator and the rotary digger—were the subject of many an argument. Lord Willoughby d'Eresby in 1850 believed he had the answer to the question of mechanised cultivation by using an endless chain. He also commissioned an expert—Daniel Gooch of the Great Western Railway no less—to design the engine which was to do the work of 16 horse-ploughs, from a portable railway.

Below: The Wallis & Stevens 'Advance' roller was a new design in the 1920s but was of limited popularity with the switch to diesel power coming a few years later.

Right: Savages of King's Lynn built most of the old-time rides with their own engine, but Tidman of Norwich brought out this compact little power unit, capable of driving the gallopers. Ranking as 4 h.p. with duplex cylinders, it has a short stroke for even running: The chimney and exhaust pass downwards at first to discharge inside the steel centre pole on which the strength of the ride depends. The boiler-mounted donkey engine powered the organ bellows, having its own cylinder. This set is a three-abreast of about 1889, owned by Mrs. Flora Bloom and can be seen operating at Bressingham on open days.

Fowler's success

Boydell's patent wheels, and many other contrivances tried out on tractors working their way across open fields, drawing ploughs, scufflers, clod breakers, mole drainers, seed drills and reapers, were not after all the answer, despite the praise some were given at first. These heavy tractors had led through sheer weight to soil panning and excessive consolidation and ran into trouble on soils made soft or sticky by rain. Finally the answer came when in 1860 John Fowler, a young and gifted Leeds engineer, perfected a special traction engine with an underslung windlass. This engine stood at one side of a field, and the implement was drawn back and forth between it and a movable anchor at the far side, engine and anchor being edged forward in unison after each traverse.

Direct traction steam engines for cultivation were now temporarily a

lost cause. John Fowler had undoubtedly benefited from the labours of his contemporaries working on the cable principle, including Howards of Bedford who were meeting with considerable success with their system. This used a portable engine working in a field corner driving a windlass, which allowed an endless cable to pass round the perimeter, drawing ploughs or cultivators. Fowler was accused of infringing a Howard patent, but was able to avoid prosecution on a technicality and his own system was soon to become a standard which was not superseded until the end of the steam era.

Savery's ploughing engines were a novelty in having the 6 foot cable winding drum revolving round the boiler, with the chimney at the rear driving end. This was one of many devices to ensure an even progress of the cable—so easily damaged by crumpling. Fowler quickly found, however, that Savery's method of using a second engine to replace the movable anchor led to greater

Above: John and Michael, a pair of Fowler 18 N.H.P. compound ploughing engines, are now owned by the Museum of Lincolnshire Life.

Right: Aveling & Porter single cylinder agricultural engine with a Salter spring balance safety valve on the cylinder block. It is now preserved at Grantham by Aveling Barford Ltd.

efficiency, as did self-propulsion instead of using portables. There were trials at Worcester in 1863 of four different cable systems, which, though not entirely conclusive, led to substantial orders for Fowler, making it necessary for him to sub-contract production under licence to other builders, including Burrells of Thetford who eventually made 118 sets.

John Fowler died in 1864 at the early age of 38, as a result of falling from his horse, but the foundations had been laid for a famous firm, which by 1890 was employing 1,600 workers producing not only ploughing engines, but other machines in a considerable range of high quality, a large proportion of which were for export. Just over 150

Fowler ploughing engines dating from 1870 to the last days of steam in 1933 are in preservation, but only seven examples of other makers. A very few are still used commercially, but at the larger annual steam rallies such as Stourpaine, Dorset and Peterborough, a 'set', of two engines and implements, can usually be seen in demonstration working.

Fowlers continued to make various improvements to their own engines and equipment until the end, by which means the firm remained supreme for the cable method using two engines. The fact of Fowler's system for using steam on the land being so widely adopted, both in Britain and around the world, tended to put a brake on the ingenuity of others.

Fowler's competitors

Other inventors were mainly concerned either with direct traction, or with engines having a built-in cultivator; some had tilling tines, others had fork or spade digging attachments. Savages of Kings Lynn, and McLarens of Leeds, built twin-boilered engines designed for broadside digging, with axles which swivelled when needed to pass along roads and through field gateways. The 'Darby Digger', of which thirty were built, was fairly efficient; it had legs of a kind for propulsion and forks to till the land provided that it was neither too wet nor too dry.

The 'Agrimotor' from Leeds, and the 'Suffolk Punch' from Garretts were late comers as steam tractors. They were versatile and compact—designed for both land and road work, with an eye on export. The former came out in 1909, but was not noticeably successful until later models with a shorter wheelbase were fitted with solid rubber tyres for road work. Even these were not built in any quantity; but the 'Suffolk Punch', which appeared in 1915, was a thoroughbred in its way, embodying several novel features. However the old bogey of excessive weight in relation to power and traction was not dispelled. And, with internal combustion tractors already looming as a cheaper, lighter means of power on the

Cab face plate of B.R. Class 7 4–6–2 Oliver Cromwell No. 70013. Built in 1951, this represents almost the ultimate in British steam locomotive development. The driver's padded seat is on the left, with main controls within easy reach. These are: the wheeled 'cut-off' used both for reversing and valve control, braking levers, a vertical regulator lever with racket painted red, above, also red, is the A.W.S. (advance warning system) for signals. The speedometer, though fitted, was considered unnecessary by most drivers, who gauged speed by timing at stations and lineside objects. Water gauge glasses are in the centre above the sliding firehole door, and above these are valve wheels for injectors and blower, along with pressure gauges. The roof ventilator, seen above, and a wooden seat for the fireman on the right were quite recent amenities.

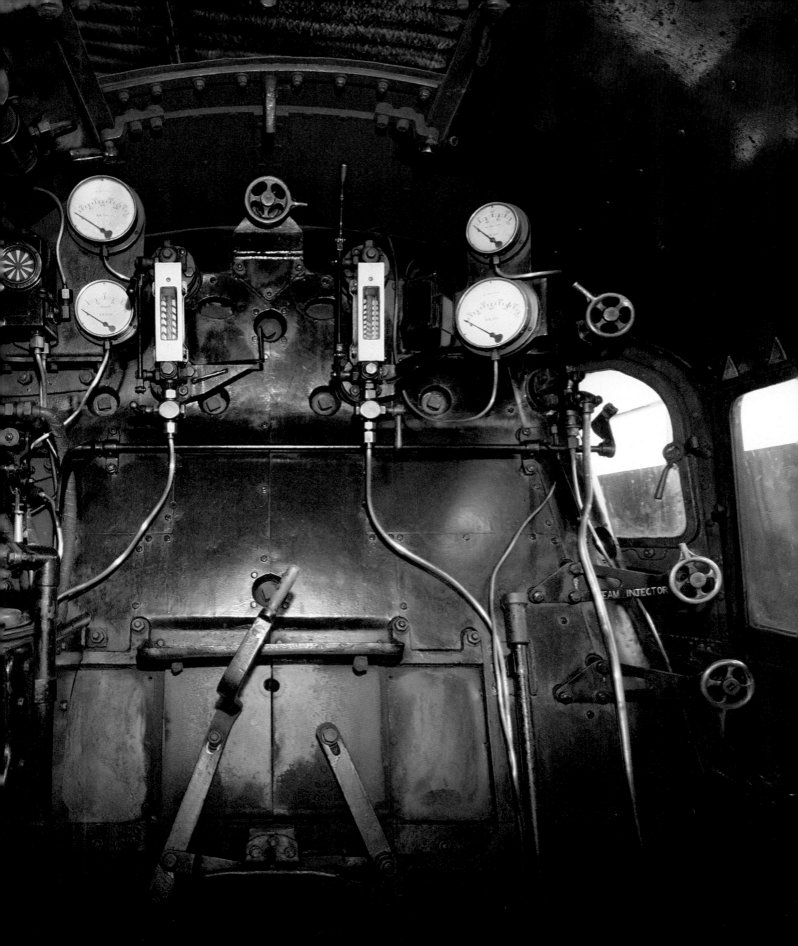

This shows the gears and motion of the single cylinder traction engine with two speeds. A lever (not visible) engages one or the other of the toothed sprockets or spur wheels seen at bottom left, into those on the crankshaft when not in motion. The belt pulley drives the governors below which can be seen the Stephenson link motion valve gear. This automatically opens and closes the ports of entry of live steam to the piston within the cylinder at the far end, whilst the piston rod turns the crankshaft bottom right. The long rod is for the regulator with its handle not visible, nor is the safety valve above the cylinder head.

land, both makes had become another lost cause by 1920.

The more outlandish steam diggers and cultivators apart from two smallish steam tractors, were confined to the 1870s and 1880s. None proved sufficiently long-lived to avoid being scrapped.

The great days of the traction engine

The heyday of the traction engine in its principal form had begun in the 1890s. The demand for general purpose agricultural engines, as well as for rollers and ploughs and portables, was steadily increasing, and English makers were achieving a splendid reputation in the four continents. Differences between makers were relatively minor, but they often retained their individuality in ways that were more superficial than real. Practically all of them turned out a range of models, varying in horsepower according to cylinder diameter. The power rating was on a formula known as Nominal Horse Power in keeping with old government regulations, ranging from about 4 N.H.P. up to 18 for the largest ploughing engines and even more for some 'Colonial' export types and for big portables. There was no accurate way of determining power, since so much depended on traction or grip, varying with surface conditions.

Compound engines became increasingly popular. A single cast iron block was bored for both high and low-pressure cylinders, the latter being much the larger of the two. Compounding made for smoother power, as well as a softer 'puff', through the chimney when the steam exhausted, than was the case with a single-cylinder 'simple' engine. Steam admission was usually by means of slide valves. Mostly the valves were operated by

Stephenson link motion, worked by eccentrics on the crankshaft moving the valve rods automatically in keeping with the stroke. Some compounds were single crank (s.c.c.)—the piston rod from the low-pressure cylinder was attached to that of the high. Other compounds had double cranks (d.c.c.) and if crossheads varied little, the housing itself over the slide bars which governed the movement of the piston rod in and out of the cylinder varied from make to make. Other valve gears than Stephenson were fitted to Wallis and Stevens engines, to some Fowlers and Marshalls, and to a very few from lesser-known makers.

Most agricultural engines were fitted with two-speed gears. These were in keeping with regulations which limited speed to 4 m.p.h. on open roads and to 2 m.p.h. in built-up areas. Since the distances they had to travel were small, even if on contract work such as threshing, these restrictions were of little consequence. In any case, the lack of springing would have courted risk of metal fracture had higher speeds been allowed. Gear changing was effected by a geared wheel being slid on its shaft to cog in with whichever size wheel on the drive shaft was appropriate to the speed required. It could

The worm drive steering gear of a traction engine is slow in operation. It can take a dozen or more turns of the steering wheel to make a 90° change of direction as the worm at the lower end of the shaft moves the spur wheel teeth. Behind this is the shaft round which the chains to the front axles are wound and unwound according to the required direction. The looped chain is to prevent a wheel coming into contact with the boiler barrel and to avoid locking. A bridged mud hole door for cleansing the boiler is seen below the gear wheel.

This illustration shows the more complex but very efficient motion of a Fowler 18 N.H.P. AA double crank compound ploughing engine. From the bottom, the driving gear shaft is seen, with an injector steam control in the centre. The pressure gauge is on the left and the regulator rod on the right, all above is firebox 'crown'. Bottom right is the gear change lever for the driving wheels, but the bevel pinion gear on the left, next to the flywheel, drives the vertical shaft for the winding drum when at work in a field. As a double crank compound, the piston rods from each cylinder—the larger being the low pressure for steam passing from the smaller one—carry balance weights as the crankshaft. Those on the left are up and alternation makes for smoother more regular working. Between are the four crankshaft eccentrics controlling the link motion valve gear to the pistons. The cylinder head dome carries safety valves and oiler, and the thin chain to the whistle can be seen.

only be changed with the motion at rest. When the gearwheel was disengaged from the drive gearing, the engine was ready for stationary work. This made the flywheel on an extension of the crankshaft into the final drive instead of the rear road wheel; a broad belt drove the threshing drum, chaff cutter or saw bench.

It was only when an engine worked as a stationary that a governor was needed, so that a constant speed on the flywheel drive could be automatically maintained.

The winch

Another power outlet that could be fitted to the rear axle inside the big iron driving wheel—usually 5 to 6 feet in diameter—was a drum with a wire rope on it. To use the drum as a winch, the driving wheels were disengaged by

pulling out heavy pins. The power of this stationary winch, once the engine was put into gear, was tremendous, and could have both dramatic and tragic results. As a boy I witnessed a house being crumpled like a house of cards, by an engine rope being passed around it and wound in. I have also used traction engines extensively for land reclamation where trees and bushes had to be pulled out bodily. When at work clearing derelict fen land, the weight of the engine was sometimes too great; if a wheel dug itself into the soft boggy earth and the engine listed dangerously, the only way out was to use the winch, anchored to a large stump or tree, by which means the engine would pull itself out on to firmer ground— provided the anchor held. I have also used the winch of a traction engine to raise two steel water towers 30 to 35 feet tall, from a nearly horizontal to a vertical position. But injury or death could occur if a wire rope snapped under strain, to snake back viciously.

The dangers of steam on the farm

On the subject of risk to life and limb it would be true to say that steam in agriculture was a greater danger there than in any other industry in which it was used, with the possible exception of the railways, if collisions and derailments were included where heavy loss of life occurred. On farms, men had

Above: The uncomplicated boiler front tube plate of a traction engine. The 35 3-in. tubes run through the boiler to the firebox and hot gases heat the water to produce steam. Tie rod ends, for extra strength, can be seen above the tubes. The whitish soot deposit is from wood, used as fuel. The exhaust pipe from the cylinders to the chimney is hidden by the smokebox rim.

Right: A close-up of the clip winding drum, or winch, of Fowler AA 7 Lion, of 18 N.H.P. The vertical shaft is driven by a bevel pinion from the main horizontal crankshaft. The clutch lever for the winch drive is seen just below the flywheel, and Fowler's patent ensured regular winding on the drum of the steel rope, which was up to $\frac{1}{2}$ mile in total length.

often no protection from exposed gears, unguarded driving belts and other potentially dangerous moving parts. Boiler explosions were not unknown and were mostly lethal to those standing near. Such fatalities occurred from various causes. A fault in the manufacture of a boiler was one of these, and a Fowler engine revealed such a fault when it exploded in 1901, causing it to burst asunder with such force that the tender and barrel were blown many yards apart in a scene of utter havoc. Explosions occurred also when scale from hard or dirty water accumulated between the firebox and its outer shell, or when a safety valve was neglected. In the early days when no pressure gauge was fitted to farm engines, a safety valve blowing off was the only indication that excessive steam had been made. But even when a pressure gauge was fitted, it was no uncommon thing for an engineman or owner to privily alter the setting of the safety valve to a figure beyond which the boiler was pressed. An extra 10 p.s.i. pressure so gained could produce greater power and output, but the risk of explosion was much increased.

One of the ploughing engines (Fowler A.A.) in the Bressingham collection caused the death of a crew member working for its former owner. The latter was so insistent on his engines being kept clean that, rather than lose precious work time, the man stood on the wooden running board polishing the boiler while the engine was on the move between one job and the next. The engine lurched suddenly, causing him to fall back into a sitting position on two large unprotected spur wheels cogging in with each other, drawing him into a mangling deathly grip. This incident should not perhaps come within the range of dangers inherent in the power of steam, but it shows only too well that human error or lack of care which is the basic cause of practically all so-called 'accidents'. It does also emphasise that pressured steam, the result of harnessing the two 'good servants but bad masters' of fire and water, becomes a more than doubly dangerous agent if not properly understood and respected.

The last of the portables

A final note should be recorded on agricultural traction engines and the portables from which they evolved. The portables spanned a larger period in commercial use than their offspring, though production of both ceased at about the same time. This was in the 1930s, when they were still at work on tasks for which they were specially suited. Oil engines were quite common by this time, but those which were portable lacked the steady power of steam, and those of equal power were neither portable nor within the reach of smaller farmers. Those who possessed a steam portable could not only undertake their own threshing and chaff cutting at the most convenient point of the farm, but could use it also for wood sawing, baling, milling and pumping.

Portables were also fitted with direct drive pumps, of all sizes up to 28 N.H.P. Others were standing engines to work machinery, while yet others were fitted with dynamos, for oc-

casions when electric power was needed. Garretts who were the pioneers of compounding for portables, even used tandem high/low pressure cylinders on some engines. Practically all engine builders offered portables as well as tractions, but they seldom departed from the early practice of having the crankshaft and flywheel behind the chimney, and the cylinders over the firebox. As with other types of engine, there was an export market and often those made specifically for overseas were designed to use straw as fuel. Steam pressures were seldom high, 120 p.s.i. was typical, and most of them would work quite well at less.

A cam-driven pump on the side of the boiler barrel was the usual means of keeping the boiler supplied with water from a tub or tank, which had itself to be supplied with water; but injectors were sometimes fitted as well. Many portables were fitted with a second flywheel at the opposite end of the crankshaft which could be employed where a machine required a different ratio of drive from a belt. Of the many thousands of portables built in England, most were shipped abroad, but sufficient remain in active retirement to be seen and appreciated for the simple, serviceable and silent power units they were. And a portable at work in good condition was practically silent.

Agricultural steam engines played a vital part in rural areas until they were pushed on to the scrap heap by tractors. As a native of one of the most intensely cultivated regions of Britain, and a farmer since 1938, I was acutely aware of the demise of steam. In 1930 tractors were already coming in for light work, but they were not powerful enough to haul and drive threshing machines, much less to compete with the mighty ploughing engines. Among the sounds villagers heard in those days was that of a threshing set on the move, perhaps a mile away, with the ringing clatter of the 10-ton engine and its iron-shod wheels. A ploughing set could be heard even farther off, for there would be two heavier engines and their equipment. When these were at work there would also be the occasional sound of their shrill whistles, indicating a need for coal or water. The portables were silent, at work or in motion; but one always knew where a threshing engine was at work, for the low moaning sound of the threshing drum itself would be carried on the wind. And wherever it was, boys would be drawn to it. Most of them came just to watch, but farmers or foremen would expect them to stand around a dwindling stack of corn with thatching spars in their hands, to slay rats and mice as they tried to escape the holocaust.

By 1939 many tractors were sufficiently powerful for farm work, and before 1945 there came an even greater threat to steam on the land. This was the combine harvester, which cut the labour costs of harvesting dramatically. A threshing operation from stacks needed at least ten men, and almost as many were needed at harvest time to cut the corn with a binder, stook, cart, stack and thatch it. The combine harvester needed but two or three men for the complete job. By 1950 steam engines were all but redundant, and with the crawler tractor replacing steam ploughing, the larger farmers and contractors hastened their exit from the scene. As on British Railways a few years later, there was a mad rush to be done with old-fashioned steam.

On my own Fenland farm, traction engines were too heavy for the soft peaty soil in winter. Most fen farmers had to wait until spring for stack threshing to be done—if they needed the money they had to thresh off the field at harvest time. Having moved on to the more solid ground of Bressingham I reverted to steam for old time's sake, with my own engine on the drum. It was nostalgic; but on working out my costs, I had to admit that it was more economic to harvest by combine, though my personal preference was still heavily in favour of steam. When my love for it led me to create a 'live steam' museum, I made sure it included a threshing 'tackle' with engine, drum and straw elevator for visitors to see in motion on open days. The number of people who stand there watching it is indication enough that interest in the steam age of agriculture, as of railways, remains undimmed. It goes well beyond mere nostalgia.

Now at Bressingham, this is the only Burrell single crank compound portable engine still in existence. The main features of No. 2363, built in 1909, are the absence of man-stand and tender, cylinders over the firebox end, a flywheel at each end of the crankshaft and a long, hinged chimney which could be folded down in transit.

The Pedrail was a fairly late attempt, by Boydell, to overcome the handicaps of road traction with iron-shod wheels. Boydell's early success did not last, and nor did the Pedrail, nearly 40 years later in 1910. The engine is a Lincoln-built Foster.

6

ROAD LOCOMOTIVES

Roads and restrictions

It is necessary at this point to refer again to the obstacles under which steam traction had laboured since 1830.

Road surfaces had steadily improved during the century, thanks to Macadam's method being more widespread. Road transport by steam, even with speed restrictions, had increased, if only to cart the granite road material from railway stations. Engines for this work differed little at first from agricultural engines, though most of them had canopies fitted which altered their appearance considerably. With the removal of the 'red flag' law in 1896, which coincided with the acceptance of the need for fledgling motor cars to be less hindered by regulations, there was an upsurge in heavy haulage by steam at greater speeds. Road steamers at this period were tractors, hauling one or more wagons, all with iron-shod wheels. Some were built to pull light loads, such as furniture pantechnicons, but others were for heavy industrial equipment and building materials, calling for the distinguishing term 'road locomotive', of up to 12 N.H.P. rating and weighing up to 16 tons. A few were fitted with cranes. Though permitted speeds only went up to 10 m.p.h., this was a big step forward.

Goldsworthy Gurney (of whom more later) had earlier appealed to no avail against the heavy road tolls and restrictions which under the Turnpike Act resulted in rank injustice to road users. The Turnpike Trusts were composed of local landowners and magistrates, empowered to levy tolls more or less as they pleased on roads they had to maintain. By and large they were against steam, one reason being that farming centred so much on the horse, and there was a profitable trade too in supplying feed and bedding for horses in towns.

Later these trusts tended to become moribund but by further Acts of Parliament restrictions on weights and speeds were again imposed, along with licence fees of £10 for each engine used for haulage. Farmers' engines were exempt, but in all cases speeds over 4 m.p.h. were prohibited on the open road, and only 2 m.p.h. was allowed in towns and villages. It was an Act of 1865 which brought the necessity of a man carrying a red flag 60 yards ahead of an engine. This reduced the scope of road transport by steam so much that, although development did not cease, it had to be almost entirely aimed at the export market, chiefly to the colonies.

One firm, however, showed great enterprise by setting up a regular service in France. McLarens of Leeds organised a road transport service in the 1880s, with a daily trip over the 70 miles between Grenoble and Lyons. Their engines working at the high pressure of 175 p.s.i. had enclosed cabs, and ran at night each way at about 8 m.p.h. Each engine was said to cover 15,000 miles a year, despite the severity of gradients along this route.

The first traction engine on the streets of London 29 July, 1858, built by Maudslay & Field, to Bray's design.

Tuxfords of Boston were amongst the many firms who tried to solve the problem of road transport. In this unusual design the motion was beneath the boiler and the transmission was geared to a single broad studded rear driving wheel. The design at the rear shows that it was intended to transport more than the three passengers sitting behind.

Engines for export

Engines of many types were built and tested in Britain, and then sent out to serve for both passenger and freight services, as well as for farming operations, in India, Africa, Australia and South America as well as in Europe. Farm engines often had specially constructed fireboxes for burning wood and even straw, but still wider adaptations were made to suit needs and circumstances not applicable to Britain. Nathaniel Grew, as early as 1860, delivered a transport engine to Russia to run in winter on a frozen river. It had sprung skids at the rear, cylinders each side of the footplate and connecting rods driving a central wheel for traction. The steering handle was connected to the front skid. In spite of a weight of 11 tons, the engine was successful enough to bring Grew another order for an engine to work on the river Neva at St. Petersburg—now

Leningrad. In this hectic period of 1860–1890, it seemed that steam power had almost limitless use.

Of the many widely differing and sometimes outlandish forms which road transport engines took, only a brief survey here can be given. Records do exist; but unfortunately relics do not. A few innovators went in for enormous driving wheels. One Fowler engine featured a wheel of 12 feet in diameter, as a means no doubt of overcoming traction problems ever present on rough or soft roads. In 1867 R. W. Thompson went back to the vertical or 'pot' boiler for engines designed mainly for overseas. He was among the first to use rubber-tyred wheels, the rubber not fitted in a continuous strip, but in close-set cross sections. When new these were quite effective, but they quickly wore out on the rough-surfaced roads over which his engines had to travel. Even so a number were built—mostly by established firms such as Robey and Burrell under patent, some doing good service for many years in the West Indian sugar plantations.

The placing of the motion

Most builders, however, had adopted the horizontal boiler by 1870, due no doubt to its success on the railways. For them the natural and most convenient place for the likewise horizontal cylinders was beneath the smokebox, which allowed direct access for exhaust steam to the chimney above. The piston and valve rods were thus in line with whichever axle was most convenient to use as a crankshaft; but with never more than two axles available on a road locomotive, all kinds of devices were invented to transmit motion—gears, pinions, chains and belts, though direct drive to a cranked axle was sometimes achieved.

According to Fletcher, whose book first published in 1894 (now reprinted) is such a mine of information on road steamers, the weekly 'Engineer' had been advocating 'undertype' engines since 1865. Fletcher himself contributed an article to the journal in January 1896, arguing that road locomotive design should follow as nearly as possible that of the very successful railway engine. He had designed one himself as early as 1872, but it does not seem to have been built. Fowler built one in 1886, with four-wheel drive—all wheels being $5\frac{1}{2}$ feet in diameter. Other firms too were producing undertype engines for tractors, making the 1890s a decade when steam engine output of all types was greater than ever before. But Fletcher appears to have been on the losing side; in 1904 he laments in a second edition of his book that practically everyone had gone over to the 'overtype' engine. The 'undertype' design was never successful for agricultural engines on land work, and the reason is easily understood. By 1870 the 'overtype' had become standard for less favourable farming conditions. But for road work, it was a different matter.

Thompson engines were also used in India, chiefly as tractors pulling both freight and passenger loads as a short train. The British Army took note, and at the instigation of R. E. Crompton (who later founded the famous electrical firm bearing his name) collaborated with Thompson in designing engines for hauling military trains on the roads. This led to a larger one being built by Robey for Woolwich arsenal and a trial in which it hauled a short train carrying 45 people at over 6 m.p.h., climbing a 1 in 9 hill at 5 m.p.h. It was named *Advance*, but it suffered from a lack of heating surface and an inadequate grate area. Thompson remedied this with his next engine, named *Chenab*—another three-wheeler designed for India. This was built by Ransome but it put up a disappointing performance.

The demand for reliable haulage power was, however, so keen that Robey, Ransome and Burrell now set about meeting it, in the belief that both rubber tyres and the locomotive-type horizontal boiler were the answer. Crompton discarded Thompson's pot boiler for the more proven 'Field' type in *Ravee* built by Ransome for India, which could pull a train of nine trucks. Orders came in to Burrell and Robey from Turkey and Greece, as well as Russia.

Ravee went on test before despatch, travelling from Ipswich to Edinburgh and back, touching 25 m.p.h. at one point but averaging only 7 m.p.h. in the 61 hours' one-way running time.

This was described by the press as an epic journey, and Crompton took the machine to India, where it performed so well that it paved the way for a fleet of similar engines to be built and shipped out. He also overcame most of the problems Thompson had encountered in using rubbered wheels, for rubber was largely an untried and unexploited commodity for transport use. The military saw its advantages, and the Royal Engineers used their new nickname of *Sapper* for an engine they ordered from Avelings of Rochester in 1871. It was relatively light at 5 tons weight, but successfully took the place of draught animals, for hauling field guns and military supplies for columns of soldiers on the march. In appearance it was ahead of its time, for engines made thirty years later were built on much the same lines. One iron-wheeled example of this type was saved by the still active Road Locomotive Society and now stands in the Science Museum, London.

An advertising photograph, heavily retouched, showing a Tasker type B1 'Little Giant'. Note the converted trailer, originally designed for horse haulage. These powerful, compound engined tractors were capable of hauling at least three such trailers.

Improved steering gear

Although steering by a man sitting in front of the chimney was still common for the older farm engines, the unrestricted development of the road locomotive for overseas sales led to several improvements, including a steering wheel at the rear or driving end, on four-wheelers with horizontal boilers. The steering shaft turned a worm gear which in turn rotated a cross-shaft. Cogs on this shaft engaged an endless chain taken round and gripping on to a channel in a flat semi-circular plate attached to the front axle. This method was copied from some farm engines in which the channel was the rim of a circular or semi-circular horizontal pan through which ran the vertical pivot or king pin for the front axle. The pan could also be a receptacle for carrying cleats, or wheel chocks. Whichever way the steersman turned a handle on the farm engines, it pulled or slackened a chain which swivelled the axle and thereby changed its direction. This method became standard for all tractors and farm engines by 1880.

Three-wheelers, for which front steering was mostly used, gave way at about this time to the more stable four-wheelers. On uneven roads, three-wheelers were more likely to topple over, if any of the wheels dropped into a deep pot hole or went too close to a down-sloping verge.

The growing importance to industry of haulage by steam, and in particular by the traction-engine type road locomotive, led inevitably to some easing of restrictions in the closing years of the century. Steam had come to stay on the roads as a vital factor in industrial development, just as it had in so many

A classic Fowler 8/10 N.H.P. heavy road haulage locomotive. The cylinders were surrounded by a steam jacket to reduce condensation and the flywheel is dished to clear the 3-speed gear pinions. A steam-driven dynamo has been mounted at a later date on the underslung belly tank to power electric headlamps.

other facets of life. The road locomotive was entering at 1900 its vital period, and became unchallenged in its capacity to transport an enormous tonnage on the roads, despite the rise of the steam wagon and other self-contained vehicles.

For sixty years engineers had been unceasingly active in eliminating faults and weaknesses in design and manufacture, and if with hindsight faults can now be found, it is quite safe to say that in the first quarter of the 20th century, road locomotives were examples of a splendid period of British engineering skill.

The refinements added to the agricultural engines on which road locomotives were based included many improvements, but they were scarcely radical. Following the 1896 Road Act, there was soon afterwards to be seen a range of smaller engines designed for lighter loads and greater speeds. Taskers of Andover were amongst the first to produce them, coming out with the 'Little Giant', of 4 N.H.P. but weighing only $2\frac{1}{2}$ tons. This diminutive newcomer was immediately popular, for it could haul quite easily 10 to 15 tons on trailer wagons, where the going was good; its lack of road-holding weight for traction rather than

its low power was the only disability. It had a tendency to rear up its front end if overloaded, which made steering difficult. Fosters brought out the *Lincoln Imp*, and most of the larger firms were also meeting the demand for this new product. Most of the engines had the solid flywheel now becoming standard for road locomotives, on which an additional brake was fitted. These brakes were more effective when going downhill than the brakes on a road wheel. But each set of brakes served a purpose, comparable with that of the footbrake and handbrake on a car.

The skills of the crewmen

As on a railway locomotive, there had to be a good understanding between the two men needed on the footplate of a large road engine. Both had to be very much on the alert, and though the driver would be in the superior position, orders from him were seldom necessary. On the road, the

steersman's task took too much of his attention for him to be fireman as well, and it usually fell to the driver to attend both to firing and to the water feed for the boiler. He also had to gauge the water reserves carried, so as to stop and replenish the tanks in good time. Drivers came to know where water was available and in steam days there would be a notice by a bridge or pond indicating that an engine could draw water there. The quality of water was important, to avoid fouling the boiler.

Belly tanks were also standard fittings, and very necessary when a shortage of water could cause a delay or even a catastrophe. The belly tanks had a connecting pipe to the tender tank and could be filled by steam-induced suction; the 300–400 gallons held in both tanks would cover about 12–16 miles of travel with a load behind. Another fitting which an agricultural engine would not have was a

blower valve, which allowed steam at low pressures to increase fire draught up the chimney and thereby accelerate the build-up of steam pressure. Water gauges were usually duplicated and better protected. Although a pump operated by a crankshaft eccentric was still sometimes fitted, the injector was the most convenient means of keeping water at the correct level in the boiler. Some engines had two injectors, one for high and one for low pressure. On all engines, a boiler face plate carried a maker's warning that it should be cleaned every 14 days of work, or after 100 hours in steam.

Compound engines were also fitted with a push rod which allowed dry, live steam into both cylinders at once. This was useful for getting the motion into action, when the high-pressure cylinder had its piston on dead centre, or when extra power was needed. Cylinders were mostly fitted with independent oilers on drip feed, as well as displacement or pump-action cylinder lubricators. Another feature on road locomotives, not included on many agricultural engines, was that of a

The gearing on the three speed heavy road locomotive The President. At the top is the gear change lever operating a sliding pinion on a counter shaft. By a simple, but quite ingenious alteration of key ways on the shaft, the drive pinion can be brought into mesh with whichever of the three large spur wheels is required. These vary the speed as they in turn engage the fixed spur or cog wheel on the driving axle, with the smallest diameter giving the highest speed of about 8 m.p.h. A change of gear can only be made from the neutral position.

balanced crankshaft. Weights opposite the thrust point made for a smoother, more regular motion, and avoided snatch on the driving gears, especially on engines with multiple forward gears.

Each cylinder on a road locomotive engine was fitted with a drain cock or relief valve. This was operated by a lever from the footplate, and was opened when raising steam to allow any condensate water remaining in the cylinders to escape. Failure to open these small valves could be dangerous on starting, if full steam pressure was admitted to the cylinder.

For road locomotives a canopy was a necessity on what was otherwise a

purely functional but thoroughbred piece of engineering. It gave some protection to the crew, though very draughty, whether or not it covered the whole engine short of the chimney. Many canopies covered only the rear half—even they were better than nothing.

The uninformed often remark on the low horsepower ratings of traction engines and road locomotives compared with those given to motor vehicles. These ratings, under the somewhat arbitrary heading of Nominal Horse Power (N.H.P.) could to some extent be equated with the number of horses needed, with drivers using whips as encouragement, to pull an equal tonnage to that of the engine on level ground. But ten heavy dray horses would not have the reserve of power possessed by a 10 N.H.P. road locomotive with a full head of steam. And in particularly difficult situations an engine could perform otherwise impossible feats by using its winch rope, as an unfailing last resort.

Below: In reality, this Fowler crane engine is dual purpose. Built as a standard Fowler road locomotive, it has a demountable winch and jib to enable it to be converted into a crane for medium lifting.

Fowler 'showman' road locomotive No. 15116 'Bertha' was built in 1920 for Jack Whyatt, an 'amusement caterer' from Stoke on Trent. It was saved from the scrapyard in 1956 and has had a succession of owners until finally coming to Levens Hall, in Cumbria, in 1960.

130

7

SHOWMEN'S ROAD LOCOMOTIVES

A chance to shine

If the road locomotive was entirely functional, it was to be transformed in appearance as a result of ideas generated by the showground fraternity. Jacob Studt, a South Wales showman, was the first to see its advertising possibilities as far back as 1889. Others soon followed suit, vying with one another in ornamentation, till by the early 1900s engine builders too were competing to produce splendidly flamboyant and majestic engines for any showman prepared to pay the extra cost.

Burrells were the first in this field, having built engines to Jacob Studt's orders, and he was also the first to use electricity, generated by a dynamo on the engine. My father used to stay with relatives living close by Burrells' works, and saw this first 'showman' on its trials.

Although other well-known builders, such as Fowler, Foster, McLaren and Garrett, included 'showmans' in their range, Burrells retained their leadership throughout. To the *Scenic* in its final form, a rear crane was fitted to an extra-high tender for handling fairground equipment.

A showman's train was often composed of several wagons, one carrying the centre steam engine for a 'ride' — usually of gallopers, invented by another firm of engine builders, Savage of King's Lynn. The arrival of a train at a fairground would alone cause great excitement.

Many showmen also owned a smaller engine with which to haul secondary equipment; but when all was erected the big engine with its brass adornments stood here magnificent with a belt on its flywheel driving the dynamo on a plate jutting out beyond the smokebox, making colourful electric light. The British Army also used this device to power portable searchlights.

The general public very often has little idea, when seeing a restored engine on display, of what is involved to achieve the transformation. This photograph shows the typical state of an engine saved for preservation. Having spent 20 years in a scrapyard, this Burrells 'showman' was rusted solid when she was brought to Bressingham Steam Museum in 1962. The chimney, dynamo, canopy and most of the non-ferrous parts and small fittings were missing. However, the result of two years' hard work can be seen on page 102.

Jacob Studt's first 'showman' set the basic pattern for the dozens more turned out by Burrells over the next thirty-five years. They built, in fact, more than all other makers combined, and naturally more of them are to be seen nowadays at rallies than of any other make. It follows too that a larger proportion of showmen's engines have been preserved in relation to the number built than of other types, simply because of their splendid appearance and first-class workmanship. The restoration of some, left derelict for years, may involve complete dismantling and rebuilding, a long, tedious task, but one which gives intense satisfaction to those concerned. The decor and livery included brass and copper, wherever burnish and polish would contribute to its splendour, and the most delicate of lining out as a finish to the paintwork. Most Burrells were crimson lake, with yellow or gold lining, and yellow wheels; but customers could order paintwork to their own design, which was whatever they believed to hold the greatest public appeal.

Having to travel a seasonal round of fairs, speed in erecting and pulling down amusements and rides, as well as in travelling, was an important factor with showmen. Their engines became capable of 12 m.p.h. but even half this speed on iron wheels made for a rough ride, despite springing. Rubber-tyred wheels became a standard feature after 1900. These allowed faster travelling, and the average speed for quite long distances was close to 10 m.p.h. with a load up to 20 tons trailing behind. With 'showmans' as with most large road locomotives, the driver needed a steersman when travelling. This man would be perched up on a fold-back iron seat, out of the driver's way, where he had a better view of the road. It was also found that double crank compounds were much superior to single crank models; otherwise, with a belt driving a dynamo, a stop on dead centre could be difficult to restart. Horsepower ratings were up to 10 N.H.P. with 8 N.H.P. most popular, and driving wheels measured 6 feet 6 inches without the rubber tyres which

built them up to 7 feet. The brass tubes from the safety valves were extended through the canopy, otherwise blowing off was embarrassing and dangerous to the driver and steersman. The chimney also protruded, and when working on a fairground a 10–12 foot extension was fitted to avoid a smoke nuisance. When travelling this extension was carried lying down in brackets on the canopy roof.

The fall– and rise– of the 'showman'

A curious but understandable change of attitude on the part of showmen occurred during the early 1930s. For more than a generation they had been intensely proud of their engines. They maintained them and their rides in immaculate condition. But a younger generation was emerging which saw greater speed and economy in the new diesel lorries. They were modern, and steam engines were old-fashioned, so it became a status symbol over the next few years to own a diesel lorry. By 1939 many a showman's engine had been laid aside, with a rapidly falling second-hand value. Wartime difficulties and restrictions brought some back into use, but when it ended the decline of steam accelerated. At a Norwich fair in 1946 only one engine was present, where twenty years earlier up to nine could have been at work. But the owner of the one in 1946 seemed ashamed of it; after using it solely for haulage, he left it tucked away and cold.

At that time, showmen's engines were being cut up for scrap (along with hundreds of tractions and portables) having been sold for a few pounds to be rid of them. £50 was seldom reached; the majority sold for much less. Then, when most of them had

vanished, the tide began to turn. By the middle 1950s traction engines of all kinds, and especially 'showmans', were being acquired by those who had a nostalgic interest in them, and the means to restore them to running order. The preservationists were by no means all engineers. Many had never before owned an engine or worked with one. The first rallies added further incentive, for they provided an excuse for a pleasurable pastime, especially when the general public showed that they too were interested, and willing to pay to see the engines come back to

life and motion. Competitions were arranged, prizes were awarded for events and for appearance. By 1960 an engine in fair order was worth up to £200—more for a 'showman'. Since then prices have steadily risen for engines of all kinds; in 1978 a fully restored 'showman' was sold for over £30,000, and no less than £65,000 was offered for a particularly fine example in late 1979.

Although the tremendous upsurge of interest in steam is manifest in showmen's engines, the showmen themselves have not resorted to them.

The number in preservation runs into three figures, but if one is seen at a fair the chances are that it belongs to an 'amateur'. At most traction engine rallies, and there are scores of them held up and down the country between April and October, there will be at least one 'showman'. At some of the larger rallies, such as Peterborough and Stourpaine in Dorset, up to a dozen may be seen in all their glory, along with fifty or more engines or steam wagons of various types, representing the less common as well as the well-known makers. It should, however, be

remembered that the 'showmans', for all their splendour, are but highly embellished road locomotives.

Its owner stands proudly by the 'showman' engine built for him in 1909. It is a double crank compound of 8/10 N.H.P. but lacks both rubber tyres and twisted brass uprights seen on most 'showmans'. Behind Mr. East are drawbars for the vehicles it hauled, and on top of the canopy is the chimney extension to be fitted when at work providing fairground light from the dynamo in front. This extension mitigated smoke nuisance and risk of fire from sparks. It appears likely that this engine began as a heavy road locomotive for heavy haulage and was adapted for fairground use.

NEWMARKET HURDLE JUMPERS.

Richard Trevithick's steam carriage. Built in 1803, it had a cylinder 5½ in. in diameter, with a stroke of 2½ ft. It was capable of speeds of 8 or 9 m.p.h. Unfortunately its trials in London ended when the engine framing became twisted. The carriage part was sold off and the engine used to drive a mill for rolling hoop-iron.

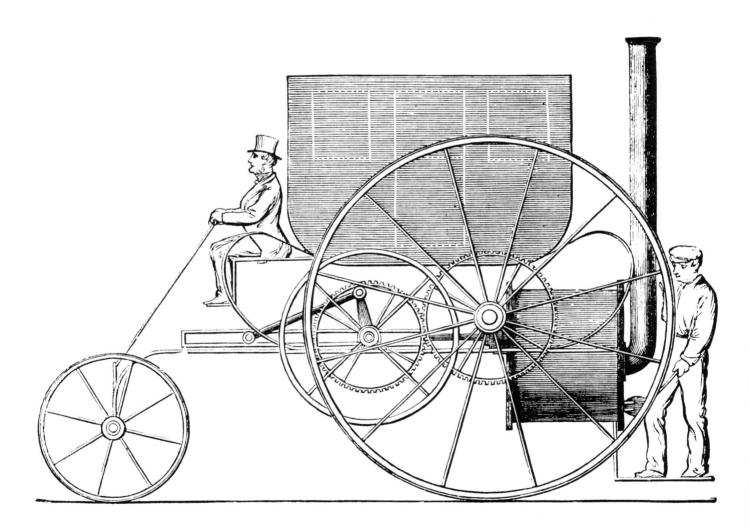

8

STEAM CARRIAGES AND MOTOR CARS

The pioneer– Nicholas Cugnot

Historical facts tend to become obscured or embellished especially if not adequately recorded at the time. Happenings which fire the public imagination become the subject of myths and legends, and this is true of steam discoveries in general and steam carriages in particular.

The term discovery is used more correctly than invention, because the pioneers in steam were simply discovering its potential. The word carriages is also used advisedly because in the early days the word 'car' had little meaning, in spite of biblical references to Elijah's ascent to Heaven in a car of flame. 'Fire engine' was in fact the term used rather than 'steam engine'. What the early pioneers were seeking was a means of propelling a vehicle along the roads, and any of the vehicles under various names being used in the early years could, they thought, be adapted to steam propulsion. Mother Shipton had predicted the arrival of the iron horse, and it was horses that steam had the power to replace.

Several myths sprang up around the work of Nicholas Cugnot, the man who built and ran the first-ever steam carriage in 1771 in Paris. There is no need to mention more than the bare fact that he was commissioned to build a 'drag' or tractor for hauling cannon, but very little is known of its performance. A second, larger, drag was much more successful and is still to be seen and appreciated for its builder's ingenuity, which in detail offsets its apparent crudity. Certain boiler fittings which one would have thought essential are missing, and it remains an open question as to whether the present boiler is the original or if someone thirty years after its manufacture gave the command for a replica to be made and then left this to be preserved in working order, as the ancestor of the motor car, in the Paris Conservatoire.

Watt and Trevithick

The honour of Cugnot might belong to France, but the development of the steam carriage during the first half of the 19th century belongs almost entirely to Great Britain.

James Watt's hostility to high-pressure steam is well known. To him even 25 p.s.i. was a high pressure. It is not perhaps as well known that as early as the 1770s he was urged to invent a steam carriage. He overcame his reluctance to the extent of laying down some specifications, but was not willing to spend much time over what he believed was a dangerous project. If he had put his plans into practice, his would have been a very ponderous machine to work, of course, at low pressure; but to lessen the weight, he specified a wooden boiler, to work at 25 p.s.i. His correspondents, who included Erasmus Darwin, must have given up goading him when they realised that if his design for a carriage ran at all, it would be too large and heavy for the roads. But on the mechanical side, Watt's sketchy specifications for transmission gears embodied features which were basically similar to those used in motor cars over a century later.

Watt could not or would not get away from his own first invention of the condensing engine, but he may have seen the possibility of others doing so, with pressures high enough to make a steam carriage a reality even in his lifetime. When he retired to Heathfield Hall in old age he laid down that on no account should a steam carriage be allowed to approach it. As has been mentioned earlier, it was Trevithick who took the next forward step. His London steam carriage had a reception worthy of its merits, and if only he had found such a backer as Boulton was to Watt, he might well have bcome even more famous.

It is interesting to note that Richard Trevithick, the Cornishman now acknowledged as a genius, was not mentioned in the classic book by William Fletcher on road steam carriages and traction engines, published in 1904, entitled *Steam on the Common Roads*. It is in comparatively recent years that Trevithick's contribution has been recognised, and although several steam carriages were projected during the 1790s, he had the distinction of building one in 1803, the first to take to the English roads. It was a three-wheeler, with a carriage-type body, capable of seating eight passengers, with a pair of driving wheels 10 feet in diameter, and it was said to have achieved a speed of 12 m.p.h. with a full load.

Trevithick was by nature an impetuous man—a not uncommon trait in a creative genius, and when having demonstrated the success of his invention he failed to find a backer to provide capital, he switched his interests from roads to railways, to

"The above is a representation of a Steam-Carriage, the invention of Mr. W. H. James of Birmingham and Thavie's Inn, London. The weight of the Carriage and propelling Machinery is two tons; and the estimated power is from 15 to 20 horses. With this power it is calculated that the Carriage will travel at the rate of from 8 to 12 Miles an hour carrying six inside and twelve outside passengers."

become a successful if again ultimately disappointed designer.

During the early 1800s there were many plans laid and designs put to paper for road steamers which never became a reality. Some were from visionaries rather than engineers, but among the latter were a few who could see success not by transmitting power to the road wheels of a carriage but by emulating the push of horses' legs. At least two steam-powered pushers were actually made, in the belief that steam power applied to wheels would merely make them spin. One of the makers was David Gordon, who, having given up his first idea of a huge drum behind the coach for propulsion, devised an ingenious system of cranked pusher legs.

The other one-time exponent of mechanical legs was none other than Goldsworthy Gurney. He admitted that in deciding to make his first steam carriage propelled by pusher legs he had been influenced by eminent engineers who had proved that motion was not possible by power applied to the wheels.

There was a grotesque and amphibious steam-powered contraption

built for dredging by Oliver Evans in America during 1804. Evans apparently devised a means of making it self-propelled on land. Legend has it that its versatility ended when, after travelling the one and a half miles from workshop to water, it entered a river and sank, never to rise again. But this is only legend.

A lull of several years came before the next appearance of steam on the roads.

In Europe the Napoleonic Wars were a deterrent to venturesome projects, and at home endeavours were becoming even more concentrated on the application of steam to the rapidly expanding industries of Britain.

The early efforts of men like Trevithick were not only handicapped by lack of finance. Boilers for steam carriages needed to be so much lighter than for other types of steam engines, and the metallurgy of the time had still a long way to go. So too had the methods of raising steam within a boiler—realising the importance of increasing the heating surface, in order to utilise the full capacity of the boiler, and so obtain low fuel and water consumption.

Gurney and Hancock— a limited success

The next two champion pioneers of road steamers were Sir Goldsworthy Gurney and Walter Hancock who came onto the scene in the 1820s. Gurney's idea was simply for steam power to take the place of horses pulling a coach. In other words he planned a tractor, but Gurney called it a 'drag', and it went some way towards allaying the fears of an explosion, which seemed such a risk in a single vehicle, with its engine and boiler built in. Hancock's machine was of the latter type, but both became moderately successful and for several years provided a regular accident-free service.

Although their success was decidedly limited, both men had achieved a remarkable breakthrough in the application of steam power. They had set out to produce engines differing vastly from those used in industry, where weight and power went more or less hand in hand. Industrial engines were heavy, ponderous structures, relying on large-diameter cylinders and low-pressure steam for slow-motion power. Yet once the problems of lightweight boilers with higher pressures were tackled it took a relatively brief period of experiment for lighter, faster-working engines to be made. The maximum steam pressure in industrial engines at that time was under 50 p.s.i., but this figure was the minimum for the new road engines, and by the mid-1830s some worked at 150 p.s.i. High pressure enabled a shorter, faster stroke to be made, in cylinders only a few inches in diameter. One advantage for a steam-driven carriage was in smoother running, for with a long piston stroke a lurching motion would be transmitted all over the vehicle, to the great discomfort of passengers.

The lightweight boiler was achieved largely by the multiplicity of the tubes within, and by a greater use of copper and malleable steel, of greater strength in relation to its thickness. It was found that, if a small fire heated a much greater surface of thinner metal

through the use of tubes, steam raising was faster and more continuous than if a large furnace boiled water in a heavy boiler shell. It was also found that by keeping water levels in the uppermost heating surfaces as low as possible consistent with safety, steam production was accelerated and a greater reservoir of dry, high-pressure steam created.

In retrospect, it can be seen that, whereas the 18th century inventors' greatest concern was with the power produced by the working of a piston within a cylinder, during the first part of the 19th century interest was centred more on the boiler.

The piston/cylinder principle, using live steam as power, had become firmly established, with few avenues open for its improvement as a mechanism. Very significant improvements were, however, visualised as the new breed of innovators appeared, whose minds were uncluttered by Watt's weighty and often repeated strictures on the dangers of higher pressures. Trevithick had been one of the first rebels, and those who followed began breaking with convention in a variety of ways, with experiments on some very unconventional boilers in order to achieve high pressure and so greater power

from smaller, lighter units.

For road-using vehicles such lightweight boilers were essential, especially if they were built into a coach. It will be seen from illustrations of these early road steamers that the horsedrawn stage-coach shape was used—as indeed it was for the first railway carriages, and to some extent for motor-car bodies at the very end of the century. This was perhaps a kind of status symbol, for the use of the gentry and the affluent, but this is by the way. More important is the fact that, as reasonable success came after many a trial and error in producing safe, lightweight boilers for road vehicles, so further improvements were made in the application of the higher pressures they produced. Gurney ran a regular service with his 'drags' for several years between Gloucester and Cheltenham, usually covering the nine miles in less than an hour. On seeing a demonstration in 1829, the great Duke of Wellington remarked that "it is scarcely possible to calculate the benefit we shall derive from this invention." Between February and June 1831, this service totalled 3,500 miles without mishap, but late in June an axle broke and, although there were no serious injuries, there were sufficient other

"A Sketch of Mr. Gurney's New Steam Carriage as it appeared on the 12th of August (1829), with a Barouche attached containing the Duke of Wellington and other Persons of Distinction."

reasons for Gurney deciding to withdraw the service—the first of its kind in the world.

There is little doubt that these other reasons were either economic or springing from prejudice against his efforts. There were interests opposed to steam on the roads. These were not only the stage-coach operators, but also the wealthy gentry with their own horsedrawn vehicles who were often against steam, if for no other reason than that of fear for the horses. Accidents from frightened and bolting horses were not uncommon and a stage coach was easily overturned. The 'common people' may well have viewed the new steam vehicles with wonderment, but only as onlookers; and although the steamers had only a slightly greater axle load than horsedrawn coaches, the prevailing system of road upkeep engendered further opposition from the farmers on whom this burden fell.

Walter Hancock was more successful than Gurney, but he too was continually opposed by the horse-using fraternity. He built his first steamer in 1824 and this was followed by eleven more, against a total of six built by Gurney, including his 'drags'. Hancock was based at Stratford, then separated from London proper by fields and gardens. He saw steam as a potential servant for passenger transport in the nearby metropolis. His designs were therefore of practical, soundly-engineered vehicles to carry passengers safely and with regularity at eight to ten miles per hour in relative comfort on roads that were dusty in summer and muddy in winter. In overcoming various engineering problems, inevitable in the lot of pioneers, Hancock is outstanding and he is said also to have been a most reasonable and modest man.

His regular services were between Stratford and Threadneedle Street, and from Paddington to Moorgate, Pentonville and Islington—all to and from the then suburbs to the City of London. He also occasionally undertook much longer journeys, including runs from London to Brighton and to Marlborough. His vehicles included both the coach type, with passengers seated above and within the enclosed section, and an open-ended omnibus type with 'toast rack' seating.

Hancock went in for smartness and had his vehicles gaily painted, giving them such fanciful names as *Era*, *Automaton*, *Autopsy*, *Infant*, as well as the more appropriate *Enterprise*. Each was crewed by three men, the driver on the wheel at the front, an engineer at the rear, and a boy as stoker, using coke to minimise any nuisance from smoke.

Some data is on record of the mechanical features of Hancock's engines, and although diagrams exist of the boilers he made in his Stratford workshop, no two were alike. It is surprising that, in meeting a real need for a passenger transport service, both Gurney's and Hancock's endeavours had ended by 1840. The latter reckoned his profits on the venture amounted to 25% but the clue to his decision to give up may be found in a statement he made in defence of his convictions. 'Years of practice have not put all doubts of the economy, safety and superiority of steam on the common roads at rest when compared with horse travelling, and I have now in preparation calculations founded

Three of Walter Hancock's steamers, depicted as being in service, but doubts could be cast that this is what the artist actually saw.

on actual practice which, when published, will prove that steam locomotion on common roads is not unworthy of the attention of the capitalist, though the reverse has been disseminated rather widely of late by parties who do not desire that this branch of improvement should prosper against the interest of themselves.'

The opposition triumphant

Walter Hancock was obviously making an appeal for capital, as well as trying to convince the general public. He had also claimed that a steady 25% operating profit was to be made from such a service as his. But in spite of all this, the opposition proved to be too strong. By 1840 the first 'railway mania' period had begun. New rail routes, on which far more people could be carried at much greater speeds and at lower fares than on the common roads, had fired widespread public excitement. A paradoxical situation arose which united both the stage coach operators and the railway companies in their enmity to the road steamers; and between them they forced the road operators out of business.

There was however one further reason why, during this early period of development, the road-using steam vehicle did not prosper, despite Macadam's improvement to road surfaces. This was because, among those who tried to oust the stage coach by the use of steam, there were a few—apart from Gurney and Hancock—who had set their sights ridiculously high. They attempted to outdo each other, as well as the horses, by increased speed, and this resulted in some crazy machines taking to the roads, to the danger and subsequent anger of the public. These men, ill-equipped as engineers and with inadequate capital, eventually brought discredit on the project as a whole.

It is however on record that James Nasmyth and John Scott Russell, both

A contemporary caricature by someone who obviously feared a threatened proliferation of steam powered road vehicles, and their attendant evils.

of Edinburgh, built and ran road engines for a time. Russell ran a service from Glasgow to Paisley at hourly intervals, but allowed up to forty people to ride on a vehicle designed to carry only twenty-six. Such popularity indicated a need for transport, and although a Glasgow newspaper praised Russell's venture as a triumphant success, the Road Trustees were in active opposition. At the Glasgow end of the route, where speed was restricted to 7 m.p.h., the Trustees laid a thick coating of loose stones, hoping that this would put a stop to the steamer service. The experiment evoked considerable local interest, and to the chagrin of the Trustees those present watched the steamer forge ahead through the stones, while horses jibbed and were forced to use a diversion until the stones were cleared away. Finally, however, a wheel broke on a steam coach which threw the whole weight of the vehicle on to the boiler, and caused it to burst with fatal results. The Court of Session then ruled that steam on the

common roads was henceforth to be prohibited.

All these early road steamers were of course faulty in one way or another. This is not surprising, for their builders were still experimenters, with their enthusiasm often outweighing their practical knowledge based on experience. In spite of failures and of opposition, it is quite remarkable that, throughout the Victorian era, there was scarcely ever a time when no one was engaged in building a steam carriage in Britain. One is tempted to assume that the incentive came not only because there was a public need for better transport on the roads, but also because of enthusiasm on the part of a few individuals for steam as a source of power. No matter how outspread the railways became, they could not cater for the increasing size and population of the towns and for the need for short-run transport within them. For this traffic horses were quite inadequate, although horsedrawn trams were coming in by mid-century.

Boiler developments

Though the vision of a fully successful road steam carriage was rather like a will-o'-the-wisp, those who pursued it at least discovered more of the potentialities of steam, if only because they laboured under tighter environmental restrictions than the railway, industrial and marine engineers, who were much less hampered by problems of weight and traction. A historical study of early vehicles reveals to those mechanically minded a fascinating catalogue of variations on two basic themes—the means of raising steam in keeping with the narrow limits of weight, and of applying its power as it passed through the cylinders, to propel the vehicle. The boilers used were mostly vertical or bottle-shaped, with the chimney in the centre, above the furnace. The area allotted to water space varied considerably, in an effort to achieve the maximum heating surface. Heat from the fire above the grate was convected to the water space behind the inner boiling plating. The inner and outer plates called for stay bolts to withstand the pressure as the water expanded with heat, and experimenters with lightweight boilers were sometimes made painfully aware that very few alternatives were open to them. The most promising invention was that of multiple tubes, by which the heating surface could be increased, thereby reducing the size of the boiler.

Horizontal tubular boilers were already more or less standard for railway locomotives, but tubes were much more difficult to fit into smaller vertical boilers, which lacked an adequate smokebox below the chimney. They therefore had to be set to converge, passing through the water space, into the chimney. These made for a greater heating surface and increased the draught, as in the case of the Field boiler which was an early patent, often used for road steamers in the first half of the 19th century. Field improved on this first pattern in various ways, and there were others who experimented both in the number and diameter of tubes. They varied from an inch or two to eight or nine inches in diameter, and to ensure tight fitting, screwing, expanding and heading over the protruding ends were all practised, according to the beliefs of the boiler maker. The water space between the inner and outer boiler plating also varied in width, as did the grate area of the firebox.

A quite early development was that of the water-tube, as opposed to the fire-tube, boiler. The principle involved was that of the circulation of water through tubes, exposed to the heat of the fire, instead of the latter passing through tubes to heat the water surrounding them. Such tubes were even more difficult to fit successfully, although the principle was sound enough, but the use of water-tubes instead of cast iron for firebars proved to be impractical. The build-up of pressure inside water-tubes was a major problem, but it was eventually overcome with such success that the last make of steam vehicle to run on the roads was powered by a water-tube boiler working at a pressure of up to 400 p.s.i.. Such a pressure was inconceivable to the early experimenters, and although 150 p.s.i. had been attained by 1840, this was considered by many as excessive and dangerous.

With higher pressures in small tubular boilers came the vital need for reliable fittings. These included safety valves, water-level gauges, and water injectors to replenish loss by evaporation. The necessity of maintaining water levels was vital for all boilers. To allow fire heat on metal not backed by water was highly dangerous and Trevithick's idea of 1802 of a fusible plug was soon adopted in one form or another. It took the form of a hole in the inner boiler plate above the firebox filled with lead, or an alloy, which would melt if there was not enough water above the plate to absorb the fire heat. The lead, on melting, allowed steam to escape downward on to the fire and so an explosion was avoided.

The failure of an engineman to maintain his water levels and so allowing a plug to melt has always been a matter of shame. But three safety devices helped him to avoid such a disaster. The first was the provision of an outside gauge indicating the level of the water inside the boiler; the second was a reliable means of pumping or injecting water against the pressure within, and the third the provision of a safety valve to allow excessive steam to escape. The latter was not too difficult to apply to small boilers, but all three demanded special care and attention when fitted to the boiler of a passenger-carrying vehicle. These considerations applied just as much to such fittings as

An early experimental steam carriage, made by Rickett, led to an order for a somewhat similar one from the Earl of Caithness. The fire was behind for obvious reasons.

glands, pipe joints, and access plugs and plates for boiler cleaning.

The environment in which Gurney, Hancock and other pioneers endeavoured to make steam carriages work was simply not conducive to success. In some ways there was less public hostility to steam on the roads before 1850 than after. In the earlier period steam was still the wonder of the age. But the great majority of the population saw little of it in action. Only a fraction of the people were free of the harsh conditions of life which chained them to their place of work, mostly for twelve hours a day. Very few of them could know that conditions were even worse in France, where in 1820 only two hundred steam engines were easing manual labour, whereas in Britain

there were five thousand.

It has been said that several wealthy young men sported their own steam cars, a change from the smart horse-drawn phaetons. But this too is a myth, because there were ample reasons why small steam carriages for one or two persons were no match for a high-stepping horse in the shafts. A very few were made, no doubt, as experiments, but their use was probably confined to the makers. Walter Hancock was among these, and the reason why no two of his carriages were alike was that he was endeavouring to remedy any fault manifest in an earlier design. Such faults were largely confined to transmission. His patent boiler was very efficient, and so was his two-cylinder engine. But its power and

speed had to be geared down to suit the speed of the road wheels, and his primitive crank and chain drive was often unequal to the strain. Hancock had also to overcome stress on the wheels of his carriages, and some of his solutions to these early problems were of value long after his time.

With his short-run urban services, Hancock had less trouble with the provision of water en route than did Gurney. His was in any case a better boiler and though both were of the water-tube type, Gurney's consumed about 10 gallons per mile, and was liable to throw some of this out with the steam. But the main reason for the disappearance of steam carriages from British roads was the crippling tolls imposed by most Turnpike Trustees.

Very little is known of this quaint vehicle, now at the National Motor Museum, Beaulieu. Its construction is typical of the 1880-90s. The Thorneycroft experience in building steam launch engines is evident in the vertical boiler and the underfloor layout of the engine and crankshaft onto the chain drive.

As has been mentioned elsewhere, they were empowered to levy tolls for road upkeep—and often discriminated in favour of the horse—from 1835 onwards. It may be that both Gurney and Hancock overstated their cases in writing their own form of testimonials. If they did, it was perhaps to cover up what they might already have seen as defects. Perhaps they were glad to get out of a venture which in the circumstances could scarcely have shown a profitable return. Be that as it may, for the next twenty years what halting attempts a few enthusiasts made are not worth recording.

The steam carriage revived

The second phase of the steam carriage saga began about 1858, when Thomas Rickett of Buckingham made his first steam carriage for the Marquess of Stafford. He borrowed Trevithick's design of 1801 to some extent, but a horizontal locomotive-type boiler was fitted, with a spur gear and pitch chain transmission. This was followed in 1860 by three or four more, including one for the Earl of Caithness, who successfully drove himself and his Countess in it from Inverness to his castle near Wick, a distance of 150 miles. These engines had speeds of up to 10 m.p.h. and for the next thirty years were the prototypes in general design of those which followed.

An Act of Parliament, in 1861, reduced road tolls to a bearable level and gave impetus to more interest in steam carriages. Pressure had been building up against the folly of allowing branch lines on the railways to spread too widely. Some of these were failing to show a profit and a case was made out for fast passenger-carrying road steamers to feed the trunk railway routes. But cussedly, another act of 1865 known as the Locomotives and Highway Act came down heavily on the side of the horse and the railway

locomotive. Road steamers were to be restricted to 4 m.p.h., whether for heavy haulage of freight or the conveyance of just two passengers. All were classed as road locomotives and, what was more, each required to have not less than three persons in attendance, one of whom was to walk 60 yards ahead holding a red flag. The upsurge of enthusiasm for faster road steamers was dampened; but one surviving example of this bleak period is preserved and should therefore be mentioned.

This is known as the 'Grenville Carriage' and was built at Newton Abbot railway works in 1875 by two premier apprentices, Robert Neville and George Churchward, who later became the famous designer of Great Western locomotives. It was a three-wheeler, with a vertical boiler, and fitted with a two-cylinder engine proved to be very serviceable, capable of 18 m.p.h.. Although now static in Bristol City Museum it was put in running condition again after thirty years of neglect, and was in steam in 1938 and again in 1946. Apart from this, there were three other machines made in the 1870s which could qualify as steam cars; but they were described as J. G. Rushaw's 'jaunting car' of 1871, Mackenzie's 'brougham' of 1875, and Blackburn's 'dog cart' of 1878.

All the above were one-off jobs, but some forward-looking ingenuity had been shown by making a lightweight vehicle having a quick-start boiler heated by a petrol burner, with a carburettor preheating and vaporising the fuel by exhaust steam. Experimenters were again at work, and some were delving back into the past, picking out for re-examination first-phase developments which had been neglected for various reasons. One of these was the Ackermann steering gear which overcame the difficulties encountered by those who relied on a simple pivoted front axle. Tiller steering on carriages so fitted required uncommon strength and dexterity, yet the Ackermann steering, so much more effective and easier to manage, was not widely adopted till about 1900, nearly a century after its invention.

The first steam cars– in France

The outstanding burst of British inventiveness declined in favour of the French, and to a lesser extent the Americans, once the men of those two nations settled back to work after their respective wars of 1861–65 and 1870–71. And in the field of steam cars and carriages, they captured the lead in development with Britain barely in third place till the end of the era. British incentive had been strangled by prejudicial legislation, though it remained supreme for steam in industry, heavy transport and agriculture. The three most outstanding names in the development of steam carriages across the Channel were Amadee Bollée Senior, le Comte de Dion and Leon Serpollet. The first was an ingenious mechanic, devoted to steam, who began by using the reliable British Field boiler on a variety of 'carriages', the largest of which weighed 20 tons. He overcame the steering problem to a large extent by a complicated but effective system and for one vehicle fitted independent engines to drive each rear wheel. He also greatly improved the application of springs, which was a much-felt need in the 1880s when iron-shod wheels were still being used.

De Dion, a wealthy amateur, became interested in 1881. He was outsize in both build and mental capacity, and he used the engineering expertise of a M. Bouton to set about producing a lightweight boiler as a first essential for a steam car. This was achieved—with a multiplicity of tubes—and it powered his first car in 1883. The De Dion-Bouton partnership branched out into steam for tricycles, quadricycles, cars and carriages, and heavier road vehicles of many types. The British-made Rudge tandem steam tricycle was fitted with a Bouton boiler weighing about 100 lb. complete with fittings and water, which gave it a speed up to 25 m.p.h.

De Dion switched to petroleum and later to paraffin, as a more reliable and economical fuel than coke, but as Panhard-Levasseur and Benz were achieving success at the time with their internal combustion 'horseless carriages' he abandoned steam, and found fame with motor cars. Not so Leon Serpollet, who took out a patent in 1888 for an oil-burning steam car which eventually became popular. At first, he co-operated with Armand Peugeot; but trial runs were so uncomfortable and disappointing that Peugeot also decided petrol motor cars more to his liking. Some of De Dion's carriages, known as the 'Remarquer' type, were 'drags' or tractors fitted to tow victoria or landau-type carriages behind them. But by the 1890s his machines were beginning to take the shape of a car, with the engine and boiler out of sight under the bonnet in front.

The Stanley steamer in the USA

In America, where several attempts to make reliable steam carriages had brought out just a few with less than spectacular results, Lucius Copeland had come up with a useful oil burner for a boiler he fitted to an English-made tricycle. This took only half an hour to move off from cold. Not much is known about the steam carriage built by Achille Philion of Akron, Ohio, in 1892, except that it ran on spidery wheels and that the smoke from the vertical boiler must have been a nuisance to the driver sitting just behind it. Also in America the twin brothers F. E. and F. A. Stanley began making 'steam buggies', as they called them. Even if they were not trained engineers, luck and intuition favoured them; and at a time when they had orders for two hundred cars to fill, they sold out lock, stock and barrel for $250,000. The Stanley steam car then became the Locomobile, but although

De Dion's first experiments were on a very modest scale. This single seater steam tricycle of 1887 created little demand, but led to larger models being made.

quite large numbers were sold, with many coming to England, they proved troublesome. Little more than a year later, the brothers were able to buy back their patents when the Locomobile Company went over to gasolene cars. The repurchase price was only $20,000 and the brothers soon lived down the bad reputation of the Locomobile steam cars and restored their own good name for reliability.

After these vicissitudes, and improvements to their cars, the Stanleys settled down with a more or less standard mechanical design in 1904, which lasted till 1925. Because steam was defeated in the battle fought in the early 1900s between it and the internal combustion engine, it is not generally realised how close a fight it was. In 1902, of 909 motor cars registered in New York State, 485 were steamers. And after 1897, nearly two hundred names are on record as having made or projected the making of steam cars. Of these rather more than half were based, by fair means or otherwise, on the Stanley pattern.

The advantage these American cars had over their European competitors (based entirely on de Dion, Serpollet and Bollée designs) was their lightness. The Americans adopted the cycle-type wheel, whereas the French used a

much heavier type, although both had gone on to pneumatic tyres before 1900. Another factor was cheapness, with the American 'buggy' costing about £150, while a Serpollet of the same h.p. rating cost about £250. The latter were imported into Britain, but it became customary to add such refinements as mudguards to imports coming in from the U.S.A., especially to the poorly-equipped Locomobiles.

One distinct advantage steam cars possessed was the ability to gain speed without gear changing from a standing start. The gears of petrol cars in the early 1900s were anything but easy to engage. They caused grindings and groanings. Besides being far noisier vehicles than the steamers, the petrol cars could exhaust as much or more smoke. In appearance the two rivals steadily became more alike as time went on; but as the basic faults and weaknesses of the motor car were overcome, the steamer began to lose popularity, largely because of its need for fuel, water and—above all—the time needed to raise steam.

During the early period British steam car engineers were not idle, even if scarcely any were actually making them. Clarksons, who had made just a few steam cars at the turn of the century, soon concentrated entirely on wagons and buses; many of the latter became the National steam buses serving London. They also made condensers for the American Locomobiles, and paraffin burners to replace the less-than-safe petrol furnaces with which they were fitted. English experts devised a permanent 'torch' as a means of starting up, in place of the 'firing iron' which proved a nuisance, and made other improvements to water heating, superheaters and lubricators. No steam Locomobiles were made after 1904 and the way was open for the Stanleys and others to go ahead, but success came only to those who used the Serpollet-type flash boiler as a basic fitting. Patents were not difficult to by-pass by making slight variations.

The range of steam-car makers world-wide dwindled to four as the Edwardian period advanced. After

1907 the number made in Britain was negligible and some of these were constructed under foreign patents, though for steam wagons it was a very different story. Serpollet, who led the field in so many respects and was usually the winner in long-distance races, was still making improvements when ill-health overtook him and he sold out to Darracq in 1907. This firm, already having an order for 100 steam bus chassis for London on its books, soon allowed car production to languish. This left Stanley with only one serious competitor—the White.

The White car and the Doble

Rollin White began with a steam buggy in America in 1901 as a change from making sewing machines. It had several Stanley features. This was followed by something more like a car, with wheel steering and a tonneau body. The boiler stayed much the same throughout the nine years White was in production, while his engine was a double-acting compound with Stephenson link motion. With a prop-shaft drive to a bevel-geared axle a White ran sedately and silently at 35 m.p.h. and by the use of a device which varied the steam cut-off, so as to give the effect of a second gear, it was the most sophisticated car on the roads. Over 3,000 had been built when production ended in 1911; but the car probably priced itself out of the market. Prices ranged up to about $5,000 for a 7-seater, 40 h.p. model, which in fact cost more than the 40/50 h.p. Rolls-Royce car of the same year. It is believed that the 3,000 Whites made was probably less than a third of the number of Stanleys.

The Stanley was virtually the only make available from 1911 to 1920, and was continued till 1925, but in 1921 the Doble appeared from Detroit, Michigan. Abner Doble was a steam enthusiast who set out to improve the

Stanley to the limit. His experiments began before 1914, but a few years later he came to regret fitting a Uniflow engine. Always aiming for perfection, and believing that his customers would pay more for the perfect steam car, his achievements led to more fame than fortune. Only about sixty Dobles were made, including the early experimental models. His later Model E had a Woolff four-cylinder double-acting compound engine, and one of these was sold to Henschel of Kassel who were interested in obtaining the licence.

It was said that no two Dobles were exactly alike, and there is little doubt that, with his dedication to steam and his constant search for perfection, Abner Doble made a notable contribution to steam car history. He was well aware that the petrol engine was rapidly becoming more automatic and flexible in operation, and cheaper both to buy and to run. Henry Ford had turned out nearly 2,000,000 'Lizzies'— the ubiquitous Model T—by 1923, but Doble persisted, and as far as his engine was concerned had succeeded; but the old, old bugbear of a boiler capable of sustaining the required power remained. His 'instant' flash boiler was faster than any other, but it was still not quick enough to compete with the petrol engine.

The later Dobles are credited with having run hundreds of thousands of miles over a twenty year period, but in that time they would have needed some essential replacements. Speeds have been put at close to 100 m.p.h., at a time when only a few top-class makes of petrol cars could match it. When Abner Doble gave up in 1932, he joined Sentinels at Shrewsbury and for five years was their consulting engineer. He took with him his own E.24 steam car, and although rumours persisted that he was working on a new car design, he was in fact concerned only with improving the famous Sentinel steam wagon. With his death in 1961, after his return to America in 1952, came the end of all serious attempts by steam cars to compete with petrol cars, which by the 1930s had progressed far beyond the reach of any existing steamer.

The end of the steam car

In spite of the eclipse of steam for cars, a faithful enthusiastic few would not give up the belief that steam had merits which the petrol car did not possess. After Doble, there were attempts to replace petrol engines with steam engines, using components of old Stanleys, Whites or Serpollets, with perhaps no other motivation than to satisfy a thirst for experiment. These attempts have continued off and on since the 1930s but there is no record of anyone achieving a breakthrough. There have, however, been attempts to persuade a petrol engine to run off steam. The great General Motors Corporation in 1969 was said to be converting an Opel petrol engine into a Uniflow steamer and fitting it into a Pontiac car. This was exciting news for the steam enthusiast, but the lack of further information was a pretty certain indication that this experiment was a failure. General Motors did not give up—as late as 1974 they were still experimenting with steam cars, developed on their behalf by the Besler Corporation, which took over the Doble factory.

A few old steamers were resurrected during and just after World War II for no other reasons than the rationing of petrol—and most steamers ran on paraffin. The venerable Marquis de Dion, when over 80, brought out from retirement his 1889 steam tricar, which ran on solid fuel. He ran it around Paris, much to the annoyance of the Nazi army of occupation; which was as he had hoped. But now scarcely any of the few steam models in preservation are in running condition. Their rarity as antiques makes them almost too precious to use on the roads, and spare parts are non-existent.

The spare parts situation became a serious disability for the steam as compared with the petrol car. Once the latter was mass-produced, there were motor agents who stocked spare parts which were always within reach of the

The White steam car, like most other makes, was built in the U.S.A. They were on similar lines to the motor car of the period, but were more reliable. This shows President Roosevelt riding in his 30 h.p. model.

A future – perhaps?

motorist in need. Not so with steam cars, whose makers, with modest factories and sales organisations, were in no position to appoint agents holding spares. These had to be sent from the makers, and for British owners this meant often a long and expensive wait. And while in an engineering sense steam cars were simpler than their rivals, being gearless and with fewer complicated moving parts, they were more complicated to run. There were many critical factors, mainly concerning the supply of steam. Too much or too little could cause a lot of trouble, and the necessity to be supplied for a journey with water as well as fuel was another anxiety. Explosions, however, were less catastrophic with flash boilers, simply because they held very little water. A bursting boiler holding a quart of water at 300 p.s.i. was much less dangerous to life and limb than the explosion of a 100-gallon ordinary boiler at only 50 lb. steam pressure.

Another serious attempt to overcome the disadvantages of the steam car was made in England. Alex Moulton of Leylands had been interested in steam for twenty years, and his experiments led him to believe that if only a greater compactness of boiler and engine, with less weight, could be achieved, steam could still compete. Funds were made available for his ambitious project of making a power unit comparable in size, weight and power to that of the ordinary car. But this ideal never materialised; time and money gave out before a successful ending.

Then there was the Paxton Phoenix project, supported by McCulloch, the American chain-saw tycoon. Abner Doble assisted in the design of a low-revving double-acting compound, to bring his own classic steamer up to date. Due as much as anything to a clash of personalities, this Phoenix never rose again. But although the belief that steam cars have a future has not completely died away, the idea remains more in the minds of those still affected by its elusive magic than in the minds of expert engineers. As recently as 1977 I was approached by a visitor who claimed to have made the vital breakthrough. All he needed was finance, to produce a steam engine and boiler for cars which would outstrip the petrol engine for performance and economy. Had I been a tycoon I might have shown more interest and offered the help requested, but at the time I was too busy driving a 96-year-old locomotive with a train-load of visitors. But I wish now that I had noted his name and address, if only to give details here of what he had in mind.

I doubt even now that steam cars are a dead letter. There is a growing concern for the pollution from internal combustion engines. Some big American car makers are very well aware of this; and they know that fuel costs will inevitably rise higher and higher. They are not oblivious to the merits of steam power to ease pollution, they have the resources and they may eventually solve the problem of automobile steam power. Steam is known to be more powerful and versatile now than ever Watt or Trevithick imagined.

Tasker's Little Giant from Andover was a popular locomotive for light haulage work. This photograph was taken in 1907, at the RAC commercial motor trials at Maidenhead, although this engine was not a competitor.

STEAM WAGONS, LORRIES, TRACTORS, BUSES

A heavyweight start

In using the simile for steam of a tree-trunk with its branches, it is difficult to find a definite branch for the steam wagon. This is largely because its origins can readily be traced to such early self-propelled passenger-carrying road vehicles as those of Cugnot, Evans and Trevithick, Gurney and Hancock. In practice, if not in principle, those early iron horses were ahead of their times, and they tended to evolve towards the steam tractor, or 'drag engine'. In Britain, moreover, there were stringent restrictions for most of the 19th century against road transport by steam. When the most

severe of these restrictions were finally lifted in 1896, there was very little demand for steam passenger-carrying vehicles on the roads, for by then the railways, and urban rail systems, had become firmly established. This chapter is therefore mainly devoted to load-carrying self-propelled steamers, because they filled an important gap in the field of transport, as the true fore-runners of the motor lorry. The first steam wagon proper on record is that built for a specific purpose by John Yule in Scotland as early as 1870. No doubt special dispensation was given for Mr. Yule to carry the boilers made at his Rutherglen works to Glasgow Docks. His wagon was of necessity a sturdily-built affair capable of carrying a 40-ton boiler, its own vertical boiler (working at 50–60 p.s.i.) being moun-

ted at the rear, clear of the main chassis which was 26 feet in length. It was well designed and constructed, and although slow, it mattered little if it took two hours to cover two miles with its 40-ton load; since it had previously taken four hundred men to pull it, and forty to haul the empty trolley back from the docks. The cost of moving each boiler was finally reduced to £10, from the £40 it had cost to hire men at two shillings a head for the job.

The next successful road wagon was built at Leyland, Lancashire, to carry coal for James Sumnor from the pit-head to an engineering works, where later arose one of the great names in motor transport. This first steamer in 1884 came in for harassment by the police, and it was not until a few years later, when the Leyland firm had become known through an amalgamation as the Lancashire Steam Motor Co., that production went ahead again with designs for both wagons and vans. In their day these steamers were almost as famous as the motor lorries which, under the Leyland name, followed them. A new design of vertical boiler was used, adaptable both to coke burning and to liquid fuel. Working pressure was stepped up to 225 p.s.i., and with a horizontal compound engine having Stephenson link motion working at 425 r.p.m., a speed of 6 m.p.h. was attained by the new wagons, which won prizes and medals. These were the rewards of entering some of the trials organised by the Liverpool Self-Propelled Vehicle Association, which in itself is some indication of the interest in and need for this form of road transport at the period around the turn of the century.

For several years Leylands (the title was changed to Leyland Motors in

A Thompson engine is seen here in an experiment with an omnibus loaded with 65 passengers, about 1870 on the short-lived Edinburgh to Leith route.

An early type of steam wagon built by the Yorkshire Steam Wagon Co. Ltd., with a horizontal compound engine and a vertical boiler. It was built from 1903 onwards until superseded by the horizontal boiler with its chimney in the middle.

1907) were in the front rank of steam wagon builders. An earlier partnership as a private company registered in 1902 included William Norris as chief engineer, who became the author of several books on this specialist subject. One of these, *Modern Steam Road Wagons* of 1906, was reprinted in 1972. Apart from the mechanical details relating to various makes, there are tabulated results of the Liverpool Trials of 1898, 1899 and 1901. A contemporary insight is also given on the complexity of regulations still affecting weights and speeds on the roads of the period.

Roads were still a problem, and although much less steam was required when travelling over hard paved roads, such as the stone setts so common in northern districts, the noise created by iron-tyred wheels, even at 6 m.p.h., must have been a public nuisance. The macadam surfaces common on trunk roads in country areas were often damaged by heavy loads where the subsoil was unstable, or in wet spells. Potholes were liable to damage the wagons themselves or upset the loads they carried, since once a small pothole became a puddle, continuing traffic soon widened and deepened it.

Against such hazards, the chain-drive wagons were found to be more resilient than those with geared drive which made little headway until metal-led roads became more widespread. Some so-called roads were less than hard, and ruts were not only a menace, but could have the effect of creating a continuous gradient, from the compression by a heavy load of a road material which had failed to consolidate, such as gravel. This factor had to be reckoned with in the early days, for journeys often involved using second and third class roads. Tests and calculations were made which showed that endlessly climbing out of a 2-inch rut, created in a road surface by the weight on the wheels, could be the equivalent of a gradient of 17% to 29%, depending on the diameter of the wheels and the width of the tyres.

Leylands and their rivals

When the Lancashire Steam Motor Co. became Leyland Motors Ltd. in 1907, they bought out the nearby competition of Coulthards, at Preston. Although Leylands made their first petrol engine in 1904, they had sufficient faith in the future of steam to continue building wagons, improving them all the time. They also stuck to their own design of vertical boilers for several years, switching from fire-tube to water-tube types, and at working pressure stepped up to 250 p.s.i. The vertical boiler had certain advantages, one being that it took up less space and was lighter than the horizontal low-type boiler. It was also capable of raising steam more rapidly and could house a superheater more easily, so that in little more than half an hour from cold a wagon was ready for the road.

Some Leyland engines were horizontal, and enclosed in an oil-bath, but the vertical type was also used for a time. The design of valve motion was also changed, in line with a policy of continuous improvement to performance. In the knowledge that drivers were unlikely to be trained engineers, some fittings such as bearings were made without means of adjustment, against the risk of harmful tampering. Gearboxes allowed for two forward and two reverse changes, and steering was on the Ackermann principle— invented in 1818 but scarcely used for

An iron-tyred Foden wagon belonging to the Eastern Steam Co. is smartened up for the 1911 coronation parade of commercial vehicles at Earls Court.

the rest of the 19th century.

Five steam wagon models were available when full production resumed after the First World War. But the war had also proved that petrol lorries were faster and more versatile than steamers, and Leylands themselves set out to meet the increasing demand for them. They were pioneers of both steam and petrol lorries, and by the time the last steamer was made in 1926, Leylands were in the forefront as builders of heavy-duty motor lorries.

The firm of Merryweather should be mentioned as a company faithful to vertical boilers. As fire-engine makers they were world famous, and much of their success rested on their patent boilers, which were capable of raising steam in three minutes and having 100 p.s.i. on the gauge in less than ten. The secret lay in a simple but clever arrangement of tubes which allowed perfect heat circulation. Merryweather also built steam tram engines, but the self-propelled fire-engine may be considered here as a steam wagon, along with the cesspit evacuators Merryweather built. They came on the market in 1907, and all their boilers were oil burners, oil having the advantage over solid fuel of instantaneous combustion.

One unusual feature of the Merryweather design was the way in which the engine with its duplex cylinders was fitted vertically above the drive to make a very compact vehicle, which gave the fire-engine a short wheelbase and allowed for a 750-gallon tank on the cesspool emptier. This special vehicle had a larger coal-fired boiler, since it was not built for emergencies, but the makers claimed for it that sewage could be removed with a complete absence of nuisance.

Such a specialised vehicle would seldom be seen at work, for sewage disposal was often carried out under cover of darkness. All the same, the first quarter of the present century was the period when the sight of steam-powered engines, both road and rail, was most commonplace. It was also the most prolific period for new designs of steam wagons, and one of

several builders in the Liverpool area produced a platform lorry with everything but the chimney and driver's seat underneath the chassis. This was the Musker, and it was first seen about 1901. It was a well-designed vehicle, with good weight distribution. Muskers made boilers, both coke and oil fired, which had a series of coiled tubes allowing for 250 p.s.i., but the makers claimed that they were tested to no less than ten times that pressure. The engine had a pair of twin cylinders, each separately enclosed, and at 500 r.p.m. it gave a rating of 25 b.h.p. Two types of engine were built as prototypes, embodying features not seen elsewhere, but the wagons did badly in the 1901 Liverpool Trials owing to their being largely untested beforehand. It remained a matter of conjecture why, after further experiments and improvements, Muskers failed to exploit their product, but after a few had been sold they gave up in 1905 and parted with their patents to Savage Bros. of Kings Lynn, who made little use of them.

Among the other restrictive regulations with which operators of steam wagons had to comply was that of steam and smoke emission. Because of this, coke rather than coal was used as fuel. This was no disadvantage, however, because coke was cheaper at a time when it was more or less a waste product from the numerous coal-gas plants of the period. The price was usually between 10 shillings and £1 per ton, and from some plants lump coke could be had free for the taking. With such smokeless fuel, there still remained the problem of steam, either emitted from safety valves blowing off, or exhausted through the chimney. To overcome this, some engine builders fitted condensers of one kind and another, which not only avoided the risk of frightening horses, but served to recycle the water which was at least warm before entering the boiler again.

Interesting though it may be to make comparisons of pre-1914 costs, these are distorted by post-1940 inflation. All that need be said about the cost of new steam wagons before 1914 was that the price of most models was

Yorkshire patent steam wagons are instantly recognisable by their transverse boiler mounted at the extreme front end of the chassis. Boiler pressure is 200 p.s.i. and the enclosed compound engine drives through gears onto the chain final drive unit. There are only 5 Yorkshire wagons known to be preserved in Britain and this example, 3 ton wagon No. 940 of 1917, is at the Todber Museum of Steam.

in the region of £500. This was a considerable outlay at that time, for it must be multiplied by at least 20, based on the fall in value of the pound since then. Allowance must however be made for the fact that for such vehicles, and indeed for traction engines as well, there was no such thing as mass production on assembly lines, which would have reduced unit costs. Running costs were therefore important despite the low cost of coke, and all the

Boiler improvements

It is safe to assume that plans made in anticipation of this relaxation soon resulted in new types of wagon, and so began a boom in models using both horizontal and vertical boilers. There was too a renewed interest in the placing of engines served by horizontal boilers, to find out whether an undertype or overtype position was better. The latter meant putting the engine above the boiler—'top works' as it was called. All traction-engine makers had long since forsaken undertype motion for their machines. The general design of traction engines had become standardised by the twenty or so principal firms making them, but when they entered into the new and expanding steam wagon market, it is not surprising that their designs differed widely. All were competing to produce what they hoped would be a standard type for both home and export sales.

Variations were based on boilers of many types, some specially designed for this new purpose. Certain established traction-engine builders used vertical boilers, as well as adapting their own versions, reduced in size, of the horizontal locomotive-type boiler. They had to be shortened so as to allow a greater load capacity behind—in this respect vertical boilers had the advantage.

But one firm, the Yorkshire Steam Wagon Co. of Hunslet, came up with a hybrid. It was a cylinder-shaped boiler lying lengthways across the front of the vehicle, but with a firebox in a central position below, and the chimney directly above. Their steam lorry was one of the most successful designs; the first was made in 1903, the last, numbered 2271, in 1937. They were made for a variety of purposes, though the straight wagon predominated. One of these fascinated me, for it was the lorry used by a nurseryman at Tunbridge Wells for whom I worked in 1924. Peter Brotherhood of Peterborough also used this type of boiler for the few

tests and trials between various makes carefully recorded the fuel and water consumption. The builders of the St. Pancras Wagon, made in London, were for example proud to announce that the 1911 model with a payload of 7 tons consumed 12–14 lb. of coke per mile, at an average speed of 6 m.p.h.

To give one more example of a wagon with a vertical boiler, the 'Londonderry' is worthy of note, if only because a prominent nobleman was its instigator. The then Marquess of Londonderry had them built in his colliery workshops at Seaham Harbour. And although his idea was to provide work for his men at slack times, his wagons were so successful that his lordship decided to go into wider production. His machine was fairly typical of the design of the period, with a cab-enclosed boiler over the front axle, and

a horizontal compound engine totally enclosed beneath the wagon platform. This had slide valves, with the firm's own variation on Stephenson link motion worked by crankshaft eccentrics, and it had two speeds, 2½ and 6 m.p.h. As far as fuel consumption was concerned, it was claimed that for a journey of 84 miles, at 6 m.p.h. with a 5-ton load, the wagon burned 10 cwt. of coke—slightly more per mile than the 'St. Pancras' mentioned above.

Although vertical boilers were most often used by makers in the early 1900s, some firms already building traction engines of various types were not slow to take advantage of the easing of highways restrictions against steam by the 1905 Act of Parliament. These firms were of course more wedded to the locomotive-type horizontal boiler.

Above: Pendle Prince, No. 190708 is the only Fowler steam wagon known to exist. Built originally as a gully emptier, she is now restored as a plain wagon.

Below: Heavily retouched works photograph of a 1920s Robey double-crank compound 6 ton wagon for export to Spain. The Robey 'pistol type' boiler can be seen.

was not only a shameful, but often a frightening experience, with steam at perhaps 200 p.s.i. suddenly surging down on to the fire.

Mann and Hunslet

The steam cart idea was born in the 1880s, but it was not until 1898 that it became a reality. The first was built at Hunslet in Yorkshire by J. M. Mann whose company later became the Yorkshire Steam Wagon Co. In some respects it was a small traction engine, with a top-mounted single cylinder, rated at 4 N.H.P. All likeness to a traction engine ended to the rear of the small flywheel, for there were three rear wheels and above these was

wagons they made, but neither this nor the 'Hercules' boiler, which had two chimneys, one at each end instead of one in the centre, was taken up by other makers.

One disability inherent in the vertical boiler was its lack of water capacity above the firebox, as compared with the horizontal. The greater the heating surface, the greater the steam-raising capacity of a boiler. This lack applied especially to the smaller, narrowed vertical boilers and, although some makers introduced devices that were said to avoid trouble, they did little to lessen the more or less constant anxiety drivers felt about keeping the water in the boiler at the correct level. Over-anxiety could lead to priming, with the chimney throwing up watery steam from excess water in the boiler, and reduced pressure. But allowing the water level to fall out of sight in the gauge glass would bring immediate feelings of fear. There was then seldom any sure means of knowing by how much the crown of the boiler was water-covered; once it became dry, the fusible plug would melt and it would take hours to get on the move once more. To 'drop the plug' on any engine

carried a screw-operated tipping container, capable of holding 6–7 tons of material such as roadstone or coal. The central wheel, which took the geared drive, was broad and studded for grip, while the outside wheels were plain, as stabilising weight-carriers. A cable-winding drum was also fitted to make the cart adaptable for two-engine ploughing, and here its advantage lay in its ability to traverse soft ground without sinking in.

By 1901, the firm which had now become Manns Patent Steam Cart and Wagon Co. Ltd. claimed to have sold sixty steam carts which were giving good service. By 1908 the number had risen to five hundred, but this included a type with an open platform as well as one with a compound engine. To save space, the firehole door was placed on the right-hand side; the driver's position was cramped and the steering wheel set well forward just behind the cylinder.

In the course of time, many more varied and improved designs left the Hunslet works, including machines using enclosed oil-bath engines, both under- and overtype, with pressures up to 200 p.s.i. For the last Mann design, named the 'Express' and introduced in 1924, pressure went to 250 p.s.i. His fitting of a vertical, water-tube boiler serving an enclosed undertype engine made for quick steaming and easy servicing. The 'Express' was in fact a long-distance vehicle, capable of much higher speeds than those the firm produced for short hauls. An enclosed cab with upholstered seats, and pedal controls for steam and brakes, put the 'Express' in the forefront of steam lorries, to compete for the growing long-distance traffic demands then rapidly emerging in Britain.

Robey and Savage

The well-established firm of Robey was famous for boilers of many types, as well as engines. They were one of four firms in Lincoln specialising in steam, and entered the wagon market in the early 1900s with a vertical-boilered vehicle of fairly conventional design. In 1909 they introduced their own version of the crossways-mounted boiler of cylindrical shape, as fitted by Mann, but with a domed firebox riveted inside and without the stays which were often the source of leaks. Interesting and well designed as this boiler was, it gave way after a few years to a new horizontal boiler, with top-mounted motion, which was geared down to power a chain as final drive. This overtype eventually became their standard, sold with various improvements until the end of steam. This boiler was not quite a small locomotive-type boiler, in so far that its firebox was well below the barrel, and had a rounded shape incorporating the improvements mentioned above, which such a firm was well able to make with the experience and expertise it possessed.

Savage of Kings Lynn had a long tradition of steam. They were known as the leading makers of fairground rides, and the fact that these had a centre steam engine showed that steam was at the centre of their business activities. They too made traction engines and followed them up with wagons, some of which incorporated the Musker patent boiler. But while most of the four or five models built went for export, the firm also built to special order. Models available included a 'Sanitary Wagon' for street cleaning, and a portable electricity plant, with a large dynamo fixed to the wagon platform. As their answer to the vexed question of road wheels, they also patented a wheel fitted with wood blocks to form the tyre.

Other firms, already well known for traction engines, steamrollers, etc. who branched out into producing

wagons as well during the boom period of 1900–1910 cannot all be covered in detail. Allchin, Aveling, Burrell, Clayton, Foden, Foster, Fowler, Garrett, Howard, Ransome, and Wantage, apart from those already mentioned, were all engaged in meeting the demand. The numbers built by each varied greatly, and comparisons with modern lorry output cannot be fairly made.

The 1920s– Foden and Sentinel

Although many of them had inadequate workspace and no knowledge of mass-production techniques, most firms were busy with orders for all sorts of vehicles. Avelings, for example, if their works numbering was consecutive, had a total output between 1909 and 1924 of 5,575 engines of all types, of which about 290 were wagons. Burrells made 114 in about the same period, after 1911, but far more were made by firms specialising in wagons. Only one firm noted for its railway locomotives is known to have entered this market. This was Beyer-Peacock of Gorton, Manchester; but two concerns who started by making steamers became well-known later for motor lorries—Atkinson and Thorneycroft. The demand for steam wagons fell away sharply after the First World War, and by the late 1920s there were virtually only two firms left to compete with the internal combustion engine. One of them, Fodens of Sandbach, emerged as the last champion of the overtype, with horizontal boiler. The other was Sentinel, which with its vertical boiler and enclosed undertype engine outlasted all its rivals—and went down at last with honour, if not with flying colours. The history of these two firms can therefore be conveniently examined to exemplify the development of the steam wagon up to its final disappearance from the roads as a vehicle serving the nation's transport needs.

Edwin Foden decided to settle for himself which of the two types of boiler was best for the type of steam wagon he had in mind. This was in 1898–9, when others too were arguing about the respective merits of the locomotive-type boiler and the vertical. His first experiment was with the latter, but the whole design was unconventional in having a vertical engine too, with a front-wheel chain drive. Much smaller rear wheels took the steering from a worm-operated chain to the axle. The second experimental wagon had a locomotive-type boiler, and a cab covering the top-mounted compound engine, but it had front

T. LEIGH d
'PHONE
CHESHAM HAULAGE COM
161 CHARTRIDGE,
BUCKS.

chain steering and a long chain for the final drive to the rear wheels. Both this, and Foden's third and fourth designs, were improved in various ways, especially by shortening the boiler barrel to give more load capacity.

It was the fifth modification which became the basic prototype for the large number of steamers the firm built for nearly thirty years afterwards. It had a good start, having gained second place at the War Office trials, held in 1901. The £250 prize was of less importance than the government order which followed. The first prize went to Thorneycroft, a firm already well established with contracts for the Royal Navy, as well as being one of the leaders for reliable steam wagons and vans. Despite their high reputation which culminated in gaining them the Premium War Office Award in further trials held in 1906, Thorneycroft decided to discontinue building road steamers the following year.

Above: No. 8562 six-wheeled steam wagon built in 1931 by Sentinel at Shrewsbury. This engine can be seen in the Todber Museum of Steam.

Below left: Standard type of 12 ton overtype six wheeler made by Fodens between 1919 and 1928.

But Foden persevered and increased his production of a standard 5-ton wagon, which was a model of sturdy compactness and skilled craftsmanship as well as good design. Among its well-tried features was a short horizontal boiler of 220 lb. working pressure, serving a double-crank compound engine. The 1905 Act restricting top speed was enforced, though much depended on the attitude of local police authorities. Although wagons were rated as having a top speed of 6 m.p.h., most of them were not only capable of more but exceeded it whenever the opportunity arose. It was the First World War, however, with its greatly increased demands for transport, which paved the way for increased speeds. By 1919 the new and further improved C-type Foden was ready. This had much the same design of engine and boiler as its predecessor but it developed sufficient power to take bulkier loads; and some models had twin rear axles to make them into six-wheelers. These could be had with solid rubber tyres, while Ackermann steering gear—much more conducive to accuracy and safety at the new speed of 16 m.p.h.—was fitted as standard.

Although there was a steady increase in the number of Sentinels seen on the roads, Foden had the cream of the market during the 1920s. They were virtually without competitors if customers wanted a locomotive-type boiler with an overtype engine, and the Fodens also had the advantage of a lower initial cost compared with the Sentinels. But the latter had the advantage of greater speed and capacity, and in performance as well as in appearance compared very favourably with the internal-combustion motor lorry. It was to meet competition from the motor lorry at a time when traction-engine makers were dropping out from a rapidly shrinking market, that Foden came out with a 'Speed Six', the 'Six' referring to the number of wheels. This was a steam lorry, remarkably modern in appearance; the enclosed cab housed a novel design of water-tube boiler, serving an under-mounted engine with duplex cylinders set across the frame.

The 'Speed Six' was designed for 45 m.p.h., but proved to be capable of 60. Its power in top gear, with boiler pressure of 275 p.s.i., would take a full load of 6 tons up a gradient of 1 in $3\frac{1}{2}$;

155

and with a high engine speed, it needed less than full throttle to cruise at 45 m.p.h.

The name 'Sentinel' was given to a steam wagon in 1906, built by Alley & McClellan of Polmadie, Glasgow. In general design it was fairly typical of the vertical boiler—undermounted engine type with duplex cylinders, but it had an advantage over some rivals in reliability and manoeuvrability. Considerable numbers were sold, and in 1915 the firm decided to set up a separate factory for wagon building, away from where they made other machinery. They chose Shrewsbury as a more central position than Glasgow and acquired 65 acres for the new works. From 1917 onwards 'Sentinel' became the company's title as well as the name of its product.

The 'Super Sentinel' came out in 1923, and was exhibited at the Motor Show as a 10-ton six-wheeler, along with a 5-ton tipping lorry. The former, with a platform 23 feet long and 7 feet wide, had well above the usual carrying capacity, and made easy work of full loads at the then legal speed of 16 m.p.h., for which the engine had only to turn over at 240 r.p.m. Several new features embodied in the 'Super Sentinel' included a very well designed differential, which reduced wear and increased safety when turning corners. The boiler was carried well forward of the front axle, giving ample room for driver and fireman, behind whose seats was the water tank. The fire was fed from the top, through a chute, and the final drive was by a short chain, activating both rear axles on the six-wheeler.

As with some other makes the boiler shell could be separated for servicing into two halves, but I learned that it was a very tricky process to bring them together again. The 'Super Sentinel' had a pressure of 230 p.s.i. and was capable of using coke, coal or, in some cases, oil for fuel. Although these wagons were proving their success to the extent of being commonplace on British roads during the 1920s, a large number were also exported. But steam power on the roads was further developed in the new 'O.G.' type which

followed the 'Super'. Pressure was stepped up to 275 p.s.i., the engine became capable of 650 r.p.m., and models were available as four, six and even eight-wheelers. The imposition of a heavy tax on solid-tyred vehicles, which in 1930 crippled many a transport firm, brought Sentinels on to pneumatics to give them an even greater resemblance to the modern motor lorry. There was of course some steamy smoke exhausted from the chimney which only just projected above the cab roof, but a 'Sentinel' was practically noiseless in operation, so unlike the modern diesel lorry with its staccato exhaust beat.

The ultimate steam lorry

The final development came during the 1930s. By this time practically all the other makers of steam wagons had dropped out. But Sentinels brought out their splendid 'S' model, said to be the most advanced steam lorry ever made; it was also built in Czechoslovakia during and after World War II. Argentina took the final batch of these steamers in 1950 from the Shrewsbury works.

The 'S' type was also made in four, six, or eight-wheel models, each having a tipper alternative. The duplex-

cylinder engine however was superseded by one with four in-line cylinders in a block, working on a single crankshaft, like a car. Also following internal combustion practice, the pistons were single acting, with poppet valves in the cylinder head, and the engine was mounted low and just off-centre, so that one other innovation could be fitted. This was the Cardan drive shaft, which gave a most effective power connection to the enclosed back axle double-reduction gears. The regulations by this time had been stretched to make 20 m.p.h. the limit for heavy vehicles, but these Sentinels were easily capable of 50 m.p.h. The four-cylinder engine was made for smooth running and high speed; at 20 m.p.h. it turned over at 775 r.p.m.

It would be a serious omission not to mention the Garrett wagon, a masterpiece which came out in 1926. It was known as the 'Regal Six' and embodied many first-rate features, including hydraulic side and end tipping gear, and a powerful duplex-cylinder engine. But Garretts were an unlucky firm in many ways, and while the new wagon itself did well, it had to be taken out of production soon after 1930.

These ultimate developments in the steam lorry as built by Foden, Sentinel and Garrett show how much they had advanced beyond the steam wagons of only twenty years before. Some performance features of the Garrett 'Regal Six' are worth tabling:

Garrett 'Regal Size' 1926			
Working pressure	255 p.s.i.	Acceleration:	
Superheat up to	800°F	0–10 m.p.h.	6 seconds
Total heating surface		0–20 m.p.h.	23 seconds
of tubes and firebox	64.13 sq. ft.	0–30 m.p.h.	71 seconds
Grate area	3.9 sq. ft.	Braking to stop	
Water tank	165 gal.	(brakes steam operated)	
Water capacity of boiler	52 gal.	at 20 m.p.h.	28 ft.
Maximum evaporation rate		at 30 m.p.h.	75 ft.
(on Welsh coal) 1,600 lb per hour		Turning circle diameter	72½ ft.
Evaporation of water		Total loaded weight 23 tons	
per 1 lb of coal	5.85 lb.	12 cwt	20.9 m.p.h.
Water consumption			
per mile	4.35 gal.		
Brake Horse Power	120		

Left: This Doble-designed experimental Foden wagon (1936) represents one of the last attempts to compete with the internal combustion engine.

Below: One of the most advanced wagon designs available in the late 1920s, Garrett's 8 ton 'QL' is illustrated here in its most popular configuration.

Timber tractors

Special-purpose vehicles were made by most of the larger firms. Both Sentinel and Foden made tractors which, while not strictly wagons, are best included here. Sentinel made a small number of timber tractors, for use where trees had to be hauled out to a trailer, and loaded by means of a winch. This was highly skilled work done by timber contractors and was often undertaken using a traction engine. The Sentinel tractor, however, was very versatile, for it carried a second engine to power the rear-mounted winch. With a short wheelbase and large twin pneumatic tyres, the special Timber Tractor weighed 11 tons—but it could negotiate soft earth and awkward spaces

between trees and having made up a load of trunks, could haul it away. The engines were very powerful when they used the low gears they possessed, but the tractor itself was capable of a quiet 35 m.p.h. on the open road. A timber tractor is exhibited at Bressingham, one of the two in preservation out of only twelve made. I gave it to my son Robert as a wedding present in 1967. Its cost when new in 1930 was £2,500.

The Foden tractor could also be used for timber work, but with only one standard horizontal engine was more often called upon to haul extra large loads on trailers. Although such tractors had a variety of uses, both they and the steam wagons were penalised soon after 1930 for the solid rubber tyres which most of them had. The excuse for the greatly increased tax was that of road damage, but, whether or not this was a just accusation, many owners discarded them instead of giving them pneumatic tyres. Up to the mid-1920s, steam wagons were a boon to long-distance cyclists, myself included. Many of the wagons travelled at a convenient 10 to 15 m.p.h., and a cyclist could hang on to the tail-board fastening chain for miles, keeping an eye out to avoid the roadside verge, since for safety it was advisable to use the near side. I remember one such hitch in 1923 which took me over 30 miles on the A11; but the practice was later prohibited by law.

Steam buses

Although two Foden steam buses are known to exist, this firm did not produce any for sale. A bus body was built on a steam-wagon chassis for the use of their famous Foden Works Band; a replica of this was built much later by Mr. George Milligan, and remains in his very interesting collection, which unfortunately is not open to the public.

A Thorneycroft wagon was fitted with a double-decker horse-bus body in 1902. It ran experimentally in London, but receipts were well below the running costs of 1/6d. per mile, and the project for a service was abandoned.

This rare type of steam wagon, made by the St. Pancras Ironworks, London, took part in the coronation parade of commercial vehicles at Earls Court in June 1911. A profile of the saint was usually included on the works name plate, below the horizontal boiler, but excluded from this wagon.

A pre-1914 example of the later type of Leyland steam bus, with no protection for the driver, but at least having solid rubber tyres.

A Sentinel steam bus appeared at the Leicester Royal Show in 1924, but the body was not of their making. Its appearance was quite advanced for the time, to which its standard Super Sentinel rounded front and vee-shaped windscreen contributed. It was a 32-seater, on solid tyres, and appeared remarkable for its low operational cost of only 8½d per mile on a 100-mile trip, needing only one stop for water.

Leyland, Garrett, Yorkshire, Mann and Straker were among those who offered steam buses at one time or another. Some were quaint and some were crude but all had character. The Garrett and the Yorkshire were quite imposing, and because they were so quiet in motion, compared with the petrol vehicles of the time, a hand-operated Klaxon horn was a necessity. Several firms specialised in steam buses and coaches up to the early 1920s. As an indication of their widespread use, it is said that over two hundred steam buses were operating in London alone in 1914.

Some of these would have been Clarkson buses, since he supplied the London Road Car Company with both single and double-deckers. Thomas Clarkson was one of the pioneers in steam wagons, and was experimenting with passenger versions from 1894 to 1903. His firm is credited

with having made more buses than any other, and the last one was withdrawn from London service in 1919. A first-class steam engineer, Clarkson's final development was of his own flash-type boiler, giving steam at 300 p.s.i. (superheated to over 700°C) to serve a V-twin compound engine. This was so compact that it could be housed under a bonnet, resembling that of a motor lorry, and both wagon and bus needed

at least a second glance—or listen—to be sure it was steam-powered. Steam could be raised in ten minutes from cold once the paraffin burner was lit.

If steam wagons, buses and cars failed to meet the steadily increasing competition from the internal combustion engine, it was not because of their noise or their pollution of the air. The petrol lorries and buses of the 1920s were both noisy and smelly, and like the farm tractors made the air stink with their exhaust gases. By the time steam vehicles on the roads had begun to dwindle, their engines and boilers had reached an advanced stage of development. But the ultimate stage never came—and many people still believe that steam power could have been developed further until it competed with petrol or diesel engines. The reason why this never happened may never be explained—but it would make a revealing and interesting story.

Perhaps the main and simple reason for steam's disappearance from the roads lay in the cheapness of motor fuel in the 1920s and 1930s, coupled with the frequency with which all but the latest steam vehicles had to replenish their fuel and water supplies while the motor car and lorry could go for many miles without a stop.

A period piece—a standard Yorkshire steam wagon fitted with a bus body. Note the extra bags of coal on roof, and the water pick-up hose under the chassis.

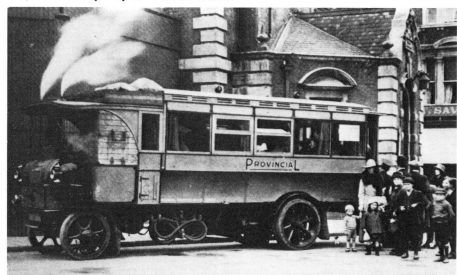

The Advance roller was developed by Wallis & Stevens to suit the finer road making materials, such as asphalt then coming into use. With these materials the pause on reversing direction which was necessary with previous rollers, left depressions in the surface, so the Advance was designed with a double-compound engine layout, which needed only a very small flywheel and could be reversed with hardly any pause. The photograph shows an Advance roller in photographic grey outside the works at Basingstoke. Several Advance rollers have been preserved.

10

STEAM ROLLERS

A late starter

The steam roller presents no classification difficulty. It also has the distinction of being the last type of steam engine to be used on the roads commercially, before giving way to diesel power long after most other forms had done so. Its development was relatively late, and its appearance in Britain seems to have sprung from a French invention of the 1850s.

At that period, the French were ahead of the British in road-making, due largely to the antiquated and fragmented system of repair and maintenance which lingered on here, in spite of Macadam's method. This method, as applied in Britain, obviated the need for rolling simply because it was left to the traffic to do it. Graded granite—crushed by steam power but hauled by horses to the road until the road locomotive arrived later in the century—was scattered over the road surface, a few inches thick, and covered with loose soil. Wheels and hooves then passed over it, and gradually the granite chips became embedded with one flat surface uppermost; a few weeks or perhaps months later, this produced a hard-surfaced road, dusty when dry, turning to mud when wet.

The author remembers this procedure still being practised on village streets and country roads as recently as 1914, with a fussy little traction engine bringing the granite from the local railway station on trailer wagons.

Horsedrawn rollers had of course been used on urban roads, but steam power had drawn a roller for roads in the Hyde Park area by 1859. This machine was one of Bray's patents, but

Fowler 10 ton d.c.c. roller, No. 9023 of 1907. Clearly seen is the characteristically massive front fork and rolls of the larger Fowlers. Several similar engines have been preserved.

by this time in France Lemoine had discovered a way of building a self-propelled roller which had eluded English designers. This led to others taking up the idea, including Gelleret, whose improvements were taken up by the Leeds locomotive builders, Manning Wardle. Ranging in weight from 15 to 30 tons, their machines were an adaptation of the railway engine with rollers beneath fore and aft. Transmission was by shaft and bevel gearing, with chains as final drive. The rolls, acting as wheels, were steered from the footplate by a worm screw on to bevel pinions and on to the sliding spindle inside each roll.

It was a complicated arrangement, but it worked—at least in Paris, where

Gelleret had eight machines on hire to the road authority. The 15-ton model was of 10 N.H.P. and had a working pressure of 90 p.s.i. Others were quick to see the need for lighter, more efficient rollers, including Clark, a municipal engineer in Calcutta. His design was passed on to the Birmingham firm of Worsdell Evans, and in 1863 the result was an improved machine which did good work for seven years in spite of a few faults. In 1867 the progressive Thomas Aveling of Rochester took up the challenge and supplied a massive three-wheeled roller to Liverpool Corporation, of 30 tons weight. It had a marine-type steering wheel on a footplate amidships, and the driving wheels were

"ROBEY" TANDEM HOT R[...]

ROBEY & CO LTD
MO 31512

14 TONS

A Robey tandem roller with Hine's patent heated rear roll, on an L.N.E.R. machinery wagon in the late 1920s.

Tandems are unusual in that an outside frame is used to carry the two full-width rolls.

7 feet 6 inches high; but as it tended to crush rather than roll the road material, his next venture had to be reduced in weight.

The first steam roller –in Paris

Aveling and his associates persevered with both design and motive power. He tried a vertical boiler on a tandem roller, and the American patent Shay gearing on a three-wheeler. He also tried tandem compound cylinders, but all these early efforts were faulty and unwieldy. Then in 1870, the final form of roller began to take shape. In large measure it reverted to the use of a simple portable or horizontal type boiler, with single or compound cylinders behind the chimney, and chain or geared drive to the rear wheels, as for the fast-developing traction engine. Steering was by worm gear and chain fixed to the protruding front roll spindle, the roller itself having a king-pin as a swivel through a plate bracket in front of the smokebox door.

It was this idea that led by degrees to the front rollers being placed well ahead of the smokebox by means of a heavy iron saddle. This became the standard pattern for all three-wheel rollers. The tandem with two rollers as wheels was less reliable and less suitable for rough surfaces, and it was prone to topple over on its side if not working on a reasonably level road, unless it was very broadly built.

All along the road of progressive invention there was a strong inclination for someone to try and remedy the faults which appeared in an earlier type. The demand for road rollers during the 1870s and 1880s was sufficient to spur on other firms besides Avelings. Several companies were taking out patents, and in spite of the failings of the tandem type, its further improvement was not overlooked, nor was the vertical boiler entirely forsaken.

An expanding marketing

It could be said that the internal combustion engine led to the proliferation of steam rollers. By 1900 motor cars were becoming so popular that at last the authorities were compelled to pay more attention to road making and surfacing. In addition there was a rapidly expanding export market, both to continental Europe and much farther afield. Many established road engine builders were meeting the demand for rollers, and there were specialist newcomers, including Green of Leeds, Allen of Cowley near Oxford and Armstrong Whitworth of Openshaw.

Although the three-wheeler with its front roll well forward under a projecting saddle remained a standard pattern, variations for special purposes came out in steady succession. Armstrong Whitworth built a tandem type with a boiler perched high above. Allen brought out the 'Waveless Roller' having rolls of barred metal strips with spaces between to avoid road material driving up in front, as sometimes it did. Green contributed an interesting variation, a cylindrical boiler amidships on an otherwise standard three-roll machine, as well as a roller with the single roll under the tender instead of out in front. In addition, there were many variations in motive power and its transmission. Weights varied all the way from 3 tons to 30, for in this sphere the weight of a roller was a vital factor and depended on the type of work for which it was designed.

As roads continued to improve, other materials than granite were adopted for surfacing. The Macadam road was quite satisfactory for slow-moving traffic, whether horsedrawn or steam-powered. Slow vehicles created no dust problem; but cars did, since they travelled at more than twice the speed. And the first car owners were people of influence as well as of affluence, able to bring pressure where it was needed. But road improvement was still a slow process. It was not until the 1920s that many village and country roads were tarred, and I remember cycling along the A11 from Newmarket to Thetford, and having to squint and duck to lessen the effect of traffic-raised dust, as late as 1921.

Steam rollers were a very common sight in those days, and like traction engines, threshing sets and ploughing engines, they were let out on hire by contractors. Some contractors owned fleets of a dozen or more, but the firm of Edison went far beyond this with nearly forty before they switched over to diesels. The use of chippings and shingle for tarring, and later of tarmac, called for lighter rollers, to supplement the heavier machines, with 16-tonners about the heaviest. The two-wheeler or tandem roller reappeared for light work, such as the final surfacing in which bituminous materials were used, where there was much less risk of keeling over.

Among the firms who brought out a special purpose tandem was Robey of Lincoln. Their 1924 design was unusual in having an inclined boiler with a rounded firebox, pressured to 200 p.s.i. but tested to 425 p.s.i. It had two cylinders, weighed 5 tons, and was steered direct on to the front roll; its final drive was by chain. The most outstanding designs came from Wallis and Stevens of Andover. Their 'Advance' of 1923 lived up to its name, for in this model most faults inherent in other makes were largely eliminated. It was manoeuvrable, could be quickly reversed and (very important) had an equal weight distribution to leave an even consolidation. It dispensed with a flywheel by having cranks set at 90°, worked by duplex cylinders. The 'Advance' was reckoned by many to be the finest and most efficient steam roller ever built, and it was available in sizes from 5 to 10 tons.

The same firm also produced the diminutive 'Simplicity' roller in 1925, with a weight of just under 3 tons. It is on record that the 'Simplicity' was designed for China, but because of its low cost and indeed its simplicity, with its easily replaceable firebox and ease of maintenance, many were sold in England. The boiler was quite sharply inclined—allowing the front roll to take more of the weight. A 'Simplicity' carried 1 cwt of coal and 75 gallons of water—sufficient, it was claimed, for a day's work.

Aveling and the last of steam on the road

Although Aveling, with their famous rampant-horse emblem on the front roll saddle, remained the first name in rollers for the longest period, there was never a time when their design stagnated, while modifications made were soon discarded if they did not please their customers. These included a built-in stone crusher, which enabled a steam roller to haul loads of broken rock to the site and crush it into small pieces for road-making. Among equipment which became standard fittings were water-trickles to clear mud packed up on the rollers, and scrapers. Many rollers were fitted with scarifiers for use where the existing surface had first to be broken up, but a heavy machine was needed to make this successful. Some rollers had a steam take-off for use in heating tar, and some makers offered 'convertibles'—a machine with a detachable front roll replaceable by a two-wheeled axle, so that by switching, a roller could become a traction engine.

Rollers, being the last steam engines in use on the road, were also the last to be acquired by those interested in preservation. During the 1950s and 1960s many were left discarded in scrap and contractors' yards which could have been bought for little more than scrap price. I bought three in good condition for under £200 in 1961; but now these would fetch around £2,000 each. Such values are due to the demand by late-coming preservationists, who have to make do with a roller, because the faster and more popular traction engines fetch even higher prices now that the supply of derelict relics is exhausted.

In spite of their lack of speed and manoeuvrability, steam rollers are to be seen at practically all the rallies, and most rallies attract enough paying visitors to enable the organisers to meet the costs of bringing in steam rollers on low-loaders. But some owners take a pride in driving their rollers to the rallies, however long it may take.

This is Burrell 6 N.H.P. 6 ton double-crank compound roller No. 3993 built in 1924. Burrell rollers always seem to have a long, low look compared with Fowlers for example, which seem pug-nosed. This particular engine was owned for many years by Doran Bros of Thetford and is now at Bressingham.

James Nasmyth was the inventor of the steam hammer, developed in 1839. The same principle was used later for steam powered pile drivers which are still at work.

11

SOME LESSER USES OF STEAM

It might have been expected that the 'railway mania' which began in 1840 would have quickly led to the employment of steam power for the vast amount of earth-moving which new railways entailed. Mechanical excavators called for no great powers of invention, at a time when the basics of steam power were well established. But if likely British inventors were not lacking in number and ingenuity, the fact was that scarcely any demand existed, mainly because there was an ample supply of manual labour. The canal diggers were coming to the end of their contracts with the advent of railways, and their labourers, nick-named 'navvies' from the word 'navigation', were seeking work, as were their employers.

Steam-powered excavators or 'steam shovels' were introduced in the early days of American railroad building, because labour there was scarce and costly; but British contractors were disinclined to invest the £1,500 which American machines, such as the 'Otis' of 1838, cost, when there were plenty of men to be had with picks and shovels. The railway 'navvies' became

The steam navvy caused many labour troubles when it was first employed to replace work of men with picks and shovels. Here one is seen digging what was to become the Manchester Ship Canal in the 1890s.

WALKING BY STEAM   RIDING BY STEAM   FLYING BY STEAM

Note .. In the Ladies Vehicle the Steam is made with a strong infusion of Gunpowder Tea   (LOCOMOTION.)   For an explanation of the Machinery see the next Number of the Edinburg Review.

Hat fashions are included in this contemporary caricature by Shortshanks, who saw the amusing as well as the dangerous aspect of steam power.

a formidable force. They lived rough and worked hard, they were quite highly paid and they would have undoubtedly resisted the introduction of machines capable of reducing their importance.

The first steam 'navvies' had limited scope. They had to be on rails, and the spoil they dug or grabbed out had still to be carried away. They were of simple construction, with a boiler on a platform, and a pipe carrying live steam to cylinders which powered a winch working a chain-hoisted shovel. This basic design lasted throughout the steam era, but as its use expanded, not only for the later railways but for open-cast mining and quarrying, so improvements followed, giving the

machine a greater capacity, reach, and ability to swivel and get rid of its spoil.

Steam excavators slowly came into their own in Britain after 1860. They were used for the Midland Railway from St. Pancras and the Great Central from Marylebone. They were also used for the Manchester Ship Canal, and the machine patented by James Dunbar for this great work was taken up by Ruston & Proctor of Lincoln. This too was rail-borne and, though very effective in eating away a bank, it had rather too limited a swivel. Smith of Rodley near Leeds produced a more versatile steam excavator in 1887. His 3-ton model was already quite popular, but the new one was designed to swivel 180 degrees, with its vertical

boiler placed to balance the jib.

Excavators on similar lines continued to work until the 1960s, nearly always using rail track for movement. Their mechanism was applied to cranes, which were extensively used for dock work as well as for other industrial purposes, and of course for railway use. Indeed, British Rail still has steam cranes at some depots ready to use for breakdowns and derailments. Their vertical cross-tube boilers can be raising steam while the breakdown train travels to the accident.

Steam hammers were common in industry for well over a century for forging, and their way of working was also used for pile drivers. Steam power raised the hammer weight, and gravity applied the punch; but wherever progressive constructional work was undertaken, the machine with its own vertical boiler had also to be self-propelling. Steam-powered pile drivers are still being used.

It is easy to imagine that the 19th century—the century of steam—led some inventive minds to go beyond the bounds of practicality. An attempt was made to produce a steam-powered submarine, but it is not surprising that as a reliable weapon of war it was not a success. Even less successful was an attempt to use steam to power a flying machine; the weight factor, being of such vital importance, was against the steam engine with its boiler and furnace. One outlandish but outstanding application of steam was to work a chiming clock. This was no doubt built as a novelty, perhaps in expectation of further orders; but it still stands, and it still works, in Vancouver, B.C.

The advantages of Stott's steam lawnmower were advertised as many, in spite of the price of £60 for the 9 cwt model, and up to £90 for the largest. One of the advantages, claimed Stott, was 'No damage to borders, no marks left by horses'.

The simple face plate of the 1883 Hunslet 0-4-0 locomotive Gwynedd (ex-Penrhyn Slate Quarries) which the author regularly drives on open days at Bressingham. The vertical chain on the left of the firehole door controls the ash pan flap as a damper. The two water level gauges are of different makes, but both are protected in case the inner case indicator tube bursts. On either side of the centrally placed regulator (or throttle) are the original Salter safety valves, spring loaded, with the whistle between and above them. The blower valve partly hides the pressure gauge on the left and the lagged pipe, passing in front of the hand brake, is for the steam brake. The control rods for the two injectors are on this side with the reversing lever but only one injector valve can be seen. 'Blow down' valves are below the water gauges.

12

THE WORKING STEAM ENGINE

The boiler

The nostalgia for steam continues to increase. To fill any need readers may have to be better acquainted with the working of steam engines, I had better take as examples those most likely to be seen in active preservation. For all engines other than the steam turbine, the basic principle of working is much the same—of water being vaporised by heat to exert its expansive power on a piston within a cylinder, which produces reciprocating and then, if desired, rotating motion.

The power centre is the boiler, where fire activates the force latent in water. From the very beginning those two elements have to be under control; they must avoid direct contact with one another and the pressure built up as steam is generated must be contained. So the boiler, in the form of a cylinder or shell, has to be strong enough, and its steel plating thick enough, to contain steam at the working pressure of the engine in question. 10 p.s.i. was ample for James Watt's slow-acting engines, but some boilers in the present century were tested up to 1,000 p.s.i.

Boiler-making was and still is a highly skilled and highly paid profession. The mild steel plate is first rolled to the required diameter, and has to include overlaps for riveting sections together. This method has been used ever since cast iron gave way to forged rolled iron, or steel, and although welded boilers became accepted in Germany during the 1930s, riveted boilers were standard in Britain until the end of the steam era. A 'wrapper plate', with a double row of rivets, is common practice.

At the end of the boiler 'barrel', as it is called, is the tube plate, riveted inside. In this, holes are bored to take the tubes, mostly of about 2 inches diameter and varying in number from about 40 for traction engines to 140 for railway locomotives. For the 'smokebox' or chimney end, the holes in the tube plate are larger than at the firebox end, so that in driving in the tubes from the smokebox, a tight fit is obtained. The tubes, having previously been 'swaged' or shrunk for the firebox end and 'belled' or expanded for the smokebox end, are then tightened further by an expanding implement, which, with a rotary motion, squeezes the wall of the tube as close as it will go to the rim of each tube plate hole to make it watertight. These small tubes are always in the lower half or two-thirds of the boiler barrel. Hot gases from the fire pass along these tubes to heat the water surrounding them, while the free space above the ranks of tubes is for the steam to build up in pressure.

Since the early 1900s most railway locomotives have been superheated. The usual method is for the upper parts of tube plates at each end to be bored to take a number of tubes of about 4 inches diameter with walls $\frac{3}{16}$th inch thick. Within these are placed the superheater elements, in clusters of four narrow steel tubes, which allow steam to travel back and forth to become even hotter and drier from the fire heat surging round them on its way to the chimney. In the smokebox the superheater 'header' converges all the elements into the main steam pipes for the steam's final passage to the cylinders. Superheating does not come into full play until the locomotive is hard at work. Water evaporates into steam at its boiling point. Such steam is at first

'saturated', but as pressure builds up it becomes hotter and, in the superheater, drier; and the drier it becomes the greater is its power on being released. The more modern locomotive boilers are 'pressed' to work at 200 p.s.i. or above, but traction engines are usually pressed for 150–180 p.s.i. and are without superheaters.

Boiler testing is a compulsory requirement for safety and insurance purposes and apart from visual examinations and 'hammer tapping' for wastage, a boiler has to be water-tested under pressure. The method used is to fill the boiler to capacity, seal off all possible outlets, and then force more water in with a special pump, until a pressure gauge shows a reading of about 50% above normal working pressure. This has to be maintained for a specific period before an inspector will issue a certificate, and he will make any observations he thinks fit as to the general condition of the boiler and pipe work.

The firebox

The firebox is an integral part of the whole boiler and is a metal box within the outer boiler plating. It is built on a 'foundation ring' although the term is a relic of early days when it was more circular in shape. The ring is solid and wide enough to allow a water space on the two outer sides and over the top, so that the fire within the box has contact only with metal plate having water beyond. The roof or 'crown' of the firebox, as well as the sides, needs to have a large number of 'stays' or double-headed rivets, with a head outside the shell as well as inside the firebox. These are to stabilise the metal plating and strengthen the whole under pressure so that the whole box may become part of the total heating surface. On British Railways locomotives copper fireboxes were fitted, as being more resilient than steel and less liable to corrode. The greater the heating surface, the more rapid is the evaporation of water. The firebars in the base of the firebox are not part of the heating surface, but the 'grate area' is part of the engine's specifications. Firebars are made of cast iron to withstand intense heat from the fire resting upon them and they are spaced to allow draught from below and for ash to fall through. The 'ash pan' has vents or flaps, both for extracting ash and to control the draught.

Safety devices

Two vital safety devices are fitted to boilers. One is the safety valve, usually placed on the highest part of the boiler to allow steam to escape automatically when pressure exceeds the maximum designated. The other is the fusible plug. It is a large short stud screwed upwards into the crown of the firebox. Because a hole has been bored through it and filled with lead, the risk of explosion or damage from a lack of water in the space above the crown is obviated. Should the space become empty of water, the lead will melt and steam will jet through very forcefully onto the fire below.

Water can be forced into the boiler by pump or injector. The latter is almost exclusively used on railway locomotives, with steam to operate it. It can work at high pressure with live steam or at a lower pressure with exhaust steam from the cylinders. Usually one injector of each sort is fitted, and water is sucked from the tender or tank through the injector to be forced past the 'clack valve'. This is simply a non-return valve fitted to the boiler. A water feed pump is fitted to most traction engines, its action being taken from the crankshaft by an eccentric gear or a cam.

The vital water level

All steam engines must have the means of the operator's seeing at a glance the water level in the boiler. These 'gauge glasses' are on the boiler 'face plate', with the valve wheels, controls and other gauges. There are usually two for safety, each consisting of a glass tube with connections to the boiler so that the boiler water level can be seen in the tube. So long as it can be seen, all is well; but if the level drops, so comes the need to use the injector or pump. To allow the water level to fall to the bottom of the glass is risky; but injecting too much water impedes efficiency. The quality of the water is important, and to avoid any corrosion or 'furring' of boiler and tubes a chemical additive is often used. Even so, boiler 'wash outs' at regular intervals are necessary, to get rid of accumulations of sludge which can be dangerous. The most vital water space to keep clear is the firebox shell, this being narrow. 'Wash out plugs' are situated at strategic points for rinsing out the boiler, usually called for every fourteen days, or after every 100 hours' work. Partial clearance can be practised by 'blowing down' through the gauge glass fitting, when the fire is dead, but the boiler still in steam.

The term 'in steam' denotes an engine having a reading on its pressure gauge, which usually has a red mark to indicate the point at which the safety valve will blow off—its maximum working pressure. A traction engine needs only 5–10 lb. pressure to set the piston and flywheel in motion, when

out of gear, but most railway locomotives will not move until about half the working pressure is reached. To avoid serious trouble from condensed steam trapped in the cylinders, 'cylinders cocks' or 'relief valves' are fitted and these are opened before new live steam is admitted. The valves are left open until all water is cleared, and the power of steam is abundantly demonstrated by the violent jets to be seen coming from the cylinder cocks as a locomotive begins to move for the first time after steam is raised from cold.

Driving an engine

The control of steam from the boiler to the cylinders is achieved by the regulator—sometimes called the 'throttle' on traction engines. It is a remote control affair, having a lever at the driver's end and a valve or port at the other, nearest the cylinder, which controls the emission of steam from the highest point on the boiler—the 'dome', or 'chest' in the case of traction engines. With the latter a minute opening is enough under full pressure to set the pistons to work, but with most locomotives there is a less rapid response to a movement of the regulator.

Compound cylinders work automatically. The high-pressure cylinder receives the steam first, and discharges or exhausts it to the adjoining low pressure cylinder which is larger to allow for the extra volume of already expanded steam. Compound traction

Traction engine drivers have steering and gearing controls as well as of steam, fire and water, on the face plate. The winch drum is just visible bottom left below the steering wheel, above which is the flywheel fixed to the main crankshaft. Next to this is the pulley for the narrow belt driving the governors and then an eccentric to drive the water pump seen to the right of the steering wheels. The valve above the oil-can controls the pump suction. The firehole door is below the heavy axle carrying the driving wheels seen in the centre and in front is the water gauge glass, with the steam pressure gauge above. Above this is the double handled regulator or throttle, which enables a driver to use one hand for steering and the other for speed control. This is a Burrell single crank compound engine (Bertha) and the pushrod allows live steam to enter both high and low pressure cylinders for extra power. The reversing lever is on the right and part of the hand brake control in the bottom right corner, below which is an injector, controlled by the valve near the pressure gauge.

engines usually have a separate control rod, enabling high-pressure steam to enter both cylinders at once in the event of extra power being needed for a short time. This may also come into use if the crankshaft happens to be on dead centre for the high-pressure cylinder, or if the piston has an equal pressure on both sides, so that even if the engine is thrown into reverse the flywheel remains motionless. A driver often has to pull on the flywheel to obtain motion, especially on single-cylinder traction engines. The letters s.c. stand for this type of engine, s.c.c. for single crank compound, and d.c.c. for double crank compound.

The other steam control is the 'reversing lever'. As a vertical lever it works in a toothed quadrant, so that it can be set in any position. Its purpose is to control the valve gear and so the steam-ports, to admit steam to one side of the piston or the other, and make the engine go forwards or backwards. It must be set for the required direction before the steam regulator is opened (although this is not necessary for a traction engine out of gear). Once the engine is at work, the reversing lever can be adjusted or 'notched' to some extent, thereby admitting live steam to the cylinders for less of the piston's stroke. This makes for more economical running; allowing a smaller amount of steam to do the same work by its expansive power. If the lever is placed in the centre of the toothed quadrant, the valve gear is in neutral, and opening the regulator will not cause the piston to move, because steam is admitted equally to both sides of the piston.

The reversing lever on the larger and more modern railway locomotives is usually referred to as a 'gear' and is in fact operated by a wheel. 'Full forward gear'—giving a long and full admission of live steam to each stroke of the piston—is needed to gain speed with a load or on a steep gradient; but on the level the driver 'notches up' as described above, with the regulator well opened, for speed and economy. On the wheeled type of gear, as distinct from one with the true 'reversing lever' in its quadrant, the degree of 'notch-

ing' is known as the 'cut off', and the railway driver at speed with a 'clear road' in front of him keeps his regulator wide open and adjusts his 'cut-off' to get the maximum speed and power out of a short or small-as-possible admission of live steam to each stroke of the piston. To reverse an engine, the wheel is wound back, well beyond the 'mid-gear' or half-way position between forward and reverse.

Pistons and valve gear

The pistons are metal discs, fitting snugly within the smooth cylinder walls with the help of piston rings, as with a car. The piston rod projects through steam-tight glands in the rear end of the cylinder to the 'crosshead' or 'little end'. This runs back and forth between parallel 'slide' or 'guide' bars which allow reciprocating motion between them. The 'crosshead' is attached to the 'connecting rod', which as its name implies is connected to the driving wheel, or the cranked driving axle on a locomotive with inside cylinders and converts the piston's to-and-fro into rotary motion. On a traction engine the piston rod is similar, but the connecting rod is joined to the crankshaft. In both, the connection to the drive is the 'big end', the joints being known as 'bearings'. All such bearings are subject to great stress and are usually of brass, lined with white metal and grooved for oiling.

The valves which regulate the supply of steam to the cylinders are operated by the valve gear mentioned earlier, which, though controlled from the driving cab, is driven by eccentrics, gears, or cranks on the motion. There were a number of different types of valve gear invented during the steam era, but for traction engines and locomotives before the present century the 'link motion' patented by George Stephenson was the most popular. This works off eccentrics, two for each

cylinder, placed on the driving axle or crankshaft, and the adjustable 'link' moves a rod which opens and closes the steam ports. Most 20th-century railway locomotive designers came down in favour of the Walschaerts valve gear, which is fitted outside the wheels and is linked to the 'big end' on the driving wheel moving in concert with the connecting rod.

To make all the driving wheels of a locomotive turn together, outside 'coupling rods' connect them with the wheels driven by the connecting rods. Balance weights, fitted between the spokes of a locomotive's driving wheels or to a crankshaft are often needed for smooth running.

Lubrication is vital to all steam engines. Cylinder oil is of a heavy grade and has to be force-fed by means of a mechanical pump. Axle-boxes each have an oil reservoir for drip feed, but on some modern locomotives a central lubricating system is fitted with copper pipes on each side leading to each axle-box or 'journal'. All the same, enginemen still use the long-spouted oil can, for every moving part must be well-oiled—and this includes the springs. Agricultural traction engines are seldom fitted with springs, and though they have mechanical cylinder-lubricators, 'oil-can feed' for all other parts is in frequent use.

Transmission and brakes

The transmission on traction engines is by means of shafts fitted with cogs or 'spur wheels', which can only be engaged by the gear lever when not in motion. The initial gear is on the opposite end of the shaft to the flywheel. The diameter of the cogwheels determines which of the two or three gears the driver selects; it is seldom necessary to change up into a higher gear, as with a car. The running gear is pre-selected and there can be up to four shafts fitted to an engine, including the crankshaft. Most trac-

The cylinder block for a Foster traction engine is topped by a spring loaded safety valve, on the 'steam chest' above the boiler. It has both a drip feed and pressure oiler, worked from the motion. The rounded weights of the governor rise with centrifugal force when working speed increases thereby reducing the steam intake to the pistons. It is driven by a belt from the crankshaft to a small pulley wheel.

tion engines also have a cable winch on a drum fitted between one of the rear wheels and the body of the engine. To operate this, a heavy pin fitted into part of the wheel hub is removed and the engine is put in gear, bringing the winch into use without the road wheel turning. Though it is a rather primitive piece of equipment, the winch with the wheels scotched can exert tremendous power; it can be also used to pull out the engine itself, should it become bogged down in mud or soft earth, by anchoring the cable and winding in. Without this winch, the traction engine would be much less versatile.

Farm engines, so often used for stationary work such as threshing, are fitted with 'governors'. These are mostly variations on that invented by James Watt. A governor works by the centrifugal force of metal weights whirling round a vertical spindle linked to the crankshaft which, in opening out as they spin faster, automatically restrict the steam inlet to the cylinders. Such a governor prevents an engine working faster or slower if for any reason the steam pressure in the boiler should fluctuate, thereby keeping the machines it powers, with a flywheel belt, working at a constant speed. As mentioned earlier, governors were necessary for all stationary steam engines.

Traction engines are not fitted with brakes like those on a locomotive. Sometimes there is one for the flywheel, controlled by a wheel; and a rather crude device working inside the rim of a rear wheel is fitted on some 'road locomotives' as distinct from farm engines. Braking is most often effected by a pull on the reversing lever, with the regulator slightly open.

Railway locomotives are fitted with powerful steam brakes, in which a direct application of steam forces the brake blocks on to the driving wheels. The tender wheels are provided with hand-operated brakes; like the hand-brake on a car they ensure that an engine, once stopped, does not roll away. In the later steam era of railways, the driver also controlled, on passenger and fast 'fitted freight' trains, continuous brakes on all the vehicles in the train. British practice favoured the vacuum system, powered by a steam-operated 'ejector' on the engine; but most foreign railways, and the Great Eastern in England, used the American Westinghouse compressed-air system, powered by steam-operated air pumps on the locomotive.

To avoid the driving wheels slipping on wet or oily rails when maximum tractive effort is needed, sanding equipment is provided. There is usually a metal box on the 'running board' above the wheels, and a lever allows a trickle of dry sand to fall ahead of the driving wheels. This too is steam-operated on the more modern locomotives.

Raising steam

It is reckoned to be good practice to bring a cold engine into steam slowly, to avoid rapid metal expansion which might lead to leaky tubes. British Rail depots began with a fire-lighter and gradually built up the fire with coal, a process which usually took six or seven hours before an engine was ready to move. I have myself, and others have too, reduced the time to three or four hours by using a quantity of firewood to begin with, with no ill results. It takes about two-and-a-half hours to register steam on the gauge, but once a few pounds pressure is showing the 'blower' can hasten matters. The blower is frequently in use whenever the engine is stationary, but when it is working there is usually sufficient draught from the exhaust, concentrated as it is through the purposely narrowed end of the 'blast pipe'.

'Firing' an engine is a highly skilled job. When a locomotive is hauling a heavy train, the fireman has to shovel in the coal, spreading it evenly over a fire which may cover 40 square feet of grate. It is also the fireman's job to keep up the water level in the boiler by using the injector. It takes close on a ton of coal just to raise steam from cold to working pressure for a large engine, such as a Pacific; while in an hour's running an express locomotive may well consume two to three tons of coal and 2,000 to 3,000 gallons of water.

It is not surprising that steam engines, despite their obsolescence, evoke admiration, awe and nostalgia. The theory I suggested in the introduction as to why the power of steam first appealed to its beholders still holds good. I believe an even greater number of people are now fascinated by steam working than was the case two centuries ago. This may well be due to the vital place in recent industrial history occupied by steam engines, and the contribution they made to Britain's greatness.

The long list of places where steam engines in one form or another are preserved is itself an indication of their importance in our national heritage. This enthusiasm for steam, translated into loving care for their relics on the part of those dedicated to steam preservation, is well-nigh boundless, but their feelings must often be tinged with sadness on two counts. One of these is that steam power in its old delightful but economically wasteful form can never return. If steam is again used for transport—and this is possible—it will almost certainly lack the visual appeal of the old railway engine or road steamer, as did its last major development, the turbine.

The other cause for sadness is the thought that, despite the very large number of engines in active preservation, their numbers must shrink as time marches on. Already restoration has become extremely costly, and safety regulations will be more stringently applied as wear and rust take their toll. This will happen especially to the large and spectacular railway locomotives. New boilers and fireboxes will be beyond the resources of most trustees, and the engines must then become merely static exhibits or be powered by some other means than steam.

Nostalgia crept in as steam was phased out. Since then the rising generations too have become affected and even infected by the magical appeal of engines seen in retirement, especially when they come to life again. This process is likely to continue, and on the principle that interest increases in proportion to rarity, ways and means are likely to be found to prolong the active lives of some engines as long as possible. Those that are static exhibits in museums will, however, always be well cared for—and a century hence they may be the sole survivors. Those who then see them in splendid mummification may envy those of us who not only saw, but heard and smelt them, and were thrilled by them when they were alive, with fire and water.

APPENDIX

Steam pioneers

THOMAS AVELING: 1824–1882. A farmer with a background in the Cambridgeshire Fens who moved to Romney Marsh in Kent, Thomas Aveling was a man who, knowing what was required, became a pioneer in the use of steam power for agriculture. He set up works at Rochester in 1850, and brought out a long series of patents for traction engines, ploughing engines and other equipment in great variety, including windlass and direct-pull ploughing engines. He was in the forefront of efforts to make engines self-propelled, but his first self-moving engine of 1857 was the conversion of a Clayton portable. His firm, under the name of Aveling & Porter, became the most famous and prolific of steam-roller builders until the late 1930s, and many of their engines went abroad.

HENRY BELL: 1767–1830. Born at Torphichen near Linlithgow in Scotland. Served his apprenticeship under several engineers including Rennie in London. When with Shaw & Hart, the Barrow shipbuilders, he conceived the idea of using steam for navigation and set up in partnership with a Mr. Paterson. Experiments began in 1798 and in 1800 he approached the Admiralty in the hope of a contract. His idea was turned down then, and again in 1803, in spite of Lord Nelson's speaking strongly in his favour. There is strong evidence that Fulton obtained some of Bell's ideas, as well as Symington's, during a visit to England the year before his successful venture on the Hudson river. Although Bell was not the inventor of the steam boat, he was among the first to realise its practical application and his *Comet* of

Robert Boyle

30 tons, powered by a 3 h.p. engine he made, was in 1812 the first to sail on a regular schedule in Europe. She was wrecked in 1820.

ROBERT BOYLE: 1627–1691. An Irish aristocrat, he had strong leanings towards chemistry, philosophy and theology, and was in contact with all the greatest men in Europe with similar interests. In 1659, with Robert Hooke, he invented the forerunner of the air pump, and conducted many experiments with the weight and elasticity of air which were of value to those who later tried out the properties of heated water, as he himself did with Denis Papin. His interests were wide-ranging and his achievements notable in many fields of science.

ISAMBARD KINGDOM BRUNEL: 1806–1859. The only son of Marc Isambard Brunel was born in Portsmouth. His interest in civil engineering projects began there, but by 1825 he was assisting his father on the first Thames tunnel from Wapping to Rotherhithe and became resident engineer. Before this was completed he saw opportunities for his genius in railway building, and in 1833 was appointed to build the Great Western Railway from London to Bristol. His tunnels, bridges and easy gradients were remarkable feats; but with characteristic disregard of convention, Brunel decided on a broad gauge of 7 feet for the GWR which in the end had to be abandoned in favour of Stephenson's 4 ft. $8\frac{1}{2}$ in. which had

become standard. As well as becoming a consultant for railways overseas, he became interested in steamships and in 1841 his *Great Western* began the first regular steam service to America. The Admiralty adopted his screw propulsion method in 1845, the year in which the *Great Britain* was launched. Her success, in spite of adversity, led to the *Great Eastern*, then the largest ship ever to take to the water. But just before she sailed on her first voyage, Brunel was stricken with paralysis and died a week later. The toll taken on his constitution by his restlessly inventive mind and the feverish energy with which he lived was said to be responsible for his death at only 53.

Below Left: Sir Marc Brunel
Below Right: Isambard Kingdom Brunel

MARC ISAMBARD BRUNEL: 1769–1849. Born in Normandy, his loyalist sympathies led to his leaving France during the Revolution and emigrating to America where he practised civil engineering. He came to England in 1799 with plans for making ships' blocks by machine which were to reduce hand labour dramatically. He married Sophia Kingdom while at Portsmouth working for the Admiralty, and began to collaborate with Henry Maudslay. His inventive mind developed in many ways; he set up his own timber milling business in Battersea and built a factory to make boots by machine. Steam navigation occupied his mind to the extent of building ships to ply along the Thames to Margate as early as 1812. Financial difficulties occurred and in 1822 he was imprisoned for debt. He was rescued by friends, who persuaded the Government to grant him £5,000 in recognition of past services for which he had been poorly paid. His plans for the first Thames tunnel were accepted in 1824, but many difficulties arose, and it was not completed until 1842. He was knighted in 1841.

CHARLES BURRELL I: 1817–1906. Under his control a country smithy became one of the leading makers of engines and agricultural machines at Thetford, Norfolk. His engines began as portables, the first in 1848 having a haystack-topped boiler. Burrell took up the Boydell patent 'Endless Railway' type of wheel—engines fitted with it were the forerunners of the tracked vehicle, used mainly for heavy haulage. If they were not a long-term success, many were built and some were exported. Charles I possessed a flair for sales-promotion demonstrations, and although Boydell had died in 1861, the Burrell/Boydell system was being widely acclaimed by 1862, and a wide range of engines and machines powered by steam was being built, making Thetford a thriving town. He was succeeded by his son, Charles II, who died in 1929, by which time events beyond the firm's control had ended a long period during which anything that bore the name of Burrell was an example of quality craftsmanship.

THOMAS COCHRANE, Tenth Earl of Dundonald: 1775–1860. Born Annsfield, Lanarkshire. Joined the Navy in 1793, aged $17\frac{1}{2}$. Was promoted rapidly, gaining his first command, of a brig, in 1800. Served with distinction throughout the Napoleonic wars; afterwards served in the navies of Chile and Brazil and commanded the Greek navy against the Turks. Gazetted Rear-Admiral 1832. In 1843 he urged the Admiralty to adopt steam power and screw propulsion for ships of the line. During 1843–1848 he was involved in the design and building of the steam frigate *Janus*. Through lack of co-operation from the navy yards, *Janus* was a failure, but the principles of her construction were acknowledged as sound and in time were generally adopted. Promoted Vice-Admiral 1841, Admiral 1851, and nominated Rear-Admiral of the United Kingdom 1854.

JOHN FOWLER: 1826–1864. The third of five sons of a well-to-do Quaker merchant of Melksham, Wiltshire. Broke away from parental business on reaching the age of 21 to work for the engine builders Gilkes, Wilson and Hopkins of Middlesbrough. A visit to Ireland soon after the potato famine of 1845–47 inspired him to experiment with drainage equipment, believing that this was the crying need for agriculture. The first of many patents for mole draining came in 1860, but the first real answer, his use of a windlass powered by a portable steam engine, did not come until 1854. Fowler then set about inventing a cable-hauled plough on much the same principle, in collaboration with a Scottish farmer, David Greig. Between them they produced the balance plough, which needed no turning-round space, and both this and the engine to belt-drive the windlass were built by Ransomes of Ipswich. He also contracted with Clayton and Shuttleworth of Lincoln, and Kitsons of Leeds, to build his inventions, including engines of up to 14 h.p., but by 1863 his own works was set up at Leeds, building engines with his patent clip drum winch which had proved most successful. Fowler's tragic death at only 38 as a result of a fall in the hunting field put an end to this inventive genius. John Fowler & Co. Ltd. continued and remained a leading firm, producing a wide range of steam-powered vehicles and equipment throughout the era of steam.

SIR GOLDSWORTHY GURNEY: 1793–1875. This remarkable inventor began his active life as a surgeon, but dissatisfaction with his results caused him to give up medicine in 1830 for scientific pursuits. While he exploited steam power his inventions also covered chemistry, gases, and artificial lighting and he was closely associated with Michael Faraday's work. His experiments produced a high-pressure steam jet which contributed much to advances in locomotion. His efforts to employ steam for road transport in the 1830s were largely frustrated by severe regulations in favour of horses and by the poor state of public highways. His inventions also included a means of purification of sewer gases by steam, and he devised the system of ventilation for the Houses of Parliament.

WALTER HANCOCK: 1799–1852. Was first apprenticed to a watchmaker and jeweller, but switched to engineering, being of an inventive turn of mind. In 1824 he made a novel steam engine, with two cylinders fashioned of layers of heavy canvas stuck together with rubber solution, to make them flexible. These bags were filled alternately with steam. The engine worked, but it is not known if it was used for the first steam-engined carriage he made at his factory at Stratford, Essex. He was an inveterate experimenter, and pioneered the Stratford–London run with *Infant* in 1831. In 1832 he built *Era* for the London and Brighton Steam Coach Co., and *Enterprise* which had a regular route from London to Paddington. Of all early attempts to sponsor steam passenger vehicles, Hancock's was the most successful, but public interest waned with the advent of railways and in 1840 he gave up, writing his narrative, *Twelve Years' Experiments with Steam Carriages on the Common Roads 1824–1836* to record and justify his activities.

JOHN HEATHCOAT: 1783–1861. This prolific inventor was the son of a Leicestershire farmer. Most of his work was concerned with machinery for the hosiery and lace industry, and when only 24 he was acknowledged creator of the most complicated textile machine ever produced. He set up a factory at Loughborough more highly mechanised than any then existing; its employment of fewer workers led to an attack by Luddites in 1816. Turning his attention to farming he patented a steam plough in 1832, but this was in advance of its time, due mainly to its lack of traction over soft earth. He became a Member of Parliament in 1832 and not only served usefully on various Committees but also founded several benevolent schemes.

WILLIAM HEDLEY: 1779–1843. Born near Newcastle-on-Tyne, his engineering ability led to an appointment at the Warbottle and then at the Wylam colliery, where he became involved with the problems of transporting coal from the pit-head to the Tyne, to meet the rapidly increasing demand for coal to be shipped by sea. Struck by the possibilities of steam power, he made use of locomotives built by Trevithick, Blenkinsop and Chapman, and patented an idea for the use of the smooth wheel and rail system in 1813. This was used at Wylam soon afterwards. In building his own locomotive in 1814, he saw the value of a blast pipe for exhaust steam, but did not perfect this method of increasing the fire draught. It was said that during a strike of bargemen in 1822 he fitted one of his engines to drive paddles for towing. It was not realised until much later that an improvement in the method of pumping water from mines, which became standard practice after first being criticised, was a Hedley invention. He was a contemporary and rival of George Stephenson.

JONATHAN CARTER HORNBLOWER: 1753–1815. Born at Chacewater in Cornwall, the fourth son of Jonathan Hornblower, engineer and inventor of the 'double-beat' valve. Was employed by Watt erecting separate-condenser engines in Cornwall, and having mastered Watt's principles set out to build a rival engine, patented in 1781, with two cylinders and two toothed piston rods attached to the same end of the beam. His patent was held by Kings Bench to be an infringement on Watt's patent in 1799. The Hornblower engine anticipated the compound principle developed by Woolf, and is acknowledged to be the first attempt to use the expansive qualities of steam. Hornblower acquired a considerable fortune as an engineer in the Cornish mines, and published many books and pamphlets on engineering matters. He died at Penryn, Cornwall.

JAMES HOWARD: 1821–1889. Born into a well-established firm of implement makers at Bedford, with his brother Frederick he made the firm large and famous. James was keenly interested in all aspects of agriculture, and bought a farm on difficult, heavy land with steep slopes, to test and demonstrate his machinery. He wrote many articles for publication, and was not only a leading agriculturalist of his day, but became a Member of Parliament from 1868–1874, and again from 1880–1885. His philanthropy included valuable help for French peasant farmers following the war of 1870–71. Altogether he took out over 70 patents, concentrating on his own system of steam ploughing and cultivating, in rivalry with that of John Fowler.

JONATHAN HULLS: Born in 1699 at Campden, Gloucestershire. Made the first practical attempt to employ steam in propelling a vessel in water, on the Avon at Evesham in 1737. His steam tug was powered by a Newcomen engine and propelled by six paddles driven by the engine through an arrangement of ropes and spindles. Despite the fact that his invention successfully converted the linear

motion of the engine into a rotary motion, the boat itself was a failure; but Hulls' writing undoubtedly influenced Symington, and through him Robert Fulton.

HENRY MAUDSLAY: 1771–1831. First worked at Woolwich Arsenal where his father was an artificer. Became involved with locks and hydraulics and started his own business off Oxford Street, London in 1798. For a time he worked with Marc Brunel at Portsmouth Dockyard. In 1807 he patented his 'Table Engine' which remained a popular steam engine for light work for 40 years. He was joined by Joshua Field, whose reputation for making boilers stood high; in 1824 they patented a method of regulating the water supply for boilers, and for eliminating brine deposit at sea. Maudslay became famous for improvements to machine tools and invented a machine to measure down to 1/10,000th of an inch. The business expanded under his eldest son Thomas (1792–1864) and third son Joseph (1801–1861) securing naval contracts for nearly 30 years. They developed the double-cylinder marine engines which were used in the first direct screw-propelled (gearless) steamship, and for the Admiralty vessel *Rattler*, and also a direct-acting annular screw-drive engine.

PATRICK MILLER: 1731–1815. Although boasting of his penurious beginnings, Miller was born into a Scottish banking family. He spent several early years at sea, but became a banker in Edinburgh in 1760. His financial interests included a large share in the famous Carron ironworks at Falkirk, but he was an inveterate experimenter with unorthodox ideas. His favourite was a design for ships or boats with two or three hulls, and paddle wheels between them. At first these were designed for hand working, but by 1787 a twin-hulled steam-powered vessel was tried out on the lake of his estate at Dalswinton, to become the first practical demonstration of marine steam. Its engine is now in the Science Museum,

South Kensington. It was built by Symington and was followed by a larger one in 1789. Disputes arose with James Watt because of patent infringement, which led Miller to abandon a scheme which promised well. After 1790 Miller devoted his time and thought to agricultural improvements.

WILLIAM MURDOCK: 1754–1839. Born at Auchinleck, Scotland. He was using coal gas for lighting his own house as early as 1792, and by 1802 his method was first used for lighting streets and houses in Soho, London. He had already experimented with higher steam pressure than was advocated by James Watt, on whose engines he made great improvements. He also made a small steam locomotive in 1784, of which few details are known, but he was the inventor of the first oscillating engine in 1784 or 1785. He worked for Boulton & Watt throughout his career, and may possibly have made three locomotives, two models and one full-size. In conjunction with John Southern he designed the first self-contained steam engine (no support from walls necessary) and various other devices. He is best known for his services to gas lighting.

MATTHEW MURRAY: 1765–1826. Was born near Newcastle and went into the flax industry to introduce several improvements in the manufacture of flax, hemp, wool and tow for the firm of Marshall. Leaving them in 1795, he jointly founded a machine-building firm in Leeds, Fenton, Murray and Jackson, and turned his attention to steam for power. The firm soon became a rival to Boulton & Watt, making significant improvements to the Watt type of engine, with a design more compact and accessible. Murray is credited with the invention of the 'D' slide valve for controlling the flow of steam to the cylinders. In 1812 Blenkinsop employed him to build locomotives to run on the Middleton Colliery rack railway to Leeds, a distance of $3\frac{1}{2}$ miles. The four locomotives built were the first to be regularly used for commerce. They were fitted with two double-acting cylinders, but no flywheel. He also built engines for boats, and was said to have invented the planing machine for metal working.

ROBERT NAPIER: 1791–1876. Born in Dumbarton, the son of a well-to-do blacksmith. Apprenticed to his father, he spent his spare time making small tools, drawing instruments, guns and gun-locks. Went to Edinburgh in 1812, and then obtained a post in the works of Robert Stephenson, but following a blunder in the construction of a boiler he returned to Dumbarton, and then purchased a blacksmith's shop in Glasgow in 1815. His business prospered and in 1823 he constructed his first marine steam engine, for the *Leven* which was to ply between Glasgow and Dumbarton. In 1826 he built the engines for the *Eclipse* on the Glasgow–Belfast run, and from 1830 supplied engines for the ships of the Glasgow Steam Packet Company. By 1836 engines of 230 h.p. were being built. In 1840 he supplied engines for the naval vessels *Vesuvius* and *Stromboli*, and also persuaded Samuel Cunard to build four ships of 1,200 tons each, with 400 h.p. engines, thus starting the Cunard Steamship Company. In the following years over 300 steamships were constructed by Napier & Sons, many of them powered by the 'steeple' engine, patented by Napier's cousin David, which was a great improvement on the previous side-lever engine.

JAMES NASMYTH: 1808–1890. Born in Edinburgh, the son of Alexander Nasmyth, the artist. Displayed great mechanical aptitude at an early age, and by 17 he was building demonstration models of steam engines and machine tools for mechanics' institutes. At 19 he was commissioned to build a steam carriage capable of carrying six people by the Scottish Society of Arts. The carriage was successfully run around Edinburgh in 1827-28. Worked under Maudslay 1829–31. In 1834 started an engineering firm in Manchester, moving to Patricroft in 1836, later going into partnership as Nasmyth & Gaskell, and building a great reputation for quality and style. He invented the steam hammer in 1839, but did not build an example or patent the machines until 1842; he built a pile driver working on the same principle in 1845. Nasmyth invented or developed many machine tools and process machines, from the nut-shaping machine to the hydraulic punch. Later in life he took up astronomy, publishing a book about the moon in 1874.

THOMAS NEWCOMEN: 1663–1729. Born at Dartmouth. An ironmonger or blacksmith by trade, Newcomen began experiments leading to the atmospheric steam engine in the later years of the 17th century, and seems to have produced a working engine by 1710. However, his engine was for many years regarded as merely an improvement on Thomas Savery's engine, and was therefore inhibited by the latter's patent. From about 1712 onwards Newcomen engines became more and more widely used, and they enjoyed a virtual monopoly until some time after the patenting of the Watt separate-condenser engine in 1769. His engines were not powered directly by the force of steam, but he, rather than James Watt, is regarded as the Father of steam power.

DENIS PAPIN: 1647–1714. This French physicist spent many years in England working on experiments with air and water to produce power. He had made contact previously both with Huygens and von Guericke on the Continent, and in England collaborated with Boyle. Although it was known before his time that power was latent in the reaction of air and water to heat, Papin was one of the first to demonstrate that a machine with a practical use was possible, and laid down the first principles of how this could be achieved. To him goes the distinction of being the first to apply steam to raise a piston, in a machine he called a 'Digester'. This included the invention of the safety valve as an essential component. With Boyle, experiments were demonstrated to the Royal Society, which led to his being elected a member in 1681.

SIR CHARLES ALGERNON PARSONS: 1854–1931.

Born London 1854, the sixth son of William Parsons, 3rd Earl of Rosse. Entered Trinity College, Dublin at the age of 17, and St. Johns, Cambridge in 1873. Leaving Cambridge he was apprenticed for four years to Sir William Armstrong & Co., then spent two years with Kitsons of Leeds, where he developed and patented a four-cylinder high-speed epicycloidal steam engine. In 1884 he acquired a junior partnership in Clarke, Chapman & Co. of Gateshead and assumed charge of their new electrical department. As a way of improving the efficiency of steam-driven electricity generators, he developed a multi-row turbine in which steam, expanding between rows of blades on a shaft, turned the shaft which was directly connected to the dynamo. The first turbo-dynamo was constructed in 1884 and produced $7\frac{1}{2}$ kilowatts at 18,000 rpm. In 1889 the firm of C. A. Parsons & Co. was founded to develop the generation of current by turbines. By 1900, 1,000-kilowatt sets were in production and by 1928 Parsons was producing turbo-alternator sets capable of generating directly at 36,000 volts.

To tackle marine propulsion Parsons formed the Parsons Marine Steam Turbine Company at Wallsend-on-Tyne, and built the 44-ton steam yacht *Turbinia* which was capable of 34 knots. In 1899 came the first turbine destroyers *Viper* and *Cobra*, and in 1901 the first turbine passenger vessel *King Edward* for service on the Clyde. In 1905 an Admiralty committee on naval design advised that turbine machinery should be used in all future warship construction, and turbine engines were the mainstay of marine motive power until superseded by diesels.

ROBERT RANSOME. 1753–1830

Robert, the founder of this firm, was born in Wells, Norfolk, and by the time he died it was famous for ploughs and other agricultural equipment, with works at Ipswich. Robert's descendants were amongst the first in England to employ steam on the land. Theirs was the first self-propelled traction engine; appearing in 1842, it was somewhat ahead of its time, but the firm had become a leading builder and exporter of engines by 1851, when they had a large and varied exhibit at the Great Exhibition. The large Orwell Works at Ipswich turned out stationary as well as mobile and marine engines. They built Fowler's first patent ploughing engine in 1850 and by 1870 were engaged on such road steamers as *Ravee*. James A. Ransome travelled widely for export orders, and as a result many agricultural engines were built and sold as straw-burners. In 1893 no less than 140 threshing sets were sold to Argentina alone, and in 1908 Russia ordered 338. By 1930 the works covered 30 acres and had 2,500 employees, and all through the steam era new patents were taken out by this enterprising firm.

THOMAS SAVERY: 1650–1715:

An engineer of Devon origin, about whose early life little is known. He became interested in using the power of atmospheric pressure to pump water from mines, and experimented with steam as a means of creating the necessary vacuum. He became associated with Newcomen in these experiments. He also invented a kind of bellows in connection with this project, as well as a mill, but like other pioneers of his time, he was hampered by the inadequate materials and tools then available.

JOHN SCOTT RUSSELL: 1808–1882.

Born at Parkland near Glasgow and trained as a civil engineer. He was interested by the first attempts at steam navigation to study the nature of waves and water resistance. As a result of his researches and findings his new design of hull was under construction in 1835, but little is known of its performance. He undertook a steam road carriage project but when this was abandoned he concentrated on naval architecture, as well as working on bridges and buildings. At times he exhibited some rather unstable characteristics. He did not however waver in his advocacy of iron-clad ships, and was joint designer of the Royal Navy's *Warrior* and the first ironclad frigate *Versatile*. He also participated in the early work connected with the Great Exhibition of 1851, and with Brunel was a partner in the construction of the *Great Eastern*.

WILLIAM SYMINGTON: 1763–1831.

Born at Leadhills, this enterprising Scot can be considered the earliest pioneer of the steam-boat. He began as early as 1783 with a working model of a steam-powered carriage, but was drawn to ship design by the greater scope existing for waterborne transport. By 1788 he had tried an engine of his own design with two 4″ cylinders to drive paddle wheels. This was so successful that he decided on a larger-scale experiment for the Forth & Clyde canal. His employer, Robert Miller was not very impressed, and though a speed of 7 m.p.h. was attained it was decided that Symington's chain and ratchet system of drive was too clumsy.

In 1801 Lord Dundas employed Symington to construct an engine having a guided piston rod driving a connecting rod direct to a crank on the paddle-wheel crankshaft. This became the standard method of propulsion, lasting almost until the end of the paddle steamer. The *Charlotte Dundas*, first to use this layout, was largely successful, but was laid up because of the damage caused by her wash to the canal banks. Symington was then employed by the Duke of Bridgewater to construct similar steam barges for his canals, but the Duke's death left Symington without financial support. Robert Fulton took advantage of his inventions to become the first successful steamship operator in America, running a service on the Hudson river.

RICHARD TREVITHICK: 1771–1833. This Cornishman's genius was very belatedly acknowledged, for it was to him rather than to George Stephenson that credit should have gone for producing the first workable locomotive to run on smooth rails. This was in 1804, but before this he had been building high-pressure stationary engines for Cornish tin mines. Having experimented with model locomotives as early as 1796, he produced the first steam carriage ever to carry passengers in 1801. His 1804 locomotive ran in South Wales and though successful, it did not work for long, due to its inadequate track. Another ran for a time on a circular track in London in 1808. Trevithick was the first to send the exhaust steam up the chimney to increase the draught of the fire, to use steam at high pressure, and to maintain that sufficient friction for haulage was possible between smooth wheels and rails. Somewhat temperamental by nature, he was strongly competitive, and athletic, having been a notable weight-lifter and wrestler in his youth. His attempt to start a Thames tunnel failed in 1809; but in 1811 he made a successful steam threshing machine. In 1816 he went to Peru where for several years he concentrated on mining engines, and later he surveyed a railway in Costa Rica. Many of his inventions, including a superheated steam boiler and a steam-driven marine propeller, were unpatented, and he died in poverty at Dartmouth.

JAMES WATT: 1736–1819. The story of how Watt discovered the power of steam from the sight of a boiling kettle lifting its lid is more legendary than factual. His first job was that of instrument maker for Glasgow University at the age of 21. Ten years later he was employed on surveys for the Firth of Clyde and Caledonian canals, and on schemes for deepening rivers for navigation. His interest in steam appears to have been secondary until about 1764. Asked to repair a model of a Newcomen pumping engine, he noticed how much power the atmospheric principle wasted in condensing the steam. He then set about constructing an engine with a separate condenser, and the result was the patented 'Watt' steam engine of 1769.

His partnership with Boulton enabled his engines to be built and to meet a steady demand for many years, protected by patent from any serious competition. His invention of the governor as an essential control feature was another great contribution to the steam age, while other important Watt inventions included the double-acting engine, the 'parallel motion', and a fuel-saving furnace. In later years he became very conservative on the question of boiler pressure, and had no faith in any greater than the low pressures he used for his own engines. He was very jealous of his authority being questioned. The popular idea of Watt being the Father of the steam engine falls down in the light of historical fact—though his standing in the Hall of Fame remains high.

JOHN WILKINSON: 1728–1808. While he can claim no credit for steam engine development, his improvements in the production and working of iron put him in the forefront of 18th-century ironmasters. His main contribution to steam technology was the invention of an accurate boring machine, used both for cylinders and cannon. Coming south from Cumberland he built his own blast furnaces at Bilston, Staffs, and it was said that Watt's first engine powered the blower at another Wilkinson works near Bridgnorth, using coal to smelt the ore instead of the less efficient charcoal. Cast iron became his speciality, and this led to a high reputation and great wealth. He had a 500-acre farm near Wrexham where he was said to have installed a steam outfit for threshing corn. He was generous to those in his good books, but quick to take offence and inclined to be hard and unscrupulous. The bulk of his immense wealth was lost in 12 years of litigation with some of his nephews and three illegitimate sons. He was buried in an iron coffin of his own make.

ARTHUR WOOLF: 1766–1837. A Cornishman, born at Camborne, he became well-known as a mining engineer. In 1796 he assisted Jonathan Hornblower when he came to London to repair a two-cylinder steam engine at the Meux brewery, and subsequently became resident engineer there. He held this post until 1806, but in 1803 he had taken out a patent 'for the improvement of heating liquids to provide steam or vapour' and was able to construct two new boilers for higher pressures than those normally used. Another Woolf patent, of 1810, was a revival of Hornblower's use of compounding, which was barred until Watt's patent expired in 1800. Woolf returned to Cornwall, where he invented a steam ore crusher and an improved mining pump, powered by two cylinders. This pump was, however, no more efficient than the single-cylinder high-pressure Trevithick design. In his later years Woolf became Superintendent Engineer for Harvey's engine-building works at Hayle, retiring in 1833.

Left: John Wilkinson
Right: James Watt

Some famous locomotive designers

JOSEPH ARMSTRONG: Locomotive, Carriage and Wagon Superintendent, Great Western Railway 1864–1877. Built many classes of both broad and standard gauge engines. His brother, two sons and a nephew all rose to high positions in the GWR. The house at Swindon built by the Great Western for Joseph Armstrong was named 'Newburn' after his birthplace in Northumberland and it remained the residence of the locomotive superintendents until 1948.

SIR JOHN A. F. ASPINALL: Chief Mechanical Engineer 1886–1899, General Manager 1899–1919, Lancashire and Yorkshire Railway. Built the Horwich works and introduced the famous *Highflyer* 7-ft Atlantics of 1899; as General Manager introduced electric traction between Liverpool and Southport in 1904. Retired 1919. One of the greatest and most forward-looking engineers of his time.

C. J. BOWEN-COOKE: After being trained at Crewe, became Chief Mechanical Engineer, London and North Western Railway, 1909–1920. Applied superheating on a large scale and produced an outstanding range of engines capable of sustained hard work. His finest locomotives include the *George the Fifth* 4-4-0s, the *Prince of Wales* 4-6-0s and the splendid *Claughton* 4-6-0s for the West Coast main line. During the First World War he organised munitions production on a vast scale at Crewe works.

O. V. S. BULLEID: Assistant to Gresley on the London and North Eastern Railway; Chief Mechanical Engineer, Southern Railway, 1936–1947. A great advocate of advanced design features, he is most famous for the 'airsmoothed' Pacifics of the *Merchant Navy*, *West Country* and *Battle of Britain* classes, and his incredibly ugly wartime Q1 0-6-0 goods engine. His unorthodox designs and almost desperate experiments during the last years of steam entitle him to a place in the Hall of Fame.

EDWARD BURY: Locomotive Superintendent of the London and Birmingham Railway, 1838–1846. Partner in the locomotive building firm of Bury, Curtis and Kennedy. Bury engines were characterised by very light construction, bar-frames and 'haystack' fireboxes. Bury obstinately adhered to these features long after they had become outmoded.

GEORGE JACKSON CHURCHWARD: Chief Mechanical Engineer, Great Western Railway, 1902–1921. Gave the Great Western a standard range of locomotive classes. His use of tapered boilers, high pressures and long-travel valves laid the foundations for a future generation of designers. His 4-cylinder *Star* class 4-6-0s were the basis of later development by Collett and Hawksworth into the *Castles*, *Kings* and *Counties*, and by his pupil Stanier into the LMS *Black Fives*, *Princesses*, and *Duchesses*. His other achievement was the establishment at Swindon of the first plant in Britain for the stationary testing of locomotives. He retired in 1921, and in 1933 was killed on the line at Swindon, run down by one of his own engines in fog.

WILLIAM DEAN: Locomotive, Carriage and Wagon Superintendent, Great Western Railway, 1877–1902. At a time when the Great Western Railway was converting from broad to standard gauge, Dean built a series of convertible engines to bridge the gap in motive power requirements during the period of conversion. His later standard gauge 4-2-2s were among the most beautiful locomotives ever built.

R. M. DEELEY: Chief Mechanical Engineer, Midland Railway, 1903–1909. During Deeley's time the Midland needed larger and more powerful engines which were robust and economical in service. These he provided. He also greatly simplified the control systems of the Johnson compounds to need less individual skill in operation, making the engines more widely available for express service. Deeley resigned in 1909 over the Midland management's short sighted 'small engine' policy, entailing the frequent use of double heading.

DUGALD DRUMMOND: Locomotive Superintendent of the North British, then the Caledonian, and lastly the London and South Western Railway, 1896–1912. He developed highly successful series of 4-4-0s, the later examples having very large boilers; but his large 4-6-0s for the London and South Western Railway were not so successful. His special features included cross water-tubes in the firebox and a patent 'steam dryer'. Built a special coupé on the rear of the frames of his *Bug* and in it he made frequent tours of inspection. In 1912 he was involved in an accident on the line and died as a result of severe injuries.

SIR HENRY FOWLER: Chief Mechanical Engineer, Midland Railway, 1909–1922, and London Midland and Scottish Railway, 1925–1930. Rebuilt many of his predecessor's designs with superheated boilers, and produced the *Royal Scot* class 4-6-0s, the large 2-8-0 freight engines for the Somerset and Dorset line and the 0-10-0 Lickey banker *Big Bertha*. He was also responsible for the Beyer-Garratt coal engines and the *Patriot* class of rebuilt *Claughtons*.

SIR DANIEL GOOCH: Locomotive Superintendent of the Great Western Railway, 1837–1864. As Brunel's right-hand man, he established Swindon works and built a fine range of broad gauge locomotives. He laid the first transatlantic telegraph cable with the *Great Eastern*. Became Chairman of the Great Western Railway in 1865 and masterminded the conversion from broad to standard gauge, completed in 1892 after his death in October 1889 at the age of 73.

SIR NIGEL GRESLEY: Locomotive, Carriage and Wagon Superintendent, Great Northern Railway 1911–1922, Chief Mechanical Engineer, London and North Eastern Railway, 1923–1941. For the Great Northern he modernised the Ivatt Atlantics and produced the A1 Pacifics (including *Flying Scotsman*); for the LNER he designed and built a splendid range of 3-cylinder engines culminating in the streamlined A4 Pacifics, one of which, *Mallard*, holds the world speed record for steam. All his many designs were outstanding examples of his knowledge and craftsmanship. He died in office in 1941.

JAMES HOLDEN: Locomotive, Carriage and Wagon Superintendent, Great Eastern Railway, 1885–1907, after precisely 20 years with the Great Western at Swindon. His most famous design was the *Claud Hamilton* 4-4-0. Experimented with oil firing. Built the

0-10-0 tank engine *Decapod* to prove that a steam locomotive could match the acceleration of an electric multiple-unit train. It could, but was far too heavy. In 1893 built the first dining cars for 3rd class passengers, on the Harwich–York service. His J.17 goods engine was reckoned to be the most powerful 0-6-0 at the turn of the century.

GEORGE HUGHES: Chief Mechanical Engineer, Lancashire and Yorkshire Railway, 1908–1922, and London Midland & Scottish Railway, 1923–1925. Developed Aspinall's 4-4-2s by application of superheating into very long-lasting engines. The original Hughes 4-6-0s were a very poor batch but were much improved when superheated after 1921. He also built several massive 4-6-4 Baltic tanks, but his most successful design was the Horwich 'Crab' 2-6-0, which did not appear until after his retirement.

HENRY A. IVATT: Locomotive Superintendent, Great Northern Railway, 1895–1911. Built the first British Atlantic 4-4-2 *Henry Oakley* in 1898. His policy of large engines with small cylinders and large boilers was the opposite of that of his predecessor, Patrick Stirling; his ideas were improved upon by Sir Nigel Gresley.

H. G. IVATT: Chief Mechanical Engineer, British Railways, 1945–1947. Son of Henry A. Ivatt. Introduced modern fitting such as hopper ashpans, rocking grates, and self-cleaning smokeboxes and tubes to B.R. locomotive designs.

SAMUEL WAITE JOHNSON: Locomotive Superintendent, Midland Railway, 1873–1903, following service with both the Glasgow and South Western and Great Eastern Railway. Built locomotives of power and style, in particular the 3-cylinder compound 4-4-0s of 1902. He carried on and am-

plified his predecessor Kirtley's policy of building relatively small but powerful, stylish and well-finished engines, often used to double-head heavy express trains.

DAVID JONES: Trained at Crewe under John Ramsbottom, he joined the Highland Railway in 1855 and became Locomotive Superintendent 1870–1896. Best remembered for his range of powerful 4-4-0s and for his 'Big Goods' 4-6-0 of 1896, the first 4-6-0 ever to run on a British railway. He retired in 1896 following an accident on the footplate of one of his engines in which he was badly scalded. He died in 1907, aged 72.

MATTHEW KIRTLEY: Joined the Stockton and Darlington Railway at the age of 13, was a fireman on the London and Birmingham and eventually became Locomotive Superintendent of the Midland Railway 1844–1873. His engines were characterised by outside frames, robust construction and extreme longevity. Some were still in service as late as 1930.

R. E. L. MAUNSELL: Locomotive, Carriage and Wagon Superintendent, Great Southern and Western Railway (Ireland) 1911–1913, Chief Mechanical Engineer, South Eastern and Chatham Railway 1913–1922, Chief Mechanical Engineer, Southern Railway 1923–1937. On the South Eastern and Chatham he produced the remarkable class E1, a rebuild of Wainwright's 4-4-0, and on the Southern he built the *King Arthur* and *Lord Nelson* 4-6-0s, and the powerful 'Schools' class 4-4-0s. The latter were acknowledged to be the finest 4-4-0s ever built, and were the most powerful in Europe.

J. E. McCONNELL: Locomotive Superintendent, London and North Western Railway Southern Division, 1846–1864. Introduced the famous *Bloomer* 2-2-2s, and the *Patent* 2-2-2s of 1852 which were designed to run between London and Birmingham in 2 hours, a speed hardly exceeded until electrification of the line in the early 1960s.

SOME FAMOUS LOCOMOTIVE DESIGNERS

JOHN FARQUHARSON McINTOSH: Locomotive, Carriage and Wagon Superintendent, Caledonian Railway, 1895–1914. Built the superb *Dunalastair* series of 4-4-0s between 1896 and 1904, also the massive *Cardean* class 4-6-0s for the Anglo-Scottish expresses on the West Coast route.

JOHN RAMSBOTTOM: Chief Mechanical Engineer, London and North Western Railway, 1862–1871. Organised Crewe works and built the railway's steelworks, the first in the world to produce steel by the Bessemer process. His engine designs included the *Newton* and *Samson* 2-4-0s, the DX 0-6-0 goods, and the *Lady of the Lake* 2-2-2s. He patented the safety-valve arrangement which bears his name, and the split piston-ring, and also laid down the first water troughs in the world, enabling locomotives to pick up water at speed using the tender-mounted scoop which he devised. He retired in 1871 and did consultancy work, including the laying out of Horwich works for the Lancashire and Yorkshire Railway. He died in 1897, aged 80.

SIR VINCENT RAVEN: Chief Mechanical Engineer, North Eastern Railway, 1910–1922. Developed a system of audible and visual cab signalling, and built a fine range of 3-cylinder engines, culminating in the Pacifics of 1922. He was an advocate of main line electrification, going so far as to build a prototype locomotive for the proposed electrification of the Newcastle–York main line.

R. A. RIDDLES: Principal Assistant to Chief Mechanical Engineer, London Midland and Scottish Railway. Deputy Director-General of Royal Engineer Equipment in World War II. Vice President, London Midland and Scottish Railway. From 1948 he was a member of the Railway Executive and the British Railways Board, responsible for mechanical and electrical engineering. Designed the highly capable W.D. 'Austerity' 2-8-0s and 2-10-0s, and from 1951 headed a team,

Robert Stephenson

with R. C. Bond and E. S. Cox, which produced the B.R. standard range of 2-cylinder simple locomotives which saw out the age of steam on British Railways. Retired from British Railways Board in 1954 and became Chairman of Stothert & Pitt, crane builders.

JOHN G. ROBINSON: Chief Mechanical Engineer, Great Central Railway, 1902–1923. Built some of the most handsome locomotives ever to run in Britain, including the *Jersey Lily* 4-4-2s and the *Director* 4-4-0s. Invented the Robinson superheater and the 'Reliostop' system of train control. Patented an anti-telescoping device for coaching stock and experimented with pulverised-fuel firing. Was offered the post of Chief Mechanical Engineer of the London and North Eastern Railway in 1923, but stood down in favour of a younger man— Nigel Gresley.

GEORGE STEPHENSON: Born in Northumberland in 1781, he became an engine-wright in his native coal-fields. He developed the early work of Trevithick and in 1814 built a successful locomotive, the *Blücher*, for Killingworth Colliery. Was engineer to

the Stockton and Darlington, and Liverpool and Manchester, Railways. later life was mainly concerned with the building of railways rather than of locomotives. He was elected the first President of the Institute of Mechanical Engineers, and on retirement to his home at Tapton House near Chesterfield he set out to grow better hot-house plants than his neighbour the Duke of Devonshire at Chatsworth. By all accounts he succeeded. He died in 1848 and is buried in Chesterfield Parish Church.

ROBERT STEPHENSON: Born in 1803, he was the son of George Stephenson and became his indispensable assistant. Founded Robert Stephenson and Company in Newcastle and built the *Rocket* for the Rainhill Trials in 1829. His company constructed many of the early locomotives for railways in Britain and abroad. Later he also turned to railway engineering; he was the builder of the London and Birmingham Railway, his greatest achievement, among many others. Some of his finest works are Kilsby tunnel, the Britannia bridge over the Menai Strait, the high-level bridge at Newcastle and the Royal Border Bridge at Berwick. He died in 1859, the same year as his great friend and rival, Brunel.

SIR WILLIAM A. STANIER, F.R.S.: Chief Mechanical Engineer, London Midland and Scottish Railway, 1932–1944. Trained under Churchward at Swindon, he rose to be deputy to C. B. Collett before transferring to Crewe. Perhaps his greatest achievement was to reconcile the warring factions of Derby and Crewe and produce some of the finest engines ever built in this country: the *Black Five* and *Jubilee* 4-6-0s and the *Princess* and *Duchess* Pacifics. He served on two Commissions of Enquiry into the design of Indian Railways Pacifics, and in 1944 left the London Midland and Scottish Railway to become a full-time Scientific Advisor to the Ministry of Production. He died in 1966 aged 88.

George Stephenson

PATRICK STIRLING: Locomotive Engineer, Glasgow and South Western Railway, 1853–1866; Locomotive Engineer, Great Northern Railway, 1866–1895. His famous 8-ft bogie singles embodied the essential characteristic of his work: beautiful proportions, with domeless boilers and polished brass safety-valve columns. Stirling died, still at work, in 1895.

WILLIAM STROUDLEY: Locomotive Engineer, London, Brighton and South Coast Railway, 1870–1889. Introduced the celebrated *Gladstone* 0-4-2 express engines and the famous yellow livery, which he described as 'an improvement on engine green'. During his time at Brighton Works, engineering design and production standards were second to none. While attending the trials of one of his *Gladstone* engines in 1889 he caught a chill from which he died.

ARCHIBALD STURROCK: Trained at Swindon under Daniel Gooch, he became Locomotive Engineer to the Great Northern Railway from 1850–1866. Advocated large engines, high boiler pressures and advanced design. In 1853 he constructed a 4-2-2, No. 215, to illustrate the practicability of an 8-hour run from London to Edinburgh. For freight work he built 70 engines with powered tenders supplied with steam from an extra-large boiler on the engine proper. His thinking was ahead of his time and his successors dismantled his powered tenders. He retired in 1866, and died in 1909 aged 92.

ROBERT W. URIE: Locomotive Superintendent, London and South-Western Railway, 1912–1922. Went against contemporary multi-cylinder trend by building robust 2-cylinder

simple engines. This policy was later followed for the British Railways standard locomotives under Riddles after nationalisation in 1948. Several of his designs were continued by Maunsell as Southern Railway standard engines. His son was Locomotive Superintendent, Highland Railway, and later Superintendent of Motive Power on the London Midland and Scottish Railway.

FRANCIS W. WEBB: Chief Mechanical Engineer, London and North Western Railway, 1871–1903. A born organiser, he introduced production-line techniques at Crewe, ultimately turning out up to 6 new main-line locomotives per month. He designed signal-box interlocking frames, a radial axle-box, and a system of standard jigs for the erection of locomotives. His penchant for generally unsuccessful compound engines has overshadowed his fine range of smaller, less spectacular engines such as the *Precedents*, the *Cauliflower* goods locomotives and his 0-6-2 coal tank engines.

T. W. WORSDELL: Locomotive Engineer, North Eastern Railway, 1883–1890. He developed the Von Borries system of 2-cylinder compounding, and built several speedy 4-2-2 engines before retiring in 1890, to be succeeded by his younger brother.

WILSON WORSDELL: Locomotive Engineer, North Eastern Railway, 1890–1910. Brother of the above, he reverted to simple-expansion engines. He built several good 4-4-0s and went on to produce larger 4-4-2s and 4-6-0s as well as 0-8-0s for heavy freight trains. A record run was achieved by an M Class 4-4-0 during the 1895 race to the north, with an average of 66 mph from Newcastle to Edinburgh. Both brothers had gained early practical experience with the Pennsylvania Railroad, and both returned to Crewe before taking up appointments on the North Eastern Railway.

Museums, steam centres and preserved railways

KEY TO ABBREVIATIONS

M	Marine engines, or steamships
Misc	Miscellaneous
Rly	Railway engines, standard gauge
Rly (ng)	Railway engines, narrow gauge
P	A working railway carrying passengers
Rd	Road-using engines
*S**	Stationary engines preserved *in situ*
S	Stationary engines in museums

AVON
Bristol Industrial Museum, Prince's Wharf, City Docks, Bristol. *Rd, Rly, S*
Bitton Railway Centre, Bitton, Bristol, *Rly*
Somerset Railway Museum, Bleadon and Uphill Station, Weston-super-Mare. *Rly*
S.S. *Great Britain*, Great Western Dock, Bristol. *M*

BEDFORDSHIRE
Leighton Buzzard Narrow Gauge Rly, Pages Park Station, Billington Road, Leighton Buzzard. *P, Rly, (ng)*
Whipsnade and Umfolozi Light Rly, Whipsnade Zoo, Dunstable. *P, Rly, (ng)*

BERKSHIRE
Museum of English Rural Life, University of Reading. *Misc*
Englefield Sawmill, Englefield, west of Reading. *S**

BUCKINGHAMSHIRE
Quainton Railway Centre, Quainton Road Station, north-west of Aylesbury. *Rly*

CAMBRIDGESHIRE
Nene Valley Rly, between Wansford Station, off the A1, Nr. Peterborough, and Orton Mere. *P. Rly*
Cambridge Museum of Technology, Cheddars Lane, Cambridge. *S**
Stretham Old Engine, Stretham, south of Ely. *S**

CLEVELAND
Stockton and Darlington Railway Museum, Bridge Street, Stockton. *Rly*

CORNWALL
Wendron Forge, north of Helston. *S, M*
Wheal Martyn Museum, Carthew, St. Austell. *S, Rly*
Holman Bros. Museum, Camborne. *S*
East Pool Mine, Pool, Camborne. *S**
Levant Winding Engine, Geevor Tin Mine, St. Just. *S**
Parkandillick Clay Pit, St. Austell. *S**

COUNTY DURHAM
North of England Open Air Museum, Beamish Hall, Stanley. *Rly, S*
Darlington North Road Station Railway Museum, Station Road, Darlington. *Rly*

CUMBRIA
Lakeside and Haverthwaite Rly, between Haverthwaite and Newby Bridge, on Lake Windermere. *P, Rly*
Levens Hall Steam Collection, Kendal. *S, Rd*
Windermere Steam Boat Museum, Grayrigg Road, Windermere. *M*
Ravenglass and Eskdale Rly, between Ravenglass,

south of Whitehaven, and Dalegarth. *P. Rly (ng)*

DERBYSHIRE
Dinting Railway Centre, Dinting Lane, Glossop. *Rly*
Midland Railway Centre, Butterley Station, Ripley. *Rly*
Klondyke Mill Recreation Centre, Draycott-in-the-Clay, Sudbury, east of Uttoxeter. *Rd*
The Donington Collection, Donington Park, Castle Donington, south-east of Derby. *Rd*
Bamford Mill, Bamford, near Hathersage, west of Sheffield. *S**
Leawood Pumping Station, Cromford, Matlock. *S**
Middleton Top Winding Engine, Wirksworth, south of Matlock. *S**

DEVON
Dartmouth Museum and Newcomen Engine House, the Butterwalk, Dartmouth. *S*
Dart Valley Railway, Buckfastleigh, west of Newton Abbot. *P, Rly*
Exeter Maritime Museum, The Quay, Exeter. *M*
Broad Gauge Locomotive *Tiny*, Newton Abbot Station. *Rly*
Torbay and Dartmouth Rly, between Queens Park Station, Paignton and Dartmouth. *P, Rly*
Saltram House Industrial Museum, Plympton, west of Plymouth. *S, Rly*
Alscott Farm Museum, Shebbear, Nr. Holsworthy. *Rd*
James Countryside Museum, Bicton Gardens, north of Budleigh Salterton. *Rd, Rly (ng)*

DORSET
Southern Steam Trust, Swanage Station. *Rly*

ESSEX
Stour Valley Railway Preservation Society, Chappel and Wakes Colne Station, north-west of Colchester. *Rly*
Colne Valley Railway Co., Castle Hedingham Station, north-west of Halstead. *Rly*

GLOUCESTERSHIRE
Dowty Railway Preservation Society, Ashchurch, east of Tewkesbury. *Rly*
Dean Forest Railway Society, Norchard Steam Centre, Norchard New Mills, north of Lydney, south-east of Monmouth. *Rly*

GREATER MANCHESTER
Bury Transport Museum, Castlecroft Road, Bury. *Rd, Rly*
Northwestern Museum of Science and Industry, 97 Grosvenor St, Manchester. *S*
Mill Engine Museum, Bolton. *S*
Monks Hall Museum, Eccles. *S*
Dee Mill and Fern Mill, Shaw, near Oldham. *S**
Diamond Rope Works, Royton, near Oldham. *S**
Leigh Spinning Mill, Leigh. *S**

HAMPSHIRE
Hollycombe House, Nr. Liphook, west of Haslemere. *Rd, Rly (ng)*
Mid-Hants Railway, 'The Watercress Line', between Alresford and Ropley, south-west of Alton. *P, Rly*

Southampton Maritime Museum, Wool House, Bugle St. Southampton. *M*
Eastney Pumping Station, Henderson Rd., Eastney, Portsmouth. *S**
National Motor Museum, Beaulieu, *Rd*

HEREFORD AND WORCESTER
Bulmer Railway Centre, Whitecross Road, Hereford. *Rly*
Severn Valley Railway, between Bewdley (west of Kidderminster) and Bridgnorth, Salop. *P, Rly*
Herefordshire Waterworks Museum, Broomy Hill, Hereford. *S*
Broomy Hill Waterworks, Hereford. *S**

HERTFORDSHIRE
West Park and Wintergreen Rly, Knebworth House, south of Stevenage. *P. Rly (ng)*

HUMBERSIDE
Hull Transport Museum, 36 High St, Hull. *Rd, Rly*
Lincolnshire Coast Light Rly, Humberstone, south of Grimsby. *P, Rly (ng)*
Springhead Pumping Station Museum, Hull. *S**

ISLE OF MAN
Isle of Man Railway, Douglas to Port Erin. *P, Rly (ng)*
Port Erin Railway Museum, Strand Road, Port Erin. *Rly (ng)*

ISLE OF WIGHT
Isle of Wight Steam Railway, Havenstreet Station, near Hyde, south of Ryde. *P, Rly*
Albany Steam and Industrial Museum, Roest Road, Newport. *Rd, S*

KENT
Kent and East Sussex Railway, Tenterden Station, south-west of Ashford, to Wittersham Road. *P. Rly*
Sittingbourne and Kemsley Light Railway, The Wall, Milton Regis, Sittingbourne. *P, Rly, (ng)*
Romney, Hythe and Dymchurch Rly, between Hythe and Dungeness. *P, Rly (ng)*

LANCASHIRE
Lytham Motive Power Museum, Dock Road, Lytham. *Rly*
Steamtown Railway Museum, Warton Road, Carnforth, north of Lancaster. *Rly*
Todber Museum of Steam, Gisburn, north of Burnley. *Rd*
West Lancashire Light Railway, Hesketh Bank, south-west of Preston. *P, Rly (ng)*

LEICESTERSHIRE
Great Central Railway, between Loughborough Central Station, Quorn, and Rothley. *P, Rly*
Midland Steam Centre, 106a Derby Road, Loughborough. *Rly, Rd, M, S*
Leicestershire Museum of Technology, Abbey Pumping Station, Leicester. *S**, Rd*
Market Bosworth Light Railway, Shackerstone Station, Market Bosworth, north-west of Leicester. *P, Rly*

LINCOLNSHIRE
Dogdyke Pumping Station Preservation Trust, Bridge

Farm, Tattershall, south-east of Lincoln. *S**
F. A. Smith Collection, 50 West End Road, Frampton, south of Boston. *Rd*
All Saints Brewery, Stamford, *S**
Pinchbeck Marsh Pumping Station, north of Spalding. *S**

LONDON
H.M.S. Belfast, moored above Tower Bridge *M*
The London Transport Collection, Covent Garden. *Rly, Rd*
The Maritime Trust Historic Ship Collection, St. Catherine's by the Tower, City of London. *M*
National Maritime Museum, Romney Road, Greenwich. *M*
Paddle-steamer *Tattershall Castle*, Victoria Embankment. *M*
Science Museum, Exhibition Road, South Kensington. *Rd, Rly, S, M, Misc*
Kew Bridge Engines, Green Dragon Lane, Brentford, S.W. London *S*, Rd*

MERSEYSIDE
Merseyside County Museum, William Brown St., Liverpool. *Rly, Rd*
Steamport Transport Museum, Derby Road, Southport. *Rly*

NORFOLK
Bressingham Steam Museum, Bressingham, west of Diss. *Rd, P, Rly, Rly (ng) Misc, S*
North Norfolk Railway, between Sheringham and Weybourne. *P, Rly*
The Thursford Collection, Thursford Green, northeast of Fakenham. *Rd, Misc, Rly (ng)*
Bridewell Museum, Bridewell Alley, Norwich. *S*
Forncett Industrial Museum, Forncett St. Mary. *S*
Strumpshaw Hall Museum, *Rly (ng), Rd*

NOTTINGHAMSHIRE
National Mining Museum, Lound Hall, north of East Retford. *S*
Popplewick Pumping Station, south of Ravenshead, Mansfield. *S**
Nottingham Industrial Museum, Wollaton Park, Nottingham. *Rd, Rly*

OXFORDSHIRE
Great Western Society, Didcot Railway Centre, Didcot. *Rly*
Combe Sawmill, near Bladon, north-west of Oxford. *S**

SHROPSHIRE
Cambrian Railway Society Ltd., Oswestry Depot, Oswestry. *Rly*
Ironbridge Gorge Museum Trust, Telford. Includes the Iron Bridge, Coalbrookdale, Coalport China Works, and Blists Hill. *S, Misc*
Coleham Pumping Station, near Shrewsbury. *S**

SOMERSET
East Somerset Railway, Cranmore, east of Shepton Mallet. *Rly*
West Somerset Railway, Minehead to Bishop's Lydeard (north of Taunton). *P, Rly*
Somerset & Dorset Railway Museum Trust, Washford, south of Watchet. *Rly*
Somerset County Museum, Taunton Castle. *S*
Allery Moor Pumping Station, Alle, Taunton. S*

STAFFORDSHIRE
Foxfield Light Railway, Dilhorne, Blythebridge, east of Stoke-on-Trent. *P, Rly*
Staffordshire County Museum, Shugborough, east of Stafford. *Rly, S*
Bass-Worthington Museum, Burton-on-Trent. *Rly, S*
Cheddleton Flint Mill, Cheddleton, south of Leek. *S*
Gladstone Pottery Museum, Longton, Stoke-on-Trent. *S**
Chasewater Light Railway, Chasewater Pleasure Park, Near Brownhills, south-east of Cannock. *P, Rly*

SUFFOLK
Museum of East Anglian Life, Abbots Hall, Stowmarket. *Rd*

SUSSEX
Bluebell Railway, between Sheffield Park Station, near Uckfield, and Horsted Keynes. *P, Rly*
Brighton and Hove Engineerium, off Nevil Road, Hove. *S*, Misc*

TYNE AND WEAR
Bowes Railway, Springwell Village, south of Gateshead. *Rly*
Monkswearmouth Station Museum, North Bridge St., Sunderland. *Rly*
Newcastle Museum of Science and Engineering, Exhibition Park, Newcastle. *M, Rd, Rly, S*
Ryhope Engine Museum, Ryhope Pumping Station, south of Sunderland. *S**
Washington F. Pit, Washington New Town, west of Sunderland. *S**

WEST MIDLANDS
Birmingham Museum of Science and Industry, Newhall Street, Birmingham. *Rd, Rly, S*
Birmingham Railway Museum, Warwick Road, Tysely, Birmingham 11. *Rly*
Black Country Museum, Tipton Road, Dudley. *S*

WILTSHIRE
Great Western Railway Museum, Faringdon Road, Swindon. *Rly*
Claverton Pumping Station, Kennet and Avon Canal, Claverton, east of Bath. *S* (Waterwheel)*
Crofton Pumping Station, Kennet and Avon Canal, Crofton, near Gt. Bedwyn, south-west of Hungerford. *S* working beam engines*

NORTH YORKSHIRE
National Railway Museum, Leeman Road, York (near B.R. station). *Rly, S*
North Yorkshire Moors Railway, between Grosmont and Pickering. *P, Rly*
Yorkshire Dales Railway Museum Trust, Embsay, north of Skipton. *Rly*

SOUTH YORKSHIRE
Abbeydale Industrial Hamlet, Abbeydale Road South, Sheffield. *S*
Cusworth Hall Museum, Cusworth, Doncaster. *S*

WEST YORKSHIRE
Worth Valley Light Railway, between Keighley, Haworth and Oxenhope. *P, Rly*
Middleton Railway Trust, Tunstall Road, Leeds 11. *Rly*
Bradford Industrial Museum, Moorside Road, Bradford. *Rly, Rd, S*
Tolson Memorial Museum, Ravensknowle Park, Huddersfield. *S*

SCOTLAND
Strathspey Railway, between Boat of Garten and Aviemore, Highlands *P, Rly*
The Royal Scottish Museum, Chambers St., Edinburgh. *Rd, Rly, M*
The Scottish Railway Preservation Society, Wallace St., Falkirk, Central. *Rly*
The Comet, Town Centre, Port Glasgow, east of Greenock, Strathclyde. *M*
Glasgow Museum of Transport, 25 Albert Drive, Glasgow. *Rly, M*
Paddle-steamer *Waverley*, New Waverley Terminal, Stobcross Quay, Glasgow. *M*
Lochty Private Railway, west of Crail, Fife. *P, Rly*
Preston Grange Museum, Morrisonshaven, Prestonpans, east of Edinburgh. *S*, Rly, Misc*
Lothian Region Transport, Shrubhill Depot, Leigh Walk, Edinburgh. *Rd*
Industrial and Social History Museum, Forth House, Kirkcaldy, Fife. *S*
Glenruthven Mills, Auchterarder, Perth. *S**

WALES CLWYD
Llangollen Railway Society Ltd., Llangollen Station. *Rly*

WALES DYFED
Vale of Rheidol Railway, between Aberystwyth and Devil's Bridge. *P. Rly (ng)*

WALES GLAMORGAN
Caerphilly Railway Society Ltd., Van Road, Caerphilly, north of Cardiff. *Rly*
Gwili Railway, Bronwydd Arms Station, north of Carmarthen. *P, Rly*
Welsh Industrial and Maritime Museum, Bute St., Cardiff. *S, Rly, M*
Swansea Industrial and Maritime Museum, Alexandra Road, Swansea. *S, Rly, M*

WALES GWYNEDD
Bala Lake Railway, between Llanuwchllyn Station and Bala. *P, Rly (ng)*
Conway Valley Railway Museum, Betws-y-Coed. *Rly*
Fairbourne Railway, between Beach Road, Fairbourne and Barmouth Ferry. *P, Rly, (ng)*
Festiniog Railway, between Porthmadog and Tanygrisiau. *P, Rly (ng)*
The Narrow Gauge Railway Centre of North Wales, Gloddfa Ganol, Blaenau Ffestiniog. *Rly (ng)*
Llanberis Lake Railway, Llanberis, east of Caernarfon. *P, Rly (ng)*
Penrhyn Castle, near Bangor. *P, Rly*
Snowdon Mountain Railway, Llanberis to summit. The only steam rack railway in the British Isles. *P, Rly (ng)*
Talyllyn Railway, Wharf Station, between Tywyn and Nant Gwernol. *P, Rly (ng)*
Narrow Gauge Railway Museum, Wharf Station, Tywyn. *Rly (ng)*
Welsh Highland Light Railway, Porthmadog. *P, Rly (ng)*

WALES POWYS
Welshpool and Llanfair Light Railway, between Sylfaen (Welshpool) and Llanfair Caereinion. *P, Rly (ng)*

A detailed guide to all preserved standard- and narrow-gauge railways of Great Britain is available from the Association of Railway Preservation Societies Ltd., Sheringham Station, Norfolk. A leaflet entitled 'Great Little Trains of Wales' is published by the Narrow Gauge Railways of Wales Joint Marketing Panel, Wharf Station, Tywyn, Gwynedd.

Details of special steam excursions on B.R. track can be obtained from B.R. main line stations or from the Steam Locomotive Operators Association, 44 Stafford Road, Lichfield, Staffs.

Bibliography

I am grateful to the authors for the invaluable help I found in the following publications:

Evers, H. *Steam and the Steam Engine (1877)* (William Collins Sons & Co. 1877)

Galloway, R. L. *The Steam Engine and its Inventors* (Macmillan & Co. 1881)

Hoblyn, R. D. *Manual of the Steam Engine* (Scott, Webster & Geary 1842)

For further reading I recommend the following titles:

Allen, Cecil John *The Great Eastern Railway* (Ian Allan 1971)

Allen, J. S. The Steam Engine of Thomas Newcomen (Moorland Pub Co. 1977)

Barton, D. B. *The Cornish Beam Engine: Its History and Development* (D. B. Barton 1965)

Beaumont, Anthony *Traction Engines and Steam Vehicles in Pictures* (David & Charles 1969)

Beaumont, Anthony *Traction Engines Past and Present* (David & Charles 1974)

Bellwood, J. & Jenkinson, D. *Gresley and Stanier* (H.M.S.O. 1976)

Bloom, Alan *Steam Engines at Bressingham. The Story of a Live Steam Museum* (Faber & Faber 1976)

Body, Geoffrey *British Paddle Steamers* (David & Charles 1974)

Bonnet, Harold *The Saga of the Steam Plough* (David & Charles 1972)

Cardwell, D. S. L. *Steam Power in the Eighteenth Century* (Sheed & Ward 1963)

Cox, E. Stewart *British Standard Railway Locomotives* (Ian Allan 1973)

Cox, E. Stewart. *Locomotive Panorama* (2 volumes) (Ian Allan 1974)

Davison, C. St. C. B. *Steam Road Vehicles: Historical Review* (Science Museum 1970)

Garrett, Colin D. *Symphony in Steam* (Blandford Press 1970)

Haining, J. & Tyler, C. *Ploughing by Steam: A History of Steam Cultivation over the years.* (Model & Allied Pubns. 1970)

Hambleton, F. C. *Famous Paddle Steamers* (Model & Allied Pubns. 1971)

Hardy, Richard *Steam in the Blood* (Ian Allan 1976)

Hayes, G. *Stationary Steam Engines* (Shire Pubns. 1979)

Hughes, William Jesse *Century of*

Traction Engines (David & Charles 1970)

Lane, Michael R. *Burrell Showman's Road Locomotives* (Model & Allied Pubns. 1971)

Nock, Oswald Stevens *Railway Enthusiasts Encyclopedia* (Arrow Books 1970)

Nock, Oswald Stevens *The Great Northern Railway* (Ian Allan 1974)

Nock, Oswald Stevens *The Great Western Railway Stars, Castles and Kings* (David & Charles 1975)

Nock, Oswald Stevens *The London and North Western Railway Precursor Family* (David & Charles 1966)

Norris, William *Modern Steam Road Wagons* (David & Charles 1972, Goose & Son 1972)

Rolt, L. T. C. *Isambard Kingdom Brunel* (Longman, Penguin 1970)

Spratt, H. Philip *Transatlantic Paddle Steamers* (Brown Son & Ferguson 1968)

Thorley, W. G. *A Breath of Steam* (Ian Allan 1975)

Watkins, G. *The Stationary Steam Engine* (David & Charles 1968)

Whitehead, Robert Arthur *Garretts of Leiston* (Model & Allied Pubns. 1973)

Index